Stilson Hutchins, Joseph West Moore

The national capital, past and present

The story of its settlement, progress, and development

Stilson Hutchins, Joseph West Moore

The national capital, past and present
The story of its settlement, progress, and development

ISBN/EAN: 9783337229108

Printed in Europe, USA, Canada, Australia, Japan

Cover: Foto ©Andreas Hilbeck / pixelio.de

More available books at **www.hansebooks.com**

THE

NATIONAL CAPITAL

PAST AND PRESENT.

THE STORY OF ITS SETTLEMENT, PROGRESS,
AND DEVELOPMENT.

WITH PROFUSE ILLUSTRATIONS

OF ITS HISTORICAL OBJECTS, PUBLIC BUILDINGS, MEMORIAL
STATUARY, AND BEAUTIFUL HOMES.

BY

STILSON HUTCHINS,
EDITOR OF THE WASHINGTON POST.
AND
JOSEPH WEST MOORE,
AUTHOR AND JOURNALIST.

WASHINGTON:
THE POST PUBLISHING COMPANY.
1885.

CONTENTS.

CHAPTER I.

CHAPTER II.

CHAPTER III.

CHAPTER IV.

CHAPTER V.

CHAPTER VI.

CHAPTER VII.

CHAPTER VIII.

CHAPTER IX.

CHAPTER X.

CHAPTER XI.

CHAPTER XII.

CHAPTER. XIII.

CHAPTER XIV.

CHÁPTER XV.

CHAPTER XVI.

CHAPTER XVII.

CHAPTER XVIII.

CHAPTER XIX.

CHAPTER XX.

CHAPTER · XXI.

CHAPTER XXII.

CHAPTER XXIII.

ILLUSTRATIONS.

CAPITOL HILL. AS SEEN FROM THE NATIONAL MUSEUM.

THE NATIONAL CAPITAL.

CHAPTER I.

THE CITY OF WASHINGTON—SELECTING THE PERMANENT SEAT OF THE GOVERNMENT —THE LONG CONTEST IN CONGRESS—PRESIDENT WASHINGTON'S CHOICE OF THE POTOMAC SITE—THE LEGISLATIVE BARGAIN MADE—JEFFERSON'S LITTLE DINNER-PARTY—ACT OF CONGRESS DEFINING THE FEDERAL TERRITORY.

THE city of Washington can be likened to a splendid century-plant set on the banks of the Potomac by the Father of his Country, and which has now blossomed for the first time. For nearly one hundred years the capital of the American nation has had an existence, but it is only within a few years that it can be said to have awakened to a vigorous life. At first it was a promising settlement animated by extravagant visions of a sudden, grand development, but when these hopes and dreams were dispelled it settled down into a slothful, dreary, repulsive town,—a sort of tattered fringe on the national garb. And for a long time it was content to be, as M. de Bacourt wrote, "neither a city, nor a village, nor the country, but a building yard placed in a desolate spot wherein living is unbearable." But Washington now is bright and beautiful and progressive, and gives abundant promise of becoming the grandest capital of the world.

Soon after the Revolutionary war the question of a permanent seat for the American government began to be agitated. The Continental Congress had been compelled to hold its sessions in eight different places, and the Congress of the Confederation was driven from Philadelphia, after sitting there during five years, to Princeton, New Jersey, because its proceedings had been interrupted by a mob of turbulent soldiers, who were not promptly checked by the authorities of the city. "This untoward event," it is stated, "led to much unfavorable comment, and exercised undoubted influence in determining against the location of the ultimate seat of Con-

WASHINGTON IN 1813.

gress and the government in any large city." On the 23d of December, 1784, a resolution was adopted by the Congress of the Confederation for the appointment of commissioners to lay out a district on the Delaware river, near the Lower Falls, for "a Federal town, a Federal House for Congress, and for the executive officers thereof, and houses for the President and the Secretaries of Foreign Affairs, War, the Marine, and the Treasury." It was moved to substitute "Georgetown on the Potomac" as the site of the Federal town, but all the States except Virginia voted against the motion. The resolution for some unknown reason was not carried into effect, and the whole matter remained quiescent until May 10, 1787, when an effort was made in Congress, then sitting in New York, to take up a resolution for the erection of government buildings at Georgetown. This effort did not succeed, and nothing further was done in the Congress of the Confederation toward establishing the permanent seat of the government.

During the session in Philadelphia in the summer of 1787, of the convention to revise the Federal system of government, it was proposed that the new Constitution of the United States should provide "against choosing for the seat of the general government any city or place where a State government might be fixed," as it was believed that disputes would continually arise concerning jurisdiction. The matter was generally discussed, and when the draft of the Constitution was being considered a motion was made by James Madison that the following clause be added to the enumerated powers of Congress: "To exercise exclusively legislative authority at the seat of the General Government, and over a district around the same not exceeding —— square miles, the consent of the State or States comprising the same being first obtained."

The motion was adopted, and the proposed clause went to the committee on style, and was arranged in the form it now has in the Constitution: "To exercise exclusive legislation, in all cases whatsoever, over such district (not exceeding ten miles square) as may by cession of particular States, and the acceptance of Congress, become the seat of government of the United States."

The First Congress of the United States under the Constitution assembled in New York on the 4th of March, 1789, but it was not until a month later that it was ready for business. Within a short time after the session had begun numerous memorials were received praying for the settlement of the question of the permanent seat of the government. The claims of New York, Philadelphia, Baltimore, Reading, Germantown, Alexandria, Georgetown, Harrisburg, Lancaster, Carlisle, Trenton, and other places were urged with pertinacity, and Congress was soon "divided into schools of opinion hard to reconcile." The Eastern members would not agree to the location of the capital in Maryland or Virginia, and were hardly inclined to look with favor upon any place except the city of New York, which had provided Congress with ample and suitable accommodations

THE CAPITOL WHEN FIRST ERECTED.

free of cost. Nearly all the Southern members were in favor of the
Potomac site, claiming that it possessed advantages which made it superior
to all other places. Every place proposed had its strong advocates, and
for a long time it seemed as if it would be impossible for Congress to
decide upon any location. The Maryland legislature, on December 23,
1788, had passed " an act to cede to Congress and the United States any
district not exceeding ten miles square which the Congress may fix upon
and accept for the seat of government of the United States;" and the
Virginia legislature, in 1789, passed a similar act.

A stubborn contest over this important matter was begun in the
House of Representatives on August 27, 1789. A motion was made
" that a permanent residence ought to be fixed for the general government
of the United States at some convenient place as near the centre of wealth,
population, and extent of territory as may be consistent with convenience to the navigation of the Atlantic ocean, and have due regard to the
particular situation of the Western country."

The debate was opened by Roger Sherman, of Connecticut, who made
an elaborate argument against the motion, contending that as the Union
of the States was not completed, Rhode Island and North Carolina not
being represented in Congress, a question so important as this one should
be postponed to the next session. He declared, also, that the government
could not establish a Federal town, as it was not possessed of sufficient
resources.

Some of the Southern members argued that the establishment of a
capital would be a strong bond of union, and would greatly aid the nation
in its progress and development. Fisher Ames doubted " whether the
government could stand the shock of such a measure, which involved as
many passions as the human heart could display." Finally the question
was made the special order for the 3d of September following, and on
that day and the next the debate was renewed with increased earnestness.

An Eastern member moved to locate the capital at " some convenient
place on the east bank of the Susquehanna river in Pennsylvania." A
substitute was offered by a Virginia member, which provided for " a place
as nearly central as a convenient communication with the Atlantic ocean
and an easy access to the Western territory will permit." The substitute
motion was lost, and the motion for the Susquehanna location was carried
by a vote of 32 to 18.

Then ensued a long and bitter wrangle. The Eastern members were
charged with having conspired with the members from Pennsylvania to
prevent the Potomac site from being chosen, and with a disposition to
force a decision in a single day. It was declared that Virginia would not

PENNSYLVANIA AVENUE FROM THE TREASURY.

have entered the Union if it had been believed in her convention that the interests of the Southern States were to be sacrificed. Time was demanded for a free and full debate, and that all the facts be gathered concerning the various sites proposed.

The Eastern and Pennsylvania members indignantly denied the charge of conspiracy. They believed the Susquehanna was nearer the centre of population than the Potomac, and that it had a much better climate. One declared that the climate of the Potomac region "was very unhealthy and exceedingly destructive to northern constitutions." A motion to substitute the Potomac for the Susquehanna was voted down, and then a resolution for the appointment of commissioners to report the most eligible site on the Susquehanna was adopted by 28 yeas to 21 nays.

Three days were occupied by the Senate in discussing the matter, but no record of the debate has been preserved. At last it was decided not to accept the Susquehanna site, and on September 26, 1789, the Senate passed a bill by 10 to 7 locating the capital on the Delaware river at Germantown, Pennsylvania. The bill was sent to the House the same day, and, after a rather stormy debate, was agreed to by a vote of 31 to 24.

The House, however, inserted in it a proviso for the continuance of the Pennsylvania laws in force in the district to be ceded to the United States until Congress should otherwise provide, and sent it back to the Senate for concurrence. It was within forty-eight hours of the close of the session, and as there were many important matters to be acted upon, the Senate postponed the further consideration of the bill until the next session.

The second session of the First Congress began January 4, 1790, but both houses were completely engrossed with bills concerning the revenue and public debt, and no mention was made of the capital question until the last day of May. At that time a bill was introduced in the Senate by Pierce Butler, of South Carolina, to locate the permanent seat of the government on the eastern bank of the Potomac. It was referred to a select committee, which afterwards made a favorable report, but the Senate rejected the bill by a vote of 9 to 15. Wilmington and Baltimore were then proposed, but were also rejected by a large majority. No one seemed to care to take up the Germantown bill, and not the slightest reference was made to it.

It was well known that President Washington desired the capital to be located on the Potomac, and that, in fact, it was his pet project, and one for which he had labored zealously for a long time. From early manhood he had noted the wide, undulating plain on which the national capital is now located, its special adaptation to the purposes of a large city, and had even ventured a prediction that one day it would contain a large community. He held the great Arlington estate, on the Virginia side of the river, as guardian for the Custis children, and sitting on its high eastern bank with his sweet wife on many a pleasant summer afternoon enjoying the sweeping view of valley and hill and river, he is said to have conceived and elaborated the idea of having the seat of government located where it is. He had nearly the full support of the Southern members of Congress in this matter, but was unable to secure the necessary aid of the members from the Eastern and Middle States.

Two weeks passed before Congress again took up the momentous question. On the 28th of June, 1790, a bill came before the Senate locating the seat of government "on the river Potomac, at some space between the mouths of the Eastern Branch and Conococheague." The Southern Senators all voted for it, and they were supported by two Senators from Pennsylvania, one from New Jersey, and one from New Hampshire, the vote standing 16 yeas to 9 nays.

The House acted on the bill on the 9th of July, after debating it for three days. A strong effort was made to substitute Baltimore, but when

STATUE OF GENERAL JACKSON IN
LAFAYETTE PARK.

it was found to be of no avail, the
bill as it came from the Senate
was passed by a vote of 32 to 29.
In passing it the Southern members were aided by votes from the
Pennsylvania and New Jersey dele-
gations. The bill provided that
Philadelphia should be the capital
city until 1800, when the seat of government should be located permanently on the banks of the Potomac.

Thomas Jefferson has written what may be considered the "inside"
history of the passage of the bill. It appears that a legislative bargain
was made. At that time there was before Congress Alexander Hamilton's funding bill, which has been designated as a "monument of states-
manship," and which provided for the payment by the general government
of the twenty millions of indebtedness incurred by the various States
during the Revolution. The bill had met with great opposition from the
Southern members, and the House had rejected it. The Eastern States
held a majority of the war claims, and it was feared they would withdraw
from the Union if the government did not assume the indebtedness.

In reference to this Mr. Jefferson says, " I proposed to Hamilton to
dine with me, and I would invite another friend or two and bring them

into conference together, and I thought it impossible that reasonable men consulting together coolly could fail, by some mutual sacrifices of opinion, to form a compromise which was to save the Union.   The discussion took place.   It was finally agreed that, whatever importance had been attached to the rejection of the funding proposition, the preservation of the Union and of concord among the States was more important, and that therefore it would be better that the vote of rejection should be rescinded, to effect which some members should change their votes.   But it was observed that this pill would be peculiarly bitter to the Southern States, and that some concomitant measure should be adopted to sweeten it a little to them.   There had been before propositions to fix the seat of government either at Philadelphia or at Georgetown on the Potomac ; and it was thought by giving it to Philadelphia for ten years, and to Georgetown permanently afterwards, this might act as an anodyne, and calm in some measure the ferment which might be excited by the other measure alone. So two of the Potomac members agreed to change their votes, and Hamilton undertook to carry the other point.   In doing this the influence he had established over the Eastern members effected his side of the engagement, and so the Assumption was passed."

By this sagacious plan, which, it is believed, originated with Jefferson, the funding bill and the bill locating the seat of government, the two measures which had disturbed the harmony of the "infant nation" and had seriously threatened the continuance of the Union of the States, were disposed of satisfactorily.

The following is the "Act for establishing the temporary and permanent seat of the government of the United States," as passed by Congress on the 9th of July, 1790 :

"SECTION 1.—*Be it enacted by the Senate and House of Representatives of the United States of America in Congress assembled*, That a district of territory not exceeding ten miles square, to be located as hereafter directed, on the river Potomac, at some space between the mouths of the Eastern Branch and Conococheague, be, and the same is hereby accepted for the permanent seat of the government of the United States : *Provided, nevertheless*, that the operation of the laws of the State within such district shall not be affected by this acceptance until the time fixed for the removal of the government thereto, and until Congress shall otherwise by law provide.

"SECTION 2.—*And be it further enacted*, That the President of the United States be authorized to appoint, and, by supplying vacancies happening from refusals to act or other causes, to keep in appointment as

STATUE OF GENERAL MCPHERSON.

long as may be necessary, three commissioners, who, or any two of whom, shall, under the direction of the President, survey, and by proper metes and bounds define and limit a district of territory under the limitations above mentioned ; and the district so defined, limited and located shall be deemed the district accepted by this act for the permanent seat of the government of the United States.

"SECTION 3.—*And be it enacted*, That the said commissioners, or any two of them, shall have power to purchase or accept such quantity of land on the eastern side of the said river within the said district as the President shall deem proper for the use of the United States, and according to such plans as the President shall approve said commissioners, or any two of them, shall prior to the first Monday in December, in the year one thousand eight hundred, provide suitable buildings for the accommodation of Congress, and of the President, and for the public offices of the government of the United States.

"SECTION 4.—*And be it enacted*, That for defraying the expense of such purchases and buildings, the President of the United States be authorized and requested to accept grants of money.

"SECTION 5.—*And be it enacted*, That prior to the first Monday in December next, all offices attached to the seat of government of the United States shall be removed to, and until the first Monday in December, in the year one thousand eight hundred, shall remain at the city of Philadelphia, in the State of Pennsylvania, at which place the session of Congress next ensuing the present shall be held.

"SECTION 6.—*And be it enacted*, That on the said first Monday in December, in the year one thousand eight hundred, the seat of the government of the United States shall by virtue of this act be transferred to the district and place aforesaid, and all offices attached to the said seat of government shall accordingly be removed thereto by their respective holders, and shall, after the said day, cease to be exercised elsewhere ; and that the necessary expense of such removal shall be defrayed out of the duties on impost and tonnage, of which a sufficient sum is hereby appropriated.

"July 16, 1790.   (Approved.)

"GEORGE WASHINGTON,

" *President of the United States.*"

CENTRAL QUARTER OF THE CITY OF WASHINGTON.

CHAPTER II.

EARLY HISTORY OF THE DISTRICT OF COLUMBIA—THE FIRST EXPLORERS AND SET-
TLERS—ANCIENT TOWNS OF ALEXANDRIA AND GEORGETOWN—THE OLD CHRIST
CHURCH—GEORGETOWN COLLEGE—THE BOUNDS OF THE DISTRICT AS PROCLAIMED
BY WASHINGTON—L'ENFANT'S DESIGN OF THE NATIONAL CAPITAL—THE CAREER
OF THE UNFORTUNATE FRENCH ENGINEER.

HE region now known as the District of Columbia, or the
Federal Territory, was partially explored by Captain John
Smith in 1608. He was the first white man to sail up the
"Patawomeke," as he calls it in his letters, and he found its
waters full of luscious fish and its shores inhabited by savage tribes.
Fifteen years later, in search of furs, Henry Fleet, the doughty English
trader, followed nearly in the course described by Captain Smith, and
made himself, and afterwards the world by means of graphic letters,
familiar with what he enthusiastically termed "the most healthful and
pleasantest region in all this country." Fleet was a capable writer as well
as an enterprising fur-trader and explorer, and he wrote interesting descriptions of the "fair and fertile lands" traversed by him in Maryland and
Virginia. He went fearlessly among the ferocious Indians, and once was
held a captive by them. Some forty years after he had made the Potomac
country well known in England, a party of emigrants, mostly from Scotland and Ireland, settled in that portion of Maryland now included in the
District of Columbia. They found a productive soil and genial climate,
and their farms were bordered by a river on which snow-white swans
gracefully floated. Documents relating to three tracts of land, all lying
within the boundary of the city of Washington, have come down to the
present time from these early occupants of the district. One, bearing
date of June 5, 1663, describes by metes and bounds what is now Capitol
Hill. The tract was owned and occupied by Francis Pope, and he called
it Room or Rome. The small, sluggish stream flowing at the western
base of the hill was named by him the Tiber river. Another of the
documents is dated June 5, 1663, and refers to a tract laid out for Captain
Robert Troop, and designated as "Scotland Yard." This is believed to

be the land now constituting the southeastern part of Washington. The third document has the date of 1681, and describes a tract possessed by William Lang, and known as the "Widow's Mite," which it is believed was in the western part of the city. Of these settlers scarcely anything is known. For a hundred years they and their descendants lived doubtless in peace and comfort "far from the busy haunts of men," little dreaming that on their fields would eventually stand the fair capital city of the great American republic.

In 1748 the town of Bellhaven was founded on the Virginia side of the Potomac, five miles below what is now the city of Washington. A few years afterwards its name was changed to Alexandria. This ancient town had a promising early career. It rapidly became an important port and developed an extensive foreign trade. It was well known in the great English commercial cities. General Washington, Governor Lee, and other prominent Virginians interested themselves in its development, and at one time it was thought it would become a greater city than Baltimore. Warehouses crowded with tobacco and flour and corn lined its docks, and fleets of merchant vessels filled its harbor. Its claims were strongly advanced as a suitable place for the location of the permanent seat of the national government. On November 21, 1792, the publication was begun of a semi-weekly newspaper named the *Columbian Mirror and Alexandria Gazette*, and this journal for a number of years was the only one published in this section of the country. It was taken by all the opulent families, and was read regularly by Washington. Recently, in making repairs at the Mount Vernon mansion, a copy of this paper of the year 1799 was discovered in a niche in the roof.

Alexandria is now a city of fifteen thousand people,—a dull, uninter-

ALEXANDRIA FROM THE POTOMAC.

cating place, all its ancient glory having departed. Like many other promising cities in the early years of the nation, it has simply advanced in population but has retrograded in commercial importance. From 1791 to 1846 it was a part of the District of Columbia, but in the latter year Congress retroceded it, with all the lands of the district on the western bank of the Potomac, to the State of Virginia.

The old Christ Episcopal Church in Alexandria is a special object of interest. It was constructed of English bricks, and dedicated in 1765. Here Washington worshipped for many years, and he was a member of its vestry. A writer says, " The good people and gentry of the vicinage were wont to loiter about the church door each Sunday morning until Washington's equipage appeared. When he and his stately wife descended from their capacious carriage, very like a modern stage-coach, honest, modest farmers stood abashed, with uncovered heads, while the greatest man of any age or country was formally greeted by the ' nobility' of the district. Washington and his household led the way, and then the throng entered the sanctuary, in which the services of the Church of England were most reverently celebrated."

Washington's family pew in the venerable church is preserved. It has a high back and three seats, two of which face each other, and the third is against the wall. Washington always occupied the wall seat, and it is stated that it was his custom to "sit bolt upright and face the congregation instead of the pastor."

By act of the Maryland legislature, in 1751, the laying out of the town of Georgetown on the Potomac, above the mouth of Rock creek, was authorized, but the town was not incorporated until thirty-eight years later. Many suppose it derives its name from George II., as it came into existence during his reign ; but others aver that it was named after George, the son of Ninian Beall, who originally held patents for the land on the " Rock of Dumbarton," upon which a considerable portion of Georgetown is built. It was known as the "town of George" many years before it was incorporated. At present it is called West Washington, as it is a part of the capital city. On its steep heights are numerous fine mansions and various institutions. Formerly great ships from every quarter of the globe sailed into its harbor and its foreign commerce was extensive, but now in place of this are large shipments of coal, grain, and flour to domestic ports. It was in Georgetown that the plans and arrangements for the laying out of the city of Washington were made, and the ancient borough may be called the godmother of the capital.

The Georgetown College is an important institution. Its history goes back to the past century. Founded by Bishop John Carroll in 1789,

OLD CHRIST CHURCH IN ALEXANDRIA—WASHINGTON'S PEW.

made a university in 1815, it has advanced steadily, until at present it is the largest and most prominent Catholic institution of learning in the United States. It is under the control of the Jesuits, and its students are mainly from the Southern States. Besides its collegiate departments it has schools of law and medicine. The college buildings are situated on the brow of a hill overlooking the Potomac, and the grounds cover more than one hundred acres.

On January 24, 1791, six months after Congress had passed the act locating the permanent seat of government, President Washington issued a proclamation defining the territory he had selected. By his request Congress amended the act, March 3, 1791, so as to include a section of country below Alexandria, and on March 30 the President issued an amendatory proclamation, in which the Federal Territory was described as follows:

"Beginning at Jones' Point, being the upper cape of Hunting creek in Virginia, and at an angle of 45 degrees west of the north, and running in a direct line ten miles for the first line; then beginning again at the same Jones' Point and running another direct line at a right angle with the first; then from the terminations of the said first and second line, running two other direct lines of ten miles each, the one crossing the Eastern Branch and the other the Potomac, and meeting each other in a point."

The President proclaimed that "the territory so to be located, defined, and limited shall be the whole territory accepted by the said act of Congress as the district for the permanent seat of the government of the United States." It was ten miles square, or one hundred square miles, and contained 64,000 acres. It included one county in Maryland and one in Virginia, with the Potomac flowing between. Georgetown to the north and Alexandria to the south were in the district.

Three commissioners were appointed to run the lines and survey and lay out the new Federal Territory. They were General Thomas Johnson and Hon. Daniel Carroll, of Maryland, and Dr. David Stuart, of Virginia. General Johnson had served with Washington all through the Revolutionary war, and had proved a gallant soldier and trusty intimate. Rather brusque and impetuous and given often to "strange oaths," he was, nevertheless, of an exceedingly kind disposition, and an earnest, faithful worker. Washington counted him among his most devoted friends, and sometimes declared he believed "the General" would go "through fire and water" to serve him. Daniel Carroll was a young man not thirty years of age. He was one of the distinguished and numerous Carroll family of Maryland, and a good deal of an aristocrat, holding a large estate and giving grand entertainments at his manor-house. He was a member of Congress, and had given hearty support to the bill locating the capital on the Potomac. Dr. Stuart practised medicine in Alexandria, and was the leading physician in that section of Virginia. He had married the widow of Major John Parke Custis, the son of Martha Washington by her first husband, and was Washington's family physician. He was a benevolent elderly gentleman, and a great admirer of the classic poets, constantly interlarding his conversation with quotations from them.

These three men entered upon their duty at once, and on April 15, 1791, they laid the first boundary stone of the district at Jones' Point, in Virginia, after the Masonic form. An Alexandria lodge of Masons con-

GEORGETOWN, SHOWING THE AQUEDUCT BRIDGE.

ducted the ceremony, which was witnessed by several thousand people from all the country round. The commissioners named the district the " Territory of Columbia," and it retained this name for a number of years ; and the " Federal City" to be founded they decided should be known as " The City of Washington."

The plan of the city was drawn by Major Pierre Charles L'Enfant, a French engineer, who had come to the United States from Paris in 1777, and had served during the Revolutionary war in the French contingent under the Count D'Estaing. When the French troops departed from the country L'Enfant remained, and became a major of engineers in the Federal army. He had charge of the reconstruction of the old City Hall in New York when it was prepared as a " Federal House" for the First Congress, and had also arranged the building in Philadelphia occupied for the same purpose. He had constructed for Robert Morris, the wealthy merchant and statesman of Philadelphia, a mansion having the first mansard roof ever seen in America, and had also designed and attended to the manufacture of the gold badge of the Society of the Cincinnati. In the latter part of 1790 he was commissioned by President Washington to prepare the plan of the new government city, and in March, 1791, Secretary of State Jefferson wrote to him " to proceed to Georgetown, where you will find Mr. Ellicott employed in making a survey and map of the Federal Territory." When L'Enfant arrived in the district, he " viewed the ground on horseback" in company with the President and commissioners, and immediately set to work to perfect his plan, which he had begun some months before.

3

In those days there was in Georgetown a famous tavern known as Suter's, to which the wealthy planters of the neighboring country resorted for entertainment. It was a long, low wooden building with a slanting roof and wide porch, and was kept by a Scotchman named John Suter. As he was an honest, jovial host, and always provided a bountiful table, his tavern was a favorite resort. Here, day after day for several weeks, Washington, L'Enfant, and the commissioners met to confer about the plan of the capital city, and here also they met the proprietors of the land, and arranged with them for its transfer to the government. Washington generally rode from Mount Vernon to Suter's on a spirited horse, which would come galloping up the Alexandria turnpike at a very rapid pace to the ferry from the Virginia shore to Georgetown. When the details of L'Enfant's plan had been arranged he made a finished drawing of it, and it was approved by the President, and formally adopted by the commissioners. L'Enfant was appointed to superintend the execution of the plan, and he selected a corps of assistants, among whom was Andrew Ellicott, a young Pennsylvanian of marked ability as a surveyor. Ellicott afterwards received the title of " Geographer General."

In the office of the Architect of the Capitol is a torn and dingy paper, yellow and faded with age. Some of its lines of ink have entirely disappeared, and others are almost invisible. One can see, however, that it was once an elaborate, elegantly finished design drawn with great skill. It is the original plan of the city of Washington made by L'Enfant's own hand, and his writing upon it is as fine and perfect as copper-plate. The government never published the plan, as L'Enfant carefully kept it until his death, but instead had engraved and widely circulated a plan made by Ellicott in 1792. The Ellicott plan was drawn by him from sketches

he had made of L'Enfant's plan and from information he had obtained while surveying the city under L'Enfant's direction. It differs from the original plan only in what may be called minor details.

Why the government adopted the Ellicott plan can thus be told: When L'Enfant began his work of laying out the city he felt the importance of his position and believed he had the entire control of affairs. He arranged a certain system of construction, and would not permit any one to deviate from it. The city was first thoroughly surveyed and all the lines established in an accurate manner.

PIERRE CHARLES L'ENFANT.

SUTER'S TAVERN IN 1791.

No one was allowed to build until the survey was completed. The government reservations were all indicated, the public buildings located, the streets and avenues marked out, and the whole city was divided into squares as nearly as possible of equal size. L'Enfant had trouble at once with the landholders, who did not like the precise system he had adopted in regard to the streets and buildings. He also became involved in quarrels with the commissioners, who resented his dictatorial manner and assumption of authority. They tried to check and control him, countermanded his orders, and called him erratic and insubordinate. One of them even began the erection of a house directly across an avenue, cutting it in two and spoiling it. L'Enfant pulled down the house, and this arbitrary act added fuel to the flame of disfavor in which he was held. At last the commissioners demanded that he should submit his plan of the city to them, in order that it might be engraved and published for the benefit of those intending to buy lots at the government sales. L'Enfant refused to do this, and defended his action by asserting that if his plan was published speculators would purchase the best land in his "vistas and architectural squares and raise huddles of shanties which would permanently disfigure the city." In consequence of this refusal the President dismissed him from the public service March 1, 1792, and Ellicott was directed "to go on and finish the laying off the plan on the ground and the surveying and platting the district." Ellicott was also directed "to prepare a plan for publication, using the materials gathered and the information acquired while acting as surveyor." This plan was engraved in the summer of 1792 by Thackara & Vallance in Philadelphia, and circulated by the government all over the United States and in England and France. Some time before his dismissal L'Enfant had marked out the streets and avenues in the greater part of the city, and had indicated where the Capitol, the

L'ENFANT'S GRAVE

President's House, and the other public buildings were to stand, so that it was really very little labor for Ellicott to make a plan in close imitation of L'Enfant's.

On the 6th of March, 1792, Secretary of State Jefferson wrote to the commissioners in regard to L'Enfant's dismissal, and said, "It is now proper that he should receive the reward of his past services, and that he should have no just cause of discontent, I suggest that it should be liberal. The President thinks $2500 or $3000, but leaves the determination to you." Eight days afterwards the commissioner sent a letter to L'Enfant informing him that they had ordered five hundred guineas to be paid to him by a banking firm, and had also recorded a lot in the city in his name as compensation for his services. L'Enfant replied as follows: "Without inquiring the principle upon which you suggest this offer, I shall only here testify my surprise thereupon, and in testimony of my intention to decline accepting of it I hasten expressing to you my wish and request that you will call back your order for the money and not take any further trouble about the lot."

So, refusing to receive any compensation, the designer of the national capital, at the age of thirty-seven, retired from "the work of beauty which was to him a work of love," a mortified, disappointed man. And for twenty years there is but little definite record of him. Alexander Hamilton occasionally wrote to him, and President Madison once sent him a commission as professor of engineering at West Point, but the commission was returned inscribed, "Not accepted, but not refused." During the war of 1812, L'Enfant was chosen by James Monroe, then Secretary of War, to construct what is now known as Fort Washington, on the Potomac. He planned the work and carried it on for a time, but failing to agree with the War Department on some details of construction, he was dismissed.

After this L'Enfant spent the remainder of his life at the manor-houses of the Digges family in Maryland, a pensioner on their bounty. About six months before he died he resided with Dudley Digges on the Chellum Castle estate near Bladensburg, and about five miles from Washington. Here, on the 4th of June, 1824, he died in the seventieth year of his age, and was buried in the garden of the estate, but no stone was placed above his grave. And to-day the last resting-place of this unfortunate man of genius is marked only by a tall cedar-tree inclining over a bank covered with myrtle.

L'Enfant in his latter years was occasionally seen in the streets of the city he had designed, and is remembered as a man of medium height, with a bright, intellectual face and courteous manner. He usually wore a blue frock-coat of antique fashion and a bell-crowned hat. Time has fully established the great merit of his plan, and it is a recognized fact that by means of it Washington has been able to develop into a beautiful metropolis.

GEORGETOWN COLLEGE

CHAPTER III.

THE ORIGINAL LANDHOLDERS OF WASHINGTON—THEIR AGREEMENT WITH THE GOVERNMENT—DAVID BURNS AND HIS DAUGHTER—GENERAL VAN NESS—THE LANDS OF NOTLEY YOUNG, GEORGE WALKER, AND SAMUEL DAVIDSON—DUDDINGTON MANOR—DANIEL CARROLL'S DREAM OF WEALTH—SPECULATIONS IN CITY LOTS—ERECTING THE PUBLIC BUILDINGS—WASHINGTON IN 1800, WHEN THE GOVERNMENT TOOK POSSESSION.

T is not difficult to conceive of the embarrassment under which President Washington and the commissioners labored in dealing with the proprietors of the land lying within the bounds of the Federal City, and one can readily believe that the President must have frequently gone to his Virginia home after a day's conflict with these rapacious persons thoroughly disgusted with their narrow-mindedness and entire lack of public spirit. The records very clearly show that, with one or two exceptions, they were a grasping set, bent only on their own personal advantage, and that every concession to the public good had to be drawn from them by "main strength." They were mostly small planters who had inherited their lands from the first settlers of the district, and whose lives had been exceedingly common and obscure until the location of the capital had brought them into notice. Their lands were of no special value, and before the coming of the government among them could probably have been purchased for a small sum; but as soon as they ascertained that the splendid prize so eagerly contended for by the prominent cities was within their grasp they became inflamed with a raging fever for wealth and aggrandizement, and this fever constantly increasing by the oft-repeated stories that the national city was likely in a short time to exceed New York in population and importance, consumed all their generous feelings and left them sordid and difficult to deal with. For weeks there was a conflict over the lands, and almost daily Suter's tavern was the scene of bitter contentions between the commissioners and land-owners, which even the presence of Washington did not abate. David Burns, a vulgar old Scotchman, who was one of the largest owners, took occasion one day to insult the President by saying, in reply to one of his arguments in favor of the proposed transfer of the lands to the government, "I suppose, Mr. Washington, you think people are going to take every grist from you as pure grain; but what would you have been if you hadn't married the rich widow Custis?" History fails to record Washington's reception of this piece of impertinence, but it is recorded that he would never have anything further to do with "that obstinate Mr. Burns," as he designated the audacious planter.

Finally, after a great deal of toil and trouble, the principal proprietors of the lands signed the following agreement, and it was recorded by the commissioners, April 12, 1791:

"We, the subscribers, in consideration of the great benefits we expect to derive from having the Federal City laid off upon our lands, do hereby agree and bind ourselves, heirs, executors, and administrators, to convey in trust, to the President of the United States, or commissioners, or such person or persons as he shall appoint, by good and sufficient deeds, in fee simple, the whole of our respective lands which he may think proper to include within the lines of the Federal City, for the purposes and on the conditions following:

"The President shall have the sole power of directing the Federal City to be laid off in what manner he pleases.

"He may retain any number of squares he may think proper for public improvements or other public uses; and the lots only, which shall be laid off, shall be a joint property between the trustees on behalf of the public and each present proprietor; and the same shall be fairly and equally divided between the public and the individuals, as soon as may be, the city shall be laid off.

"For the streets the proprietors shall receive no compensation, but for the squares or lands in any form which shall be taken for public buildings, or any kind of public improvements or uses, the proprietors, whose lands shall be taken, shall receive at the rate of 25 pounds per acre (sixty-six and two-thirds dollars), to be paid by the public."

Thomas Beall and John Mackall Gantt were named by the President as trustees under the agreement, and the lands were conveyed to them. In effect the proprietors agreed to give the government all the lands required for the highways, and to sell the lands selected for public buildings and reservations for twenty-five pounds (Maryland money) per acre. One-half of the amount realized at the government sales of lots was also to be paid to them. Certain of their lands, after the city had been laid out and the public reservations established, were conveyed back to them.

Twenty years before the capital was located in this district two attempts had been made to found hamlets on the eastern bank of the

DAVID BURNS' CABIN AND THE VAN NESS MANSION.

Potomac, a short distance south of Georgetown. Jacob Funk, a German farmer, in 1770, had laid out a tract he possessed near where the Naval Observatory now stands, but had succeeded in getting only a few people to settle on his land. The hamlet was called Funkstown at first, and afterwards Hamburg, but it was little more than a Southern " four corners," and its inhabitants were retired sailors and farmers. About two miles below Hamburg, beginning at what is now Greenleaf's Point, and extending along the Anacostia or Eastern Branch of the Potomac, Charles Carroll, the father of Daniel Carroll, had started a settlement. He had surveyed and platted one hundred and sixty acres of land pleasantly situated on the river-bank, but as far as can be ascertained, had been unable to induce more than a half-dozen families to reside in what he had named Carrollsburg. These small settlements were embraced in the area selected for the capital of the nation, but they were not encumbrances to its location.

There were nineteen prominent land-owners in the district when it was taken by the government and a considerable number of small owners, but nothing of consequence can be learned of any of them except David

Burns, Daniel Carroll, Notley Young, George Walker, Samuel Davidson, and two or three others, and only scanty records of these men have survived the passage of time. The houses of Burns and Carroll are standing, and are about the only memorials remaining of that by-gone age. Burns from all accounts was a coarse, illiterate planter of a surly disposition, and hard, obstinate, and selfish in his dealings with his fellows. His plantation comprised the land extending from the Potomac near the present site of the Washington Monument to what is now New York avenue, and covered the square on which the White House and Treasury are located, and when his broad acres were platted into "city lots" he became a very rich man. His elevation to wealth did not cause him to change his manner of living, and until his death, in 1799, he continued to occupy the mean little cabin on the edge of the river where he had lived all his life. Burns was fond of fiery potations, and it has been said that the only change seen in him after he had plenty of money was that "he took his bottle to Georgetown oftener."

He had a daughter, Marcia, a lively, beautiful girl, with frank, engaging manners. She received a good education in Baltimore, and was said to have been the only person who could induce "Crusty Davie" to yield a particle when he had made up his mind about anything. She was born in 1782, and was an only child. All the Burns' estate came into her possession when she had reached her majority, and she was looked upon as a great matrimonial prize, suitors from far and near seeking her favor. She found a husband to her liking in the person of General John P. Van Ness, the son of Peter Van Ness, a Hollander and well-to-do farmer of Kinderhook, New York. General Van Ness was a member of Congress when he married Marcia Burns in 1802, but a year later he was expelled from the House of Representatives because he had accepted the commission of general of the militia of the District of Columbia which had been tendered him by President Jefferson. He became a resident of the district and continued so during his long life, taking a leading part in its business, political, and social affairs, and doing a great deal to advance its prosperity. He was mayor of Washington in 1830, and held other offices of trust and honor.

MARCIA BURNS VAN NESS.

Van Ness was a dashing, brilliant, free-

DUDDINGTON MANOR-HOUSE.

hearted man, could sing well and tell a
good story, and was a favorite in society.
He built a fine mansion on the grounds
where Burns' cabin was and within a few feet of it, and gave grand entertainments, which were the social sensations of the day. Latrobe, the
famous architect, constructed the mansion at a cost of $35,000, and laid
out the grounds after the English style of landscape gardening. Presidents and statesmen and eminent foreigners were entertained, and the
proceeds of many a city lot vanished in high living. Mrs. Van Ness
was a fascinating woman, with a heart full of love and kindness for all
creatures. She would never allow the old cabin in which her father had
lived to be removed, and was so little ashamed of it and her humble
origin that she would frequently invite her distinguished guests to inspect
its low, narrow rooms. In 1815 she founded the Washington Orphan
Asylum, which has been successfully continued to this day. She died in

1832, but her husband survived her fourteen years, dying at the age of seventy-nine. As there was no direct issue, what was left of the Burns' estate passed to collateral heirs.

Another of the land-owners who acquired wealth was Notley Young, a retired English sea-captain, whose estate comprised much of the river front below Long Bridge and extended to the centre of the city. He leased a large part of his land on good terms, and had a fine revenue from the leases. He lived in a spacious brick mansion situated in the southern quarter of Washington, on an elevation near the river, and around the mansion for a long distance was a beautiful lawn filled with beds of flowers and trees with expansive foliage. After his death his heirs transferred the building to the government, and it was demolished in order to extend a street.

George Walker and Samuel Davidson were Scotchmen; and one was a farmer and the other a merchant at Georgetown. Walker's farm comprised about four hundred acres in the northeast quarter of the city, and some of it was sold at large prices at first. He erected a fine residence, married the daughter of Daniel Craufurd, a wealthy planter of Prince George's County, Maryland, and began to live in luxury. He believed he could become a millionaire by land speculations, so he mortgaged his farm and purchased other lands at fancy prices; but his lovely young wife died; he became involved in lawsuits with the commissioners, his speculations proved disastrous, and he was stripped of the greater part of his property. Mourning over blighted hopes and affections he returned to Scotland, where he soon after died.

Davidson closely attended to his little shop at Georgetown and escaped the fever of speculation prevailing at the time. His lands ranged over what is now the fashionable West End, at that time, and even for seventy years afterwards, a dreary, valueless region of marshes and hillocks. He owned the land on which Lafayette Park is situated, and had a fierce and prolonged contest with the commissioners when they determined to reserve it for a park. He desired to have it platted and sold for building lots, well knowing that its location, opposite the front of the President's House, would enable him to realize a large amount of money. But the commissioners were inexorable, and fortunately saved this attractive spot for public use. Davidson died in 1810, and his heir straightway traded the West End property for land in another section which was never worth the taxes upon it.

The most prominent and also the most unfortunate of all the original land-owners was Daniel Carroll, of Duddington Manor, and his career is a remarkable exemplification of the truth of the French saying, " The un-

COMMODORE DECATUR'S HOUSE AND TOMB.

expected always happens." Carroll expected to accumulate millions: he died almost a pauper. He had the largest estate of any of the land-owners, and plenty of ready money to begin operations with when the city sprang into being, and was an educated, capable man with strong social and political influence. He had labored and schemed to have the seat of government fixed on the Potomac, and, as a member of the First Congress, made great efforts and used all his family influence to accomplish this result. He was one of the first commissioners, and therefore in a position to impel the affairs of the city towards his own interests. He was able to have the southeastern quarter of Washington, where his lands were situated, made for a time the principal quarter, and also able to locate the Capitol on the brow of a hill which he owned. None of the other original proprietors started in the race for wealth so thoroughly equipped, and none made such a calamitous finish. David Burns, who is said to have been greatly exasperated because the government came to disturb his peace and destroy his farm, and who was the longest to hold out against the transfer of the lands, died very wealthy. Notley Young, Samuel Davidson, and George Walker were raised from limited means to affluence, and the other proprietors, or their heirs, reaped a golden harvest. But Daniel Carroll, the statesman and polished gentleman, and the land-owner who had the greatest expectations, was completely distanced in the race by illiterate farmers and fishermen, who had never made an effort to secure the location of the capital on their lands.

At first Carroll's prospects were bright. He sold a portion of his estate to speculators for a round sum, partly in promissory notes, which were mostly repudiated afterwards, and erected a great brick mansion which he called " Duddington," and furnished it in a style of magnificence unusual in those days. A sanguine speculator offered him half a million dollars for the remainder of his property, but he laughed at the offer and named ten times that amount as the price. The hamlet of Carrollsburg, which his father had founded, and the spacious fields he had planted with corn and wheat, Daniel platted into narrow lots, affixed high prices to them, and confidently waited the coming of a throng of purchasers. Not content with his own estate, ample as it was, he made speculative investments in other city property, gave notes and mortgages, and assumed heavy obligations. And then he was too willing to "help a lame dog over a stile." He was too good-natured, and could seldom say no when embarrassed speculators asked him to endorse their notes or become responsible for them. He was but a young man when all this land fever was raging,—a rather conceited, showy youth, but with a good brain and kind heart,—too kind, indeed, to be a match for the host of sharpers who had come from the great cities to the new capital seeking whom they might devour. Carroll was ambitious to be an aristocrat after the manner of other members of the prolific Maryland family, and he gave splendid dinners and balls at Duddington, and with his wife went full tilt into the fashionable lists. They wasted a great deal of money in entertaining dignitaries and leaders of society, and he lived to see the time when the sum he had often carelessly expended for a single entertainment would have saved him from severe distress.

The high prices for Carroll's lots on Capitol Hill kept purchasers away. Those who wanted land for actual settlement and not for speculation went into the northwestern section of the city, and made their purchases of Burns and Young and others for less money, set up their homes and stores, and so, after a while, this section became the centre and popular part of Washington. Carroll's lots remained on his hands. His taxes were high, and the interest on his obligations was an enormous burden. He struggled manfully month after month to stem the current which was flowing perilously against him. He transferred his manor-house and the square of four acres on which it was situated, to a relative in order to save a shelter for his family, and after a desperate effort to retrieve his fortune was forced to relax his hold of the great estate, and it passed into other hands.

Carroll lived until 1849, the last survivor of the original proprietors of Washington, long life being granted to him even if riches were denied. Latrobe built the " Duddington House" in 1792, and it is now standing in good condition. The father of Carroll was a relative of Charles Carroll of Carrollton, and Bishop John Carroll, who founded the Georgetown College, was Daniel's brother.

Many other men besides Carroll were ruined in the land speculations in the early years of the city, and among the prominent ones were James Greenleaf, Samuel Blodget, Thomas Law, and James Lingan. And it is not strange that men were ruined, for everybody predicted that this new government metropolis would be a great and splendid place in a very short time ; that it would have at least 150,000 people in ten years, and probably half a million before a third of the nineteenth century had rolled away. No prediction was too extravagant for belief ; no story of future greatness too romantic to be listened to. Even the sober, sagacious Father of his Country was affected by the enthusiasm that prevailed, and wrote glowing predictions that have not been fulfilled. Men who owned land, or could buy it no matter at what price, were considered sure to be wealthy, and those who would not invest in the swamps, hills, and gulleys which then constituted the principal part of the city, were looked upon as very stupid persons. At the government sales of lots, which began October 17, 1791, and continued at short intervals for a number of months, there were crowds of speculators from different sections of the United States, and large prices were obtained.

THE PRESIDENT'S HOUSE IN 1800.

STATUE OF GENERAL NATHANIEL GREENE.

When the government had secured a considerable sum of money from the sales, the erection of the public buildings was begun. The city had to be ready for the use of Congress and the government officials in 1800, and there was much to be done in a few years. On the 13th of October, 1792, the corner-stone of the President's House was laid, and on the 18th of September, 1793, that of the Capitol. The construction of these important buildings was carried forward as rapidly as possible, but there were delays at various times on account of a lack of funds. Congress made little effort to aid the President in the building operations, and had it not been for the gifts and loans made by the States of Maryland and Virginia, the work would doubtless have been indefinitely suspended. Hardly anything was done to make the city attractive, and when the government took possession of it there was nothing to indicate in the

" dismal wilderness" that Washington then was that it was ever likely to
be "a city of unparalleled magnificence," as had been enthusiastically
predicted.

No better description of Washington as it appeared in 1800 can be
given than that written by John Cotton Smith, at that time a member
of Congress from Connecticut. He wrote: " Our approach to the city
was accompanied with sensations not easily described. One wing of
the Capitol only had been erected, which, with the President's House,
a mile distant from it, both constructed with white sandstone, were
shining objects in dismal contrast with the scene around them. Instead
of recognizing the avenues and streets portrayed on the plan of the city,
not one was visible, unless we except a road, with two buildings on each
side of it, called the New Jersey avenue. The Pennsylvania avenue,
leading, as laid down on paper, from the Capitol to the Presidential
mansion, was nearly the whole distance a deep morass covered with
elder bushes, which were cut through to the President's House; and
near Georgetown a block of houses had been erected which bore the
name of the ' six buildings.' There were also two other blocks consisting of two or three dwelling-houses in different directions, and now
and then an insulated wooden habitation; the intervening spaces, and,
indeed, the surface of the city generally, being covered with scrub-oak
bushes on the higher grounds, and on the marshy soil either trees or
some sort of shrubbery. The desolate aspect of the place was not a
little augmented by a number of unfinished edifices at Greenleaf's
Point, and on an eminence a short distance from it, commenced by an
individual whose name they bore, but the state of whose funds compelled him to abandon them. There appeared to be but two really
comfortable habitations in all respects within the bounds of the city,
one of which belonged to Daniel Carroll and the other to Notley Young.
The roads in every direction were muddy and unimproved. In short, it
was a new settlement."

NORTHWEST QUARTER OF THE CITY OF WASHINGTON.

CHAPTER IV.

URING the month of October, 1800, the government took possession of Washington. The arrival of the officials created a great excitement among the three thousand inhabitants, many of whom had been inclined to credit a current report that the government would never leave Philadelphia, where it had been pleasantly located for ten years. When the little "packet-sloop," bringing the records and furniture of the departments, and some of the officials, was seen slowly sailing up the Potomac, most of the people of the city gathered on the river-bank and gave the vessel a hearty welcome. On the following day the chief officials arrived by stages from Baltimore, and within a short time the government was settled in its permanent home. John Adams was President; John Marshall, Secretary of State; Oliver Wolcott, Secretary of the Treasury; Samuel Dexter, Secretary of War; and Benjamin Stoddert, Secretary of the Navy. The President's House was in good condition for occupancy, and the small buildings erected for the executive departments were nearly finished. One wing of the Capitol was done and ready for Congress, which began its session in November.

The "wilderness city," as Mrs. Adams called Washington, proved to be a very lonesome place to the officials after their agreeable life in Philadelphia, and they gave free vent to their feelings of disgust in letters which were printed in the newspapers of the prominent cities. Nearly all had something to say in derision of "Washington's city on the Potomac." It was called "a city of magnificent distances" set in "a mud-hole almost equal to the great Serbonian bog." It was said to be "a capital of miserable huts," and "a city of streets without houses," and that it did not possess "one solitary attractive feature." Those who had opposed its location were merry over "its exceedingly mean and disgusting appear-

51

THE "GREAT HOTEL" IN 1793.

ance," apparently forgetting that Congress had given scant aid to the
commissioners in the work of construction, and had left them to depend
for money almost entirely on chance gifts and the proceeds of the land
sales. When one reads the record of the vexatious delays in erecting the
public buildings and improving the highways for lack of means, of the
quarrels among those in authority, of the jealousy and opposition constantly displayed, the wonder is not that the capital city was a mean,
dismal place in 1800 and only fitted to be the laughing-stock of the
country, but that its builders should have been able in the face of the
obstacles they encountered to make it bear the slightest semblance to a
city.

Satire and opposition could not prevent the city from growing. Its
growth was very slow compared to what had been expected, but it was
sure and steady for a number of years. In 1810 it had a population of
8208, and in 1820 a population of 13,474 By this time the extravagant
expectations of its friends had subsided, but the opposition of its enemies
continued without abatement. All through its early years it was obliged
to meet the sneers of Congress, the sarcasm of Northern writers, and the
general indifference of the American people, who never seemed to care
what manner of city it became.

Jonathan Elliot, who wrote more than fifty years ago the first really
good account of the city, says in his little book, " President Jefferson did
much to further the prosperity of the city by procuring grants of money
for carrying on the public buildings; he also gave encouragement to all
the improvements brought forward during his administration. He caused
Pennsylvania avenue to be opened and planted with trees. President
Madison was also friendly to the city, but owing to restrictions on commerce and the subsequent war during his administration little progress
was made in the public works. But it was in the administration of
President Monroe that the most extensive and valuable improvements

were made in every part of the city, and the public money expended on the national works with the greatest liberality."

Mr. Elliot gives also an interesting statement of the receipts and expenditures of the government on account of the city up to 1820, in order, as he says, " to correct a prevailing error that the city has been and continues to be a burden to the United States." He gives the receipts as follows : " From lots sold by the United States, $700,000; donations from the States of Maryland and Virginia, $192,000; value of 5150 building lots averaging 5000 feet each, at 6¼ cents per foot, $1,509,375 ; five hundred and forty-one acres of reserved grounds, distributed in such manner as to give the government possession of the most beautiful parts of the city, estimated at 10 cents per foot, $2,356,596; free-stone quarry, wharves, and water lots, $40,000; total, $4,898,971." The expenditures for the public buildings, etc., are given at $1,214,286, which would leave a large balance in favor of the city.

Congress assumed the jurisdiction of the District of Columbia in 1801. On May 3, 1802, an act of incorporation was granted to the city of Washington, which allowed the citizens to elect a city council, but put the appointment of the mayor in the hands of the President. As there was much dissatisfaction with this method of choosing the executive, Congress, in a few years, gave the people the right to elect their mayor. The municipal form of government was continued until 1871, when Congress repealed the city charter and established a territorial government, which remained until 1874, when three commissioners were appointed to have charge of the district. The government by commissioners under the supervision of Congress, which was the original plan adopted, has been continued to the present time.

LONG BRIDGE.

In the first decade of the city the officials of the government numbered only about one hundred persons, and the annual appropriation for the civil service was less than half a million dollars, not enough to pay the daily expenses of the host of people who now perform the government work. The President received a salary of $25,000, and the Vice-President, $5000. The annual cost of Congress was about $150,000, now it costs $3,000,000. The expenses of the Treasury Department were $55,000; of the Department of State, $6300; of the War and Navy Departments, $11,000. There were six justices of the Supreme Court, and the Chief Justice received $4000, and the associates, $3500 each. The pension list only amounted to $6000 a year, now it is $60,000,000. Truly those were the days of small things.

Before the government removed to Washington several hotels were established in the centre of the city, the largest of which was the " Union Pacific Hotel," or, as it was more commonly called, the " Great Hotel." It was erected in 1793 by Samuel Blodget, on the square now occupied by the Post-Office Department, but as he lost all his money in land speculations, he disposed of the great brick building by means of a lottery. It was not entirely finished until the government purchased it, in 1810, for the post-office and patent-office. The Thirteenth Congress held a session in it after the Capitol had been destroyed by the British, and on December 15, 1836, it was burned to the ground, the government losing by the fire all its collections of patent models which had been accumulating for many years.

There was also a " Little Hotel," erected in 1795, which had a good deal of popularity. The most popular hotel, however, was the " Metropolitan Hotel," which stood in the square on Pennsylvania avenue where the present hotel of the same name now stands. In 1820 its name was changed to " Indian Queen Hotel," and for a long time after it bore this name. In front of it was a huge swinging sign with a gaudy picture of Pocahontas. The landlord was named Jesse Brown, and he was known far and near for his ability as a caterer. His prices were low,—" one dollar per day for meals with liquors, and twenty-five cents for lodgings,"—and his table was always bountifully spread. It is stated that " the old bell that rang for meals could be heard over an extensive portion of the city." The hotel was a favorite with Congressmen, and many of the prominent ones boarded there during the first part of the century.

Before the British invasion a newspaper was published called the *National Intelligencer*, and it was continued up to quite a recent date. There was some pleasant social life in the little, struggling city, and a

OLD WAR DEPARTMENT BUILDING.

writer of that period says, "the inhabitants are social and hospitable, and respectable strangers, after the slightest introduction, are invited to dinner, tea, balls, and evening parties." The high officials gave receptions as they do now, and the leading families had "grand balls in the winter at which every species of luxury was exhibited." When the destruction of the city was threatened by the British, in the summer of 1814, there was "a great running to and fro" of its people. Some fled at once with their household goods into Virginia; others brought forth ancient fire-arms and joined the militia companies which were being hastily organized to meet the invaders. The government suspended its business, and officials and clerks enrolled themselves in the ranks of the defenders of the capital.

In a letter written by an army officer in 1814 is the following account of the condition of affairs in Washington a few days previous to its occupation by the British. He says, "I arrived in the city on Sunday, the 21st of August. At that time the officers of the government and the citizens were very apprehensive of an attack from the British, who had landed a force on the Patuxent. It was stated they numbered from 4000 to 16,000. On Sunday the public officers were engaged in packing and sending off their books and the citizens their furniture, and on Monday this was continued, and many families left the city. The specie was removed from all the banks in the district. General Winder, who was in command of the American force, was stationed southeast of the city, at a point called Wood's, with 2000 men, and it was reported he would receive reinforcements of 10,000 in a week. In the expectation that there was a very considerable force collected, President Madison, accompanied by the Secretaries of War and Navy, left the city for the camp. They arrived there late that night, and the next morning, finding but 3000 men had gathered, they returned to the city to make further arrangements. All the books and papers of the government were sent off, and the citizens generally left the place."

The British troops, commanded by General Ross, marched across Maryland to within five miles of Washington. Here, at the little town of Bladensburg, they found their march stopped by a force of about 7000 militia in command of General Winder. After a very brief engagement they dispersed Winder's force, which fled pell-mell in every direction, and then they gave battle to a few hundred sailors with cannon who were holding a hill on the turnpike to Washington. The sailors were commanded by Commodore Joshua Barney, a privateersman, and they did about all the fighting that was done by the Americans. They held their ground for some time, gallantly contesting the advance of the enemy, but at last were overpowered and forced to flee toward the city. Barney was wounded and made a prisoner, but General Ross so admired his bravery that he treated him with great respect.

After a short rest the British took up their march for Washington, and arrived on the eastern grounds of the Capitol early in the evening of August 21. The soldiers fired volleys into the windows of the building, and then marched into the wing used by the House of Representatives. General Ross escorted Admiral Cockburn, of the British naval force, to the Speaker's chair amid laughter and cheers from the officers and men. Cockburn called the assemblage to order, and shouted, " Shall this harbor of Yankee Democracy be burned ? All for it say aye !" A ringing shout went up, and the motion was declared " unanimously carried." Again and again the soldiers cried, " Fire the building !" " Fire the building !" and after consultation with his officers General Ross gave the order. A search was made for combustible material, and soon all the books and pictures in the Congressional Library were piled in heaps on the floor of the Hall of Representatives, and a lighted torch was applied to them. Quickly the flames spread through the Capitol, and in half an hour it was in ruins. The soldiers marched to the President's House and fired that, and also the other public buildings. They plundered and burned stores and houses, destroyed the workshops in the navy-yard and the fort at Greenleaf's Point, and in various ways did a great deal of

damage to the city.   They remained until the next night, when taking an
alarm they hastily retreated, " without the beat of a drum or the sound of
a bugle," to Marlboro', and in a few days went aboard their ships, which
were lying off Alexandria, and sailed down the river.   The loss to the
government by the invasion was over two million dollars, and the loss
to the citizens of Washington was about half a million.   Nearly one
hundred Americans were killed and wounded.

DEFENCES OF WASHINGTON DURING THE CIVIL WAR.

After the invasion the "capital movers," as those members of Congress were called who were ever seeking to have the seat of government transferred to some other place, tried to prevent any appropriation from being made to restore the public buildings. It was said "they were secretly glad the British had burned the buildings, thus giving plausibility to the arguments for rebuilding elsewhere without sacrificing the cost of what had been built." There were exciting debates in Congress in regard to the matter, and for a time it seemed as if the Potomac would lose the national capital; but in February, 1815, a bill was passed authorizing the Secretary of the Treasury to borrow $500,000 at 6 per cent. for the purpose of rebuilding the public edifices. Private enterprise under the inspiration of this decision was awakened, and during the next ten years Washington began to be a good deal more than "a city of streets without houses."

General Lafayette was welcomed to the city on Tuesday, October 12, 1824. Upon his arrival a salute was fired, and he was escorted to a barouche, which was decorated with the French colors and drawn by four gray horses led by grooms in white livery. A procession composed of military companies and civic societies, and which was two miles in length, marched over the city with the honored guest, and throngs of people lined the way. Arches with banners, mottoes, and floral designs were placed here and there over the streets, and on the largest arch was a huge live eagle, which is said to have bent its head and flapped its wings when Lafayette passed beneath. At a certain point the hero was met by a chariot containing twenty-five handsome maidens dressed in white muslin and blue scarfs, and with wreaths of red flowers on their heads, intended to represent the twenty-four States and the District of Columbia. The little maid who represented the district spoke a few words of welcome, and then there were addresses by the mayor and other persons, to all of which Lafayette responded in a pleasant manner. After the municipal reception he visited the Capitol, where he was welcomed as the "nation's guest" by Henry Clay, then Speaker of the House of Representatives; and also visited the White House, where President Monroe greeted him affectionately. During his stay of two weeks he was lavishly entertained by prominent families of Washington and Georgetown.

Many of the descriptions of Washington written at this period are amusing. One writer says, "Conceive, then, a daddy-long-legs whose body is scarcely visible, while his legs shoot out in all directions and are everywhere seen, and you will have a conception of this metropolis. It is no more like New York or Philadelphia than 'Hyperion to a Satyr.' The streets are filled with mud in winter and with dust in summer; and instead of splendid edifices you can see nothing but corn-fields, arid plains, dry canals, and dirty marshes, where frogs croak in most sonorous strain. The citizens build houses where there are no streets, and the corporation makes streets where there are no houses."

Another writer draws this picture of society: "The first thing that strikes a stranger is the affectation of style and fashion which seems to pervade almost every rank and class. The President opens his drawing-room every fort-night for reception of such as may please to visit him; and his cabinet secretaries give dinners and evening parties during the session of Congress. The subordinate officers of the government, clerks, etc., also follow the example, and although their salaries are small and their means

OLD FORTIFICATIONS AS THEY APPEAR TO-DAY.

limited, they fancy it would be unpardonable not to ape those above
them and be what is called fashionable, and thus they plunge into the
vortex of ruin.   They give evening parties, pay morning visits with
cards in their own carriages, or any they can procure, give routs, go to
assemblies, and, in short, exhibit every folly their superiors think proper
to practice because it is said to be *haut ton*, and they cannot think of
being unfashionable, whatever may be the result."

Every one who lived in what was called the "court end" of the city
kept a carriage of some kind, and it was said "many persons would even
ride to church when the distance was not more than a hundred paces."
Members of Congress were in great request for all the parties, and the
prominent ones could not accept half the invitations they received.   Outside of its fashionable life, however, the city was apparently in "a long,
dead calm of fixed repose," and its development year by year was very
slow.   It was not until 1830 that Pennsylvania avenue, the central
thoroughfare, was paved, and then it was done cheaply and badly.
There were only two small public schools.   On August 25, 1835, the
Washington branch of the Baltimore and Ohio Railroad was opened, but
it was as late as 1851 that stages to the West ceased to run.   In 1836
the Long Bridge across the Potomac to Virginia was opened, and has
continued in use to the present day.   It was constructed at a cost of
$100,000, and is a mile in length.

In 1840 the city had 23,364 people.   On the 1st of March, 1844, a
terrible catastrophe occurred.   A large party of officials and prominent
residents visited the war-ship "Princeton," lying off Alexandria, and
sailed in her a short distance down the river.   On the return trip a cannon
burst while being fired, killing Secretary of State Upshur, Secretary of
the Navy Gilmer, and three other persons, and seriously injuring eighteen
others.   From 1840 to 1850 the gain in population was nearly 17,000;
from 1850 to 1860, over 21,000.   The census of the latter year shows a
city population of 61,122, and in the entire District of Columbia, 75,080.
Washington entered upon the trying years of the Civil War a very unat-
tractive place.   Those who had business with the government came to
the city, looked with surprise and contempt at its muddy, unpaved streets
and rude, insignificant private buildings, and went away as soon as possible   It was a capital sprawling over a great territory, but remarkable
only for its distances and discomforts and its listless daily life.

When the war began the city was without defences, and a plan was
at once adopted for protection against distant artillery fire.   On the night
of May 23, 1861, three columns crossed the Potomac into Virginia, one at
the Georgetown aqueduct bridge, one at Long Bridge, and one at Alex-

FORD'S THEATRE, WHERE LINCOLN WAS SHOT.

andria, and the next morning work was begun on several fortifications. In seven weeks the line of defences consisted of Forts Corcoran, Bennett, and Haggerty for the protection of Georgetown; Forts Runyon and Albany covering Long Bridge, and Fort Ellsworth on Shuter's hill, near Alexandria. Immediately after the battle of Bull Run a second line was constructed to fortify Arlington heights, which included Forts Craig, Tillinghast, Cass, Woodbury, Richardson, and Strong; and Forts Worth, Ward, and Lyon were added to the defences of Alexandria. About this time a line of forts was constructed along the northwestern and eastern parts of the District of Columbia, consisting of Fort Reno on the heights of Tennallytown, Fort Stevens on the Seventh-street road, and Forts Gaines, De Russey, Slocum, Totten, Bunker Hill, Saratoga, Slemmer, Thayer, and Lincoln, the latter overlooking the Anacostia. Three small forts, Kirby, Cross, and Davis, afterwards united under the name of Fort Sumner, were constructed on the heights near the receiving reservoir of the Washington aqueduct. Beyond the Anacostia, the defences were Forts Stanton, Greble, Carroll, and Mahan, to which Forts Meigs, Dupont,

Baker, Wagner, Ricketts, and Snyder were added in the latter part of 1862. At Chain bridge there were Forts Ethan Allen and Marcy.

Additions were made to the lines of defences from time to time, until, in the spring of 1863, there were south of the Potomac thirty-four forts and armed batteries with 426 guns and 60 mortars, and thirty-eight unarmed batteries for 205 guns. North of the Potomac there were forty-three forts and armed batteries with 384 guns and 38 mortars, and thirty-six unarmed batteries for 175 guns. The forts were all built of earth, rammed to the utmost degree of solidity attainable, the walls being from twenty to twenty-five feet thick at the base, and from twelve to eighteen feet thick on the parapets. The outside ditch was generally about six feet deep, and a few feet in front of the counterscarp, or outside of the ditch, a glacis was thrown up so as to bring the ground in front within the plane of musketry fire from the parapets, and on this glacis a strong abattis of pointed brush and timber was laid and secured, extending entirely around each fort. Inside magazines were dug, and bomb-proofs constructed of hewed logs, each being covered on the exposed side with from twelve to fifteen feet of rammed earth.

These fortifications and batteries, with their green sod walls and yawning embrasures, from which the black muzzles of huge guns peered out menacingly upon every exposed height, were the most prominent and suggestive features of the landscape as one approached Washington from any direction during the latter years of the war. To-day, of all these defences, only a few mounds of earth remain.

Throughout the war there was a constant fear that Washington might be invaded by the Confederates, but no really serious attempt was ever made. General Early made a dash at the city in 1864, but it has always been believed that the real object of it was to draw troops from the lines in front of Richmond. He crossed the upper Potomac into Maryland with 12,000 men, and on the 9th of July engaged a small force under General Wallace at Frederick City. After defeating Wallace he marched to Rockville, sixteen miles from Washington, and camped there on the night of the 10th. General Grant sent two divisions of the Sixth Corps under General Wright, from Petersburg, to aid in the protection of Washington, and they arrived on the 11th. Early's skirmish line advanced toward the city as far as Fort Stevens, on the Seventh-street road, on the morning of the 11th, but the guns of the fort and of Forts Slocum and De Russey opened rapid fire, and the advance was checked for a time. Late in the afternoon the Sixth Corps arrived. Early's pickets had been firing all day and shouting to the men in the forts, "Come out here, you quill-drivers and bummers, and take your dose like men!" But when they saw the well-known and greatly respected Greek cross, they ceased their taunts and yelled, " Hello, old Sixth Corps! where in thunder did you come from?" "Come from Richmond! What are you Johnnies doing here?" was the reply. "Oh, Early's brought a lot of wooden furloughs for your bummers, but they won't come out and take 'em."

On the 12th, after a good deal of picket-firing and manœuvring, General Wheaton's brigade of the Sixth Corps engaged the Confederate skirmish line and drove it back, after what has been called "a pretty little fight," which was witnessed by President Lincoln from Fort Stevens. The next morning the Confederates had disappeared, and it was ascertained that Early had crossed the river into Virginia.

The close of the war was celebrated on the night of April 13, 1865, by a grand illumination of Washington, which exceeded any previous demonstration ever witnessed in the city. The Capitol, White House, Treasury, and all the other public buildings were covered with decorations and illuminated by thousands of lights, and the greater number of the private buildings were also decorated and illuminated. President Lincoln made a speech to a great assemblage in front of the White House, in which he congratulated the country on the return of peace. Bands of music paraded the streets, and the jubilation was continued nearly all night.

The next night, Friday, April 14, President Lincoln was assassinated at Ford's Theatre on Tenth street, by John Wilkes Booth. The theatre was crowded, and all present were enjoying the performance of the comedy, "OurAmerican

HOUSE WHERE LINCOLN DIED.

Cousin." During the third act, while there was a temporary pause for one of the actors to enter, a sharp report of a pistol was heard, but it attracted no special attention and suggested nothing serious until a man rushed to the front of the box in which the President was seated with Mrs. Lincoln and two other persons, leaped to the stage with a long bowie-knife in his hand, and shouted, "Sic semper tyrannis! The South is avenged!" The audience sat spell-bound for a moment, while the assassin disappeared behind the scenes. The piercing screams of Mrs. Lincoln first disclosed that the President had been shot, and the audience rose to their feet in wild alarm, many persons rushing toward the stage exclaiming, "Hang the assassin!" "Hang him!" while others stood around the President's box petrified with horror. Booth had entered the box a few minutes before ten o'clock, and approaching the President from behind, had placed a pistol at the back of his head and fired. The President's head fell forward, his eyes closed, and he became unconscious. He was removed to a house nearly opposite the theatre, but never regained consciousness, dying the following morning at a few minutes past seven o'clock, surrounded by his wife and family and prominent officials.

At nearly the same time that the President was shot an attempt was made on the life of Secretary of State Seward at his residence, and he was seriously injured by a knife in the hands of an assassin, but subsequently recovered. Afterwards it appeared that a plot had been formed to murder all the principal officials of the government.

The news of the shooting of President Lincoln created the most intense excitement in the city, and on all sides were heard the strongest expressions of sorrow and indignation. Many wept bitterly, and the colored people were frantic with grief and dismay. All the public buildings were closed and covered with emblems of mourning, and hundreds of residences and places of business were profusely draped. The body of the President lay in state in the rotunda of the Capitol on April 20, and was viewed by thousands. The following day the funeral train left the city, bearing the body to Springfield, Illinois, where it was interred.

Booth mounted a fleet horse and made his way across the Anacostia to eastern Maryland, and thence over the Potomac. He was discovered about four o'clock on the morning of April 26 in a barn near Port Royal, Virginia, by a detachment of the Sixteenth New York Cavalry. He refused to surrender and was shot by Sergeant Boston Corbett, and died about three hours afterwards. His associates in the conspiracy were tried by a military commission, and four of them were executed. The remaining four were sentenced to hard labor at the Dry Tortugas,

GRAND MARCH AND REVIEW OF THE UNION ARMY, 1865.

where one died, and the others were subsequently pardoned by President Johnson.

The grand review of the Union Army on the 23d and 24th of May, 1865, completed the events of interest in Washington during the war period. On the first day the Army of the Potomac passed in review, and on the second day the Army of the Tennessee and the Army of Georgia. It was estimated that more than fifty thousand people from all the Northern States witnessed the review. The city was profusely decorated, and at all the prominent points there were arches, banners, and floral embellishments. In front of the White House were four stands decorated with battle-flags and flowers. The principal stand contained President Johnson and the cabinet ministers, General Grant, General Sherman, and prominent military and civil officers. In another stand were governors of the States and distinguished personages.

The troops marched from Virginia across the Potomac to Capitol Hill the night before, and early on the morning of the review. Promptly at 9 o'clock on the 23d the Army of the Potomac, under the command of Major-General Meade, began the march. All the school-children of the city with their teachers were assembled on the eastern portico and grounds of the Capitol, the girls dressed in white muslin, and the boys in black jackets and white pants, and as the soldiers passed greeted them with songs and cheers and garlands. Down the hill came the war veterans on to the broad Pennsylvania avenue, filled for a mile away with cheering throngs. First in line was General Meade, riding a few paces ahead of his escort, and the headquarters division. Then came the Cavalry Corps, commanded by Major-General Merritt; the Provost-Marshal-General's Brigade, commanded by Brigadier-General Macy; and the Engineer Brigade, commanded by Brigadier-General Benham. Following these were the Ninth Corps, in command of Major-General Parke; a division of the Nineteenth Corps, in command of Brigadier-General Dwight; the Fifth Corps, in command of Major-General Griffin; and the Second Corps, in command of Major-General Humphreys. The artillery followed each corps, and the column moved by companies closed in mass, with shortened intervals between regiments, brigades, and divisions. For the sake of uniformity the company front of the whole army was limited to twenty files, the soldiers taking the cadence step up the avenue.

It would be well nigh impossible to describe the enthusiasm that prevailed during the march. All through the day the troops passed by with their tattered flags, their odd-looking camp utensils, their pet animals and negro followers. The "boys" were clad in faded and soiled uniforms, for there had been no "brushing up" for the review, as it was intended to

ALEXANDER R. SHEPHERD.

allow the world to see the army just as it appeared in actual service. As they passed cheer after cheer rolled along the avenue. Each commanding officer received a perfect ovation; each soldier, almost, was greeted with joyful shouts. Flowers in all forms were rained on the defenders of the Union, and officers and men in many cases were burdened with them. General Custer's division of the Cavalry Corps all wore the celebrated "Custer tie,"—a red scarf about the neck, with the ends hanging down the breast nearly to the belt. When the division was passing the President's stand, a thrill ran through the vast crowd as General Custer was seen with a large wreath hanging upon his arm, his scabbard empty, and his long yellow hair waving in the wind, vainly striving to check a magnificent stallion, which was madly sweeping up the avenue. On came the horse with furious speed, thousands of people watching him with breathless suspense, which was soon followed by storms of applause at the horsemanship of the General as he mastered the frightened animal and gracefully rode back along the line.

On the second day there was a repetition of the grand scenes as Sherman's army marched in review. When General Sherman appeared at the head of the column tumultuous cheers went up. Leading the march was the Army of the Tennessee, in command of Major-General Logan. It included the Fifteenth Corps, under Major-General Hazen, and the Seventeenth Corps, under Major-General Blair. Afterwards came the Army of Georgia, in command of Major-General Slocum. This in-

cluded the Twentieth Corps, under Major-General Mower, and the Fourteenth Corps, under Major-General Davis. After the review the soldiers
marched to their camps over the Potomac, and in a few weeks the vast
army was disbanded.

It was not until 1871 that Washington began to be a beautiful city.
The movement for improving it was started by Alexander R. Shepherd,
who afterwards became governor of the district under the territorial form
of government established by Congress. The common saying is that
"Shepherd lifted Washington out of the mud," and it is undoubtedly true
that to him the credit is due for the beginning and successful continuing
of the vast improvements made in all parts of the city within a few
years after 1871. Shepherd was a man of indomitable will, and he had
determined that the National Capital should no longer be a comfortless,
repulsive place, but that it should become a metropolis in fact as well
as in name, and an object of pride and admiration to the people of the
country. He secured the friendship of President Grant, and awakened
Congress to an interest in the affairs of Washington. He gained support
in his plans from some of the prominent citizens, and he induced capitalists in the Northern cities to invest in the district bonds. Congress passed
a bill to abolish the old municipal government, putting in place of it a
territorial government, with a governor and legislature. The Board of
Public Works was organized, with Shepherd at its head, and the work
of improvement was begun. An army of laborers was set to work to
grade and pave the streets and avenues, to cut down and remove banks
and obstructions, to reconstruct the sidewalks, to cover over the old
canal, which had long been a nuisance, to set out thousands of trees, to
develop the parks, squares, and circles, to build sewers and lay water-
pipes, and to do many other things which would improve and beautify
the city.

In a few years an almost incredible amount of work had been done.
The old slovenly city had nearly disappeared. Fine business buildings
and residences, churches and school-houses, new markets, new hotels,
were erected. Shepherd's will was law, and his fierce energy pervaded
everything. At least twenty-five millions were expended in the improvements, and the result was that Washington, after three-quarters of a
century, became what had been predicted of it when it was founded,—
a magnificent capital.

STATUE OF ADMIRAL FARRAGUT IN FARRAGUT SQUARE.

CHAPTER V.

HE District of Columbia covers an area of sixty-four square
miles, and is bounded on the north, east, and south by the
State of Maryland, and on the west by the Potomac river.
The city of Washington is located on the river front of the
district, and extends over a broad, irregular valley up to the edges of a
range of thickly-wooded hills. From northwest to southeast it is about
five miles in extent, and from east to southwest about three miles. The
actual territory embraced within the city boundary is a trifle less than
ten square miles. The southwestern section borders on the Potomac,
which at this point is 116½ miles above its mouth at Chesapeake bay,
and 184½ miles from the Atlantic ocean, and the eastern section borders on the Anacostia or Eastern Branch of the Potomac. Few cities
of the United States are so beautifully situated, and few have so many
charming scenes. The national capital has become very attractive, and
its residents have a just pride in its beauty and remarkable development.

Washington grows at a very rapid rate. By the census of 1880 the
population was given at 147,307, and with the addition of Georgetown,
now West Washington, 159,885. At the present time the population is
estimated at 210,000, and in the Congressional season at 10,000 more.
The city is laid out in such a manner that it has space for half a million
people without crowding, and it is the belief that it will have this number within twenty years. The social attractions of the city are so great
that people of wealth, culture, and refinement go to it in great numbers
from all parts of the country, and many of them are induced by the genial
climate and pleasant conditions of living to become permanent residents.
L'Enfant's magnificent plan has been properly developed, and in consequence Washington to-day is one of the grandest cities in the world in

70

PENNSYLVANIA AVENUE AT ELEVENTH STREET.

its arrangement of streets and avenues, squares, parks, and public reservations. All the thoroughfares are very broad, clean, and delightfully
shaded in summer by a large variety of fine trees, and the majority of the
streets and avenues are paved with concrete or asphalt. In its architectural appearance the city is fast assuming a unique and distinctive character. Its private buildings are notable for elegance and diversity of design,
and many of its mansions are models of beauty. It is a city of brick and
marble and stone, artistically employed, and it has little of the architectural monotony of most large cities.

Within the city limits there are 6111 acres, and more than one-half
of this amount, or 3095 acres, is devoted to public uses. There are 408
acres of government reservations, 107 streets, with an aggregate length
of 279 miles, and 21 avenues named after various States. The streets
extend from north to south and from east to west, and the avenues cross
them diagonally. The Capitol marks the centre of the city, and all the
streets are laid out at right angles from it.

There are four distinct quarters of the city. The northwest quarter is
the most popular and has the largest number of people. It comprises
the business centre, and has the majority of the finest streets. It contains
the White House, the Treasury, the department buildings, the theatres,
leading hotels and mercantile establishments, and the greater number of

the churches, schools, and institutions. In that portion of it known as the "West End" are the artistic and costly mansions for which the city is famous. The southwest quarter comprises the harbor region, and contains brick, stone, and lumber yards and manufacturing concerns, and also many streets of stores and residences. The northeast quarter has the smallest population and is the least developed. The southeast quarter covers Capitol Hill, and it is fast becoming a populous section. It was here that the founders of Washington believed the majority of the residences would be located, but the tide of population flowed toward the northwest quarter, and for many years Capitol Hill was mostly vacant land. Now, however, it has a considerable population and numerous fine residences.   •

Throughout the city the streets and avenues are from 130 to 160 feet in width and have very broad sidewalks. In front of most the houses is a grass plat or garden, and beyond this is the sidewalk. There are eighty thousand shade-trees on the streets and avenues, planted within ten years, and as soon as a street is properly graded trees about thirty feet apart are set out. In a few years the boughs of the trees on many of the streets will almost touch, and Washington in the vernal season will be a perfect forest of shade-trees. Most of the trees now give a good deal of shade and a measureless amount of beauty. Carolina poplars, maples, elms, and twenty other varieties are planted, and all the trees receive great attention from the park commission.

Pennsylvania avenue is the great central thoroughfare. Its entire length is four and one-half miles, but the Treasury breaks its continuity at one point and the Capitol at another. From the Treasury, at Fifteenth street, it stretches in majesty to the Capitol, a distance of nearly a mile and a half. Over this course its entire roadway is 160 feet in width. It is paved throughout with concrete, and is considered the finest avenue in the world. Massachusetts and Connecticut avenues, which traverse the fashionable West End, are broad, long, and beautiful, and most of the other avenues are remarkable for their length and beauty. With Pennsylvania avenue the prominent business localities are Seventh, Ninth, and F streets.

Extending from the Botanical Garden, at the foot of Capitol Hill, to Fifteenth street is a broad park, or series of parks, known as the Mall. On it are located the buildings of the Fish Commission, National Museum, Smithsonian Institution, and Department of Agriculture. The improvement of the Potomac flats, now in progress, will add about 1000 acres to the Mall and extend it to the river in completed form. There will then be in the centre of the city a continuous park with shaded

STATUE OF GENERAL SCOTT IN SCOTT SQUARE

roadways for nearly two miles, and which will have an extensive river frontage.

On Pennsylvania avenue, opposite the White House, Lafayette Park is situated. It is a government reservation of about seven acres, with many ancient trees, beautiful lawns, and flower-beds. Each spring a large number of flowering plants are set out here, and many rare varieties of foreign growth are included. In this park stands an equestrian statue of General Andrew Jackson, by Clark Mills. It was cast from brass cannon and mortars captured during Jackson's campaigns, and cost nearly $50,000. Around its white marble pedestal are mounted field-pieces of antique fashion and piles of cannon-balls. The statue was unveiled January 8, 1853, Hon. Stephen A. Douglas delivering the oration.

Franklin Park, which comprises four acres, is located between Thirteenth and Fourteenth streets west and I and K streets north. It is a very pretty small park, and has a large fountain in its centre.

Lincoln Park is laid out in the square at the intersection of East Capitol street with several avenues, and is a mile east of the Capitol. It is six and one-quarter acres in extent. Here is the famous bronze group designated as "Emancipation," which was designed by Thomas Ball, and cast in Munich in 1875. It stands on a granite pedestal, upon which are two bronze tablets, the one on the front being inscribed "Freedom's Memorial. In grateful memory of Abraham Lincoln this monument was erected by the Western Sanitary Commission of St. Louis, Mo., with funds contributed solely by emancipated citizens of the United States declared free by his proclamation, January 1, A.D. 1863. The first contribution of five dollars was made by Charlotte Scott, a freed woman of Virginia, being her first earnings in freedom, and consecrated by her suggestion and request on the day she heard of President Lincoln's death to build a monument to his memory."

On the other tablet is this extract from the Emancipation Proclamation: "And upon this act, sincerely believed to be an act of justice warranted by the Constitution upon military necessity, I invoke the considerate judgment of mankind and the gracious favor of Almighty God."

The memorial represents Abraham Lincoln standing at a monolith, on which is a medallion of Washington with shields and stars. In his right hand he holds the proclamation of emancipation, and his left is extended over a negro whose manacles are broken. The group is twelve feet high and the pedestal ten feet. The bronze work cost $17,000. The ceremony of dedication took place on April 14, 1876, in the presence of a vast assemblage. Hon. Frederick Douglass was the orator.

The squares and circles are attractive features of Washington. Scott

Square, at the intersection of Massachusetts and Rhode Island avenues, Sixteenth and N streets, contains an equestrian statue of General Winfield Scott, which was erected in 1874. It was modelled by H. K. Brown, and cast in Philadelphia from cannon captured in Mexico. Its total height is fifteen feet, and its cost was $20,000. The pedestal is of granite from Cape Ann quarries, and is composed of five huge blocks, said to be the largest ever quarried in the United States. The cost of the pedestal was about $25,000. General Scott is represented in the uniform of his rank as Lieutenant-General of the army of the United States.

Farragut Square, on Connecticut avenue, has a small park, in the centre of which is a bronze figure of Admiral David G. Farragut, modelled by Vinnie Ream Hoxie. It is ten feet in height, and stands on a granite pedestal twenty feet in height. It was cast in 1880, and unveiled April 25, 1881, on which occasion the orators were Hon. Horace Maynard, of Tennessee, and Hon. D. W. Voorhees, of Indiana. The figure was constructed of metal taken from the bronze propeller of Farragut's flag-ship, the Hartford. The cost of this memorial was $25,000.

McPherson Square, on Vermont avenue, is ornamented with an equestrian statue of General James B. McPherson, which was erected by the Society of the Army of the Tennessee. It stands on a massive granite

STATUE OF WASHINGTON.

STATUE OF EMANCIPATION IN LINCOLN PARK.

pedestal, and the statue and pedestal cost nearly $50,000. The sculptor was Louis T. Robisso, and the statue was cast from cannon appropriated by Congress for the purpose. The height of the figure is fourteen feet, and the horse is twelve feet long. When the statue was unveiled, on

October 18, 1876, there was an imposing military display, and an oration was delivered by General John A. Logan.

Greene Square, on Capitol Hill, contains an equestrian statue of General Nathaniel Greene of the Continental Army, which was erected in 1877, at a cost of $50,000. H. T. Brown was the sculptor, and it was cast in Philadelphia. It stands on a pedestal of New England granite, twenty feet in height. The total height of the statue is thirty-three and one-half feet, and its length is fourteen feet.

Rawlins Square, on New York avenue, has a bronze figure of General John A. Rawlins on a granite pedestal. It was erected in 1874, was modelled by J. Bailey, and cost $12,500. It is eight feet high, and the pedestal is twelve feet high.

Judiciary Square, on Louisiana avenue, contains the District Court-House and Pension Building. A marble column surmounted by a statue of President Lincoln stands in front of the Court-House. This square has a park of about twenty acres, with handsome lawns and garden-plats.

Washington Circle, at the western end of Pennsylvania avenue, has in its centre an equestrian statue of General Washington, intended to represent him as he appeared at the battle of Princeton. It is the work of Clark Mills, and was erected at a cost of $50,000, which sum was appropriated by Congress in 1853.

Dupont Circle, at the intersection of Connecticut, Massachusetts, and New Hampshire avenues, contains a bronze figure of Admiral Samuel Francis Dupont, by Launt Thompson, which was unveiled on December 20, 1884, Hon. Thomas F. Bayard delivering the oration. The figure is of heroic proportions, and represents the admiral, in full uniform, as standing on the quarter-deck, marine glass in hand. The pedestal is of gray granite with a base of blue rock. The cost of the statue was $10,500.

Thomas Circle, at the intersection of Fourteenth street, Massachusetts and Vermont avenues, contains an equestrian statue of General George H. Thomas, on a granite pedestal ornamented with bronze tablets, upon which is the insignia of the Army of the Cumberland. The statue and pedestal are thirty-two feet in height, and they were executed at a cost of $75,000. The Society of the Army of the Cumberland erected the statue, and Congress provided the money for the pedestal. The unveiling ceremony took place on November 19, 1879, and on the occasion there was a grand military and civic parade, and Hon. Stanley Matthews delivered an oration.

Iowa Circle, at the intersection of Rhode Island and Vermont avenues, has as yet no memorial statue. There is a small park in its centre containing a fountain.

STATUE OF GENERAL THOMAS.

There are one hundred and eighty-one churches in Washington, with, it is estimated, fifty thousand communicants. Of the churches, fifty-two are Methodist, forty - five Baptist, twenty-six Episcopal, twenty-one Presbyterian, thirteen Catholic, ten Lutheran, four Congregational, two Hebrew, one Unitarian, one Universalist, one Christian, one Swedenborgian, and four non - sectarian. In the Sunday-schools there are about forty thousand scholars. Nearly one-half of the population of the city attend church,—a remarkable proportion as compared with other cities. The oldest church is the Christ Episcopal Church, near the navy-yard, which was erected in 1795. St. John's Episcopal Church, opposite Lafayette Park, on H street, was built in 1816. Many of the Presidents have attended this church.

The public school system is an admirable one. Nearly $550,000 are yearly appropriated for the schools of the district. There are numerous large and handsome school buildings provided with every convenience. The Franklin School is the most notable of the white schools, and the Sumner School of the colored. Over five hundred teachers are employed in the different schools, and there are nearly thirty thousand pupils.

There are five great public markets in Washington, profusely supplied with everything required. The Center Market is the largest, and it is also considered one of the finest markets in the United States. Its four spacious buildings were erected at a cost of $350,000, and opened in the summer of 1873. Around the market are many hucksters' stands, and on the broad street back of it can be seen every day innumerable wagons with vegetables. The Northern Liberty Market is a very large building, erected in 1875, at a cost of $150,000. By the market system the people of the city are provided with the best of meats and produce. The farmers of Maryland and Virginia bring their "truck" to the markets in great quantities, and are sure of finding a ready sale.

By Act of Congress, approved by the President on the 11th of June, 1878, the present government of the District of Columbia by three commissioners was established. The commissioners are appointed by the President for a term of three years, and consist of two civilians and one officer of the Corps of Engineers of the United States Army. They receive $5000 each per year, and have full control of the affairs of the district under the supervision of Congress. The United States assumes one-half of the expenses of the district and of the cost of all the improvements, and the annual expenditure of the government in this way is nearly two million dollars.

While Washington is devoid of large commercial and manufacturing interests, and dependent in a great measure upon the business of the government, it has during the past ten years made considerable progress in developing trade with the adjacent country, and has also begun certain lines of manufacturing which in time may be greatly increased. The city is in a very prosperous condition, and there is, apparently, nothing to hinder its advancement.

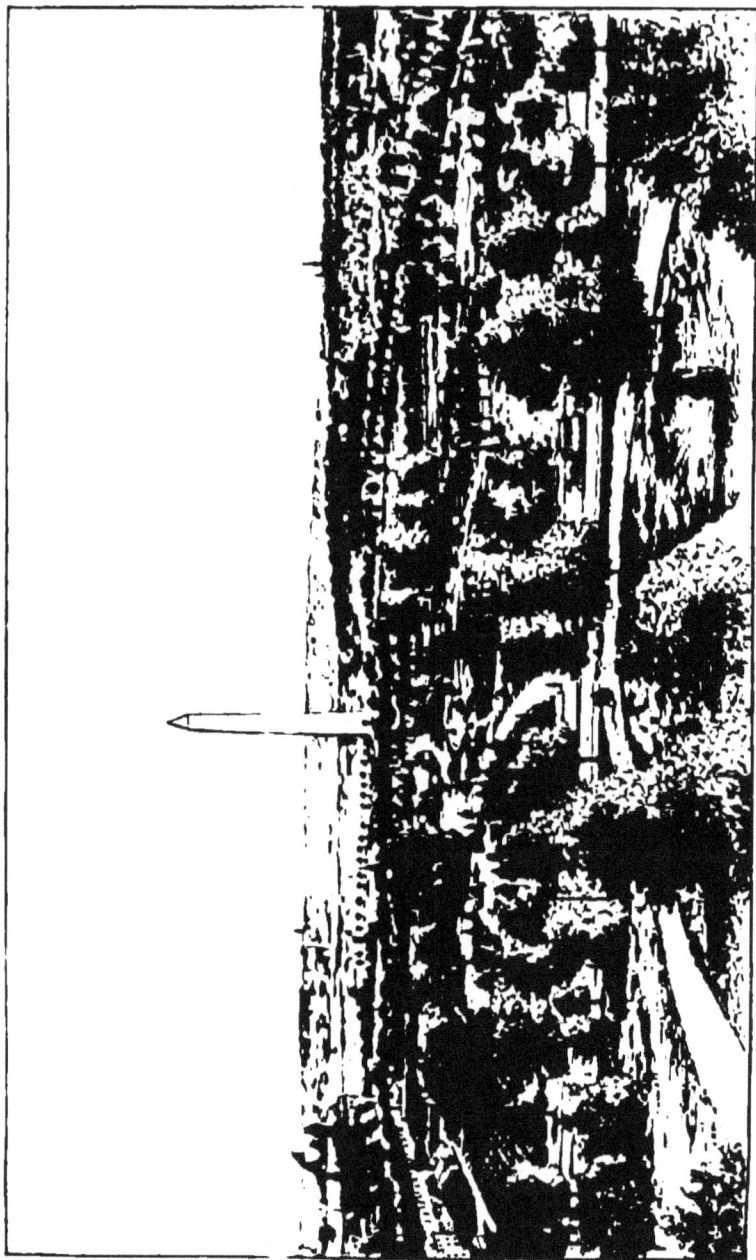

GROUNDS OF THE DEPARTMENT OF AGRICULTURE AND MONUMENT SQUARE.

CHAPTER VI.

HE Washington Monument is a massive shaft of fine white marble with a pyramidal top. It is simple in form, but has a harmony of proportion which will be likely to give it enduring beauty. Its tapering lines produce a wonderful grace and lightness, and looking at it from a distance one can hardly conceive it to be the huge structure that it is. After many years this grand memorial to the Father of His Country has been completed and dedicated, and now stands towering over the city he founded, the loftiest artificial elevation in the world. From the base-line to the aluminium point which crowns the shaft the height is exactly five hundred and fifty-five feet four inches. The shaft rests on foundations thirty-six feet eight inches deep, making an aggregate height from the foundation-bed of 592 feet. The next highest structure is the Pyramid of Cheops in Egypt, which has an elevation of 543 feet, and following this is the Cologne Cathedral in Germany, the central spire of which is 524 feet high. The Antwerp Cathedral in Belgium is 476 feet high, and St. Peter's at Rome is 448 feet. It is proposed to build the tower of the new City Hall at Philadelphia to a height of 535 feet.

The foundations of the monument, which bear a weight of 81,120 tons, are constructed of solid blue rock, and are one hundred and forty-six feet six inches square. The base of the shaft is fifty-five feet square, and the lower walls are fifteen feet thick. At the five hundred feet elevation, where the pyramidal top begins, the walls are only eighteen inches thick and about thirty-five feet square. The inside of the walls, as far as they were constructed before the work was undertaken by the government in 1878,—150 feet from the base,—is of blue granite, not laid in courses. From this point to within a short distance of the beginning of the top or roof, the inside of the walls is of regular courses of granite, corresponding with the courses of marble on the outside. For the top marble is entirely used. The marble blocks were cut or "dressed" in the most careful manner, and laid in courses of two feet by experienced and skilful workmen. There is no "filling" or "backing" between the granite and marble blocks, but they are all closely joined, the work being declared "the best piece of masonry in the world." By a plumb-line suspended from the top of the monument inside the walls to the floor, the most minute defection from the perpendicular line can be ascertained at a glance. During all the work on the enormous shaft not three-eighths of an inch defection has been noticed,—a mere trifle in a structure of this magnitude.

In the interior of the monument are eight ponderous columns of iron strongly riveted, which extend from the floor to the top. They are placed on massive stones bedded in the rock foundations, and support the iron staircase and elevator. They are so securely joined and braced that they will bear any possible weight. The elevator is suspended by steel-wire cables, which are coiled upon a great drum under the floor. During the progress of the work upon the monument this elevator was tested in every way. All the marble blocks were carried up on it, and from day to day it "elevated" greater weight than will ever be placed on it again. The staircase is wide and of easy ascent. Every fifty feet there is a platform, which extends to the elevator, so that visitors can get on or off the elevator at many different places. There are 900 steps from the beginning to the end of the staircase, and twenty minutes are required to walk to the top of the monument. The elevator goes to the top in seven minutes. The interior is lighted by electricity, as there are no openings in the shaft except the entrance door and small windows at the top.

In the rubble-stone masonry of the lower interior walls are set a number of memorial-stones, sent to the Washington Monument Society by states, corporations, and foreign governments to be inserted in the monument, but in the upper walls no such stones were set, as they would have weakened the shaft. About one hundred of these stones remain, and the greater number will be cut down to thin slabs and placed on the surface of the interior walls. Many of them are elaborately carved, and must have cost a great deal of money. They are of marble, fine granite, sandstone, and brownstone, and there is one block of pure copper. Among the finest are those inscribed "Corporation of Philadelphia," "Greece," and "Bremen." One stone is inscribed, "From the Temple of Esculapius, Island of Paros." Other stones are inscribed, "Oldest Inhabitants District of Columbia, 1870," "The Free Swiss Confederation, 1870," "Engine Company Northern Liberty, Philadelphia," "Fire De-

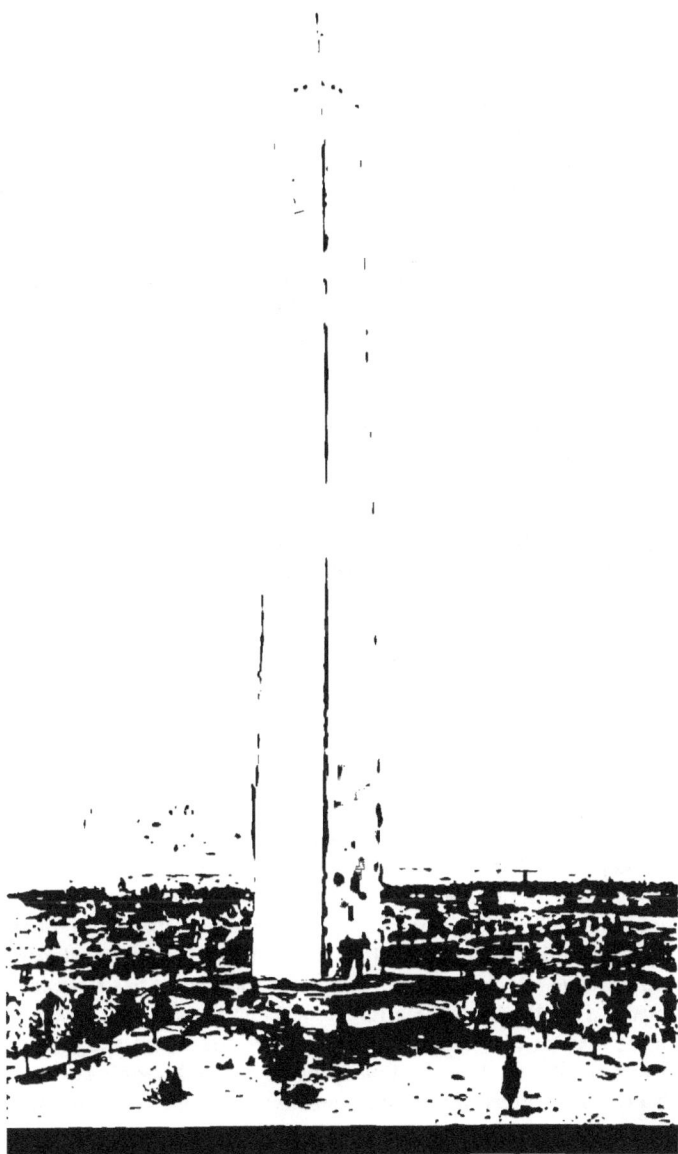

THE WASHINGTON MONUMENT.

partment, Philadelphia, 1852," "Georgia Convention, 1850," "Lafayette Masons, New York City, 1853," "Grand Lodge of Pennsylvania, 1851," "Continental Guard, New Orleans, 1856," "Jefferson Society, Va.," "Grand Division Sons of Temperance of Illinois, 1855," "The Sons of New England in Canada," "Deseret (Utah) Holiness to the Lord," "From Braddock's Field," "Battle-Ground, Long Island," "Charlestown, the Bunker Hill Battle-Ground," "Cherokee Nation, 1855," "Michigan," "Vermont," "Kansas," "Salem," "American Medical Association," "Templars of Honor and Temperance, New York," "Sons of Temperance, Pennsylvania," "Brazil," "Arabia," "China," "Nevada, 1881." Two stones sent some years before the war of the rebellion are inscribed "The State of Louisiana,—Ever Faithful to the Constitution and the Union," and "Tennessee,—the Federal Union it must be preserved." One sandstone block from Switzerland is inscribed, "This block of stone is from the original chapel built to William Tell, in 1338, on Lake Lucerne, Switzerland, at the spot where he escaped from Gessler."

One of the memorial stones received was a gift from the Pope. It was a beautiful block of African marble, which had been taken from the Temple of Concord, at Rome, and was inscribed with the simple words "Rome to America." At that time the Know-Nothing movement was rife, and a fanatical minister published an address to the Protestants of the country against placing the Pope's block of marble in the monument. Such a religious excitement was created that, on the night of March 5, 1854, the block was taken by force from the building where it was kept, and, it is supposed, thrown into the river. The Washington Monument Society offered a large reward for the apprehension of the persons engaged in this act of vandalism, but they were never discovered.

The keystone that binds the interior ribs of stone that support the marble facing of the pyramidal cap of the monument weighs nearly five tons. It is four feet six inches high, and three feet six inches square at the top. Its sides were finished in the usual shape of keystones, but above the wedge which keys and completes the arch it has a perpendicular extension to brace the interior stone blocks. When it was set two prominent Masons of Washington ascended to the top of the monument, and with a small trowel used on many occasions of Masonic corner-stone laying helped to spread the mortar which was to bind the arch under the keystone.

On the 4th of July, 1848, the corner-stone of the monument was laid, and on the 6th of December, 1884, the capstone which completed the shaft was set. The capstone is five feet two and one-half inches in height, and its base is somewhat more than three feet square. At its cap

ENTRANCE TO THE MONUMENT.

or peak it is five inches in diameter. On the cap was placed a tip or point of aluminium, a composition metal which resembles polished silver, and which was selected because of its lightness and freedom from oxidation, and because it will always remain bright. The tip is nine inches in height, and four and a half inches in diameter at the base, and weighs six pounds and a quarter.

Engraved on one side of the tip is the following inscription : "Chief Engineer and Architect, Thomas Lincoln Casey, Colonel Corps of Engineers; Assistants, George W. Davis, Fourteenth United States Infantry; Bernard R. Green, Civil Engineer; P. H. McLaughlin, Master Mechanic." On the three other sides are these inscriptions: "Corner-stone laid on bed of foundation July 4, 1848. First stone at height of 152 feet, laid August 7, 1880. Capstone set December 6, 1884." "Joint commission at setting of capstone, Chester A. Arthur, W. W. Corcoran, M. E. Bell, Edward Clark, John Newton. Act of August 2, 1876." "Laus Deo."

Nature was in a stormy mood on the day the capstone was set. It rained during the morning, but when the time arrived for the ceremony, two o'clock in the afternoon, the rain had ceased but the wind was blowing furiously. At the top of the monument the wind-gauge showed that the gale had a velocity of sixty miles an hour. Thousands of glasses were pointed at the huge shaft as those who were to participate in the setting of the capstone made their appearance on the small platform 550 feet in the air. When everything was ready each person on the platform spread some cement upon the bed of the capstone, and then the order was given to "lower away," and the 3300 pound pyramid slowly sank into position. The stone fitted exactly, and not a chip was taken from it. Cement was then spread on the shoulder on which the aluminium tip was to rest, and various coins were placed in it. The tip was then fitted to the cap and the shaft was done. A moment afterwards the American flag was hoisted above the monument and cannon below were fired.

Immediately after the cannon had announced that the mighty structure was completed members of the Washington Monument Society held a meeting at the top of the shaft and adopted this resolution : " *Resolved*, That we are thankful to have the opportunity of this occasion, and at this elevation, to congratulate the American people on the completion of this enduring monument of our nation's gratitude to the Father of His Country."

Thus after many years of delay and many years of patient labor this wonderful memorial, in many particulars the world's greatest work of construction, was successfully finished.

The view from the top of the monument is grand beyond description. In the lower course of the roof-stones on each side there are two windows, making eight windows in all from which an outlook can be obtained 517 feet above the ground. From this height the city of Washington appears spread out like a great, splendid panorama, all its broad streets and avenues, parks and buildings, being clearly outlined and displayed. The heights of Georgetown and the ranges of wooded hills on the north and east show boldly and finely. To the south and southwest the Potomac can be seen for miles winding its way through a picturesque country, and afar off the Blue Ridge mountains look like clouds of mist on the horizon. Looking down at the base of the monument a novel sight is presented. As is well known, parallel lines by the laws of perspective converge as they disappear from the sight, and looking from the top of the monument downward the

IN THE ELEVATOR

CAPSTONE OF THE MONUMENT, SHOWING THE ALUMINIUM TIP.

sides of the shaft seem to draw towards each other, and the base appears narrower than the top. The sensation of standing on a high structure which is apparently wider at the top than the bottom is peculiar.

The cost of the monument has been $1,187,710, and it will require at least $200,000 more to complete the interior and arrange the grounds. Congress has appropriated $887,710 of the amount expended, and the balance was furnished by the Washington Monument Society. The monument stands on a terrace seventeen feet high, and this terrace will be extended until its slopes gradually sink into the surrounding grounds. Trees and shrubs will be planted and walks laid out. The square of forty-one acres in which the monument is located is a part of the Mall, and is bounded by Fourteenth street and the Potomac river. On L'Enfant's plan of the city this square was designated as the site for the proposed monument to Washington which was ordered by the Continental Congress in 1783.

In 1799, directly after the death of Washington, Congress again resolved to erect a marble monument "in a pyramidal form," but failed to appropriate any money for it. In May, 1800, a select Congressional committee reported a resolution proposing an appropriation of $100,000 for beginning the work on the monument. The resolution was adopted by the House of Representatives, but was not concurred in by the Senate. From that time until 1833 nothing further was done in regard to the monument, and probably nothing would have been done to this day had it not been for a few patriotic citizens of Washington, who met in the City Hall on the evening of September 26, 1833, and organized the National Washington Monument Society. The movement was started by George Watterson, who was Librarian of Congress from 1815 to 1829, and he was aided by Peter Force, Joseph Gales, William Cranch, W. W. Seaton, and other prominent citizens. The venerable Chief Justice John Marshall, who was then eighty-five years old, was chosen as president of the society, and George Watterson as secretary. The society issued an appeal to the country for contributions, which were not to exceed one dollar from any

COMPLETING THE MONUMENT.

one person. In three years
the contributions amounted to
$28,000, and then a design for
the monument was selected
from a large number submitted
in response to an advertisement for one which would
" harmoniously blend durabil-
ity, simplicity, and grandeur."
The design made by Robert
Mills, one of the architects of
the Capitol, was accepted. It
was for a circular colonnaded
building, 250 feet in diameter
and 100 feet high, from the
centre of which there was to
be an obelisk shaft rising to
the height of 500 feet and

STAGING AT THE TOP OF THE MONUMENT DURING
THE WORK OF COMPLETION.

diminishing to forty feet square at the top. Thirty columns of massive
proportions were to surround the rotunda, and they were to be surmounted by an entablature twenty feet high and crowned by a balustrade
fifteen feet high. This design was set aside some years after, and that
of a plain shaft rising from a terrace adopted instead.

In 1847 the monument fund amounted to $87,000. The one dollar
rule had been abolished and contributions of any amount were received.
In January, 1848, Congress authorized the monument society to select
any of the unoccupied public grounds as a site for the monument, and
accordingly President Polk, who was *ex-officio* president of the society,
selected the square where the monument now stands. On the 4th of
July, 1848, the corner-stone of the monument was laid. In an account of
the event it is stated that " the ceremonies were interesting and impressive,
and were attended by an immense crowd, the largest since the funeral of
President Harrison, in 1841. It is estimated that 20,000 people must
have been present. Strangers flocked to the city and the cars were
insufficient for their accommodation. Every organization and everybody
turned out. Among the guests on the grand stand were Mrs. Alexander
Hamilton, then ninety-one years old ; George Washington Park Custis,
Mrs. Dolly Paine Madison, Mrs. John Quincy Adams, Chief Justice
Taney, Lewis Cass, Martin Van Buren, and Millard Fillmore. Not the
least prominent in the assembly was a live eagle, twenty-five years old,
which twenty-four years before had appeared in the pageant to celebrate

the arrival of Lafayette. B. B.
French, the Grand Master of
Masons, in laying the corner-stone,
used the Masonic gavel of Washington, who was a Master Mason.
Mr. French also wore Washington's
Masonic apron, and sat in the chair
which Washington occupied in the
Alexandria lodge." Hon. Robert C.
Winthrop, of Boston, then Speaker
of the House of Representatives,
delivered an oration upon the life
and character of Washington.

Work on the monument was
begun at once and carried on until
1854, when it was suspended, as the
monument society had expended all
the money it had received, and was

COL. THOMAS L. CASEY, CHIEF ENGINEER
OF THE MONUMENT.

unable to obtain more. The shaft was then 150 feet high and had cost
$250,000. Memorials were presented to Congress, from time to time,
praying that the government should assume the work and finish the
structure, but there was no practical result until July, 1876, when "the
centennial feeling" then prevailing induced Congress to make an appropriation for the monument. The government took charge of the construction, and officers of the Corps of Engineers were directed to examine
and extend the foundations of the shaft. In 1878 the entire management
of the construction of the monument was placed in the hands of a commission consisting of the President of the United States, the chief of
engineers, the first vice-president of the monument society, the architect
of the Capitol, and the supervising architect of the Treasury. Col. T. L.
Casey of the Corps of Engineers was detailed to superintend the work,
which has been carried on in a systematic and skilful manner.

On the 21st of February, 1885, the monument was dedicated with
imposing ceremonies in the presence of many thousands of persons from
all parts of the United States.

CHAPTER VII.

N the 14th of March, 1792, the following advertisement appeared in Dunlap's *American Daily Advertiser* of Phila- delphia : "Washington, in the Territory of Columbia. A premium of a lot in this city to be designated by impartial judges, and five hundred dollars, or a medal of that value at the option of the party, will be given by the Commissioners of the Federal Buildings to the person who, before the 15th of July, 1792, shall produce to them the most approved plan for a Capitol to be erected in this city ; and two hundred and fifty dollars or a medal for the plan deemed next in merit to the one they shall adopt. The building to be of brick and to contain the following apartments, to wit : A conference room, a room for the Repre- sentatives, sufficient to accommodate three hundred persons each ; a lobby or ante-chamber to the latter ; a Senate room of twelve hundred square feet area ; an ante-chamber ; twelve rooms of six hundred square feet each for committee rooms and clerks' offices. It will be a recom- mendation of any plan if the central part of it may be detached and erected for the present, with the appearance of a complete whole, and be capable of admitting the additional parts in future, if they shall be wanting. Drawings will be expected of the grand plats, elevations of each front, and sections through the building in such directions as may be necessary to explain the internal structure ; and an estimate of the cubic feet of brick work composing the whole mass of the walls."

This was the advertisement of Thomas Johnson, David Stuart, and Daniel Carroll, who were the commissioners appointed by President Washington to lay out the new Federal Territory. They were charged by act of Congress with the erection of a suitable building "for the accommodation of Congress." Major L'Enfant, in his plan of the

EAST FRONT OF THE CAPITOL.

Federal city, had given the name of "The Capitol" to the building intended for the national legislature, and this name being satisfactory to those in authority had been formally adopted. The sloping hill in the eastern quarter was nearly the centre of the city, and therefore the commissioners had decided to place the Capitol on this elevation, so that it could be seen from all points. No better site could have been chosen, and it is a very fortunate thing that the great structure—"the nation's building"—was not erected on low land, as it would have lost much of its imposing and significant appearance. It will be noticed that the advertisement for the design states that the building was to be constructed of brick. It was first intended to use this material, but the wiser "second thought" led the commissioners to select sandstone instead. Fancy the Capitol of brick!

A great number of designs were immediately submitted in response to the advertisement, but they were all very commonplace, and were promptly rejected. A building of pure classic form with a high central dome was desired, and none of the designs met the requirements. After a little time an outline of a design was submitted by Stephen Hallate, a French architect, and it being satisfactory in its general features, he was invited to confer with the commissioners about it. Hallate was a resident of New York, and had studied architecture in Paris and Rome under the best masters. He was accounted one of the most talented architects in America, and had designed a number of prominent buildings. He visited the city of Washington and thoroughly examined the site chosen for the Capitol, and then made a series of sketches for use in the elaboration of his design. The commissioners were pleased with the sketches, and

THE CAPITOL IN 1827.

directed Hallate to finish the design and they would accept it. With this understanding he returned to New York to do the work.

At that time there was living in New York an Englishman named William Thornton, who was in the service of the government as clerk of patents. He appears to have been a man of versatile talent, and had acquired a good deal of influence with Jefferson, then Secretary of State. Thornton was a fine draughtsman, and he drew a very handsome plan of the Capitol, with every part elaborated and beautifully colored, which he submitted to Jefferson. The plan was greatly admired by all the high officials, and at last President Washington wrote to the commissioners requesting them to adopt it. The commissioners notified Hallate that they should have to do this, and sent him a copy of Thornton's plan. When he saw it he declared with great indignation that it was stolen from his sketches, and was not original with Thornton. This accusation brought on a bitter quarrel between the two men, and for weeks they wrangled over the matter in public and private, and continually called each other very hard names. But finally Thornton's plan was accepted, and he received the first premium of a building lot and $500. The second premium of $250 was given to Hallate, and he was also appointed as one of the architects of the Capitol, with a salary of $2000 per year, a very large sum in those days. James Hoban, the architect of the President's House, was appointed as supervising architect.

Work was begun at once on the Capitol, and on September 18, 1793, the ceremony of laying the corner-stone was performed. In the *Columbian Mirror and Alexandria Gazette* of September 25, 1793, a copy of which is preserved in the Library of Congress, is the only report of this important event known to be in existence. The following is an exact reproduction of the report:

"GEORGETOWN, Sept. 21.

"On Wednesday last one of the grandest Masonic processions took place which perhaps ever was exhibited on the like important occasion. It was in all probability much facilitated by an advertisement which appeared many days before in several newspapers of this date. Lodge No. 9 and Lodge No. 22 with all their officers and regalia appeared on the southern bank of the Grand River Potomack; one of the finest companies of Volunteer Artillery parading to receive the President of the United States who shortly came in sight with his suite, to whom the artillery paid military honors, and his Excellency and suite crossed the river and were received in Maryland by the officers and brethren of No 22 Virginia, and No 9 Maryland, whom the President headed and preceded by a band of music with the rear brought up by the Alexandria Volunteer

MAIN ENTRANCE OF THE CAPITOL.

Artillery with grand solemnity of march proceeded to the President's Square in the city of Washington, where they were met and saluted by Lodge No. 15 of the city in all their elegant regalia headed by Bro. Joseph Clark Rt. W. G. M. and conducted to a large lodge prepared for the purpose of their reception. After a short space of time the brotherhood and other bodies were disposed in a second procession which took place amidst a brilliant crowd of spectators of both sexes according to the following arrangement: The surveying department of the city of Washington; Mayor and Corporation of Georgetown; Virginia Artillery; Commissioners of the city of Washington and their attendants; Stone Cutters; Mechanics; Two Sword Bearers; Masons of the First Degree; Bibles, etc., on Grand Cushions; Deacons with Staffs of Office; Masons of the Second Degree; Stewards with Wands; Wardens with Truncheons; Secretaries with Tools of Office; Past Masters with their Regalia; Treasurers with their Jewels; Band of Music; Lodge No. 22 of Virginia, disposed in their own order; Corn, Wine, and Oil; Grand Master P. T.; George Washington; W. M. No. 22, Virginia; Grand Sword Bearer.

" The procession marched two a breast in the greatest solemn dignity, with music playing, drums beating, colors flying, and spectators rejoicing, from the President's Square to the Capitol in the city of Washington, where the Grand Marshal ordered a halt, and directed each file in the procession to incline two steps, one to the right, and one to the left, and face each other, which formed a hollow oblong square, through which the Grand Sword Bearer led the van followed by the Grand Master P. T. on the left, the President of the United States in the centre, and the Worshipful Master of No. 22, Virginia, on the right. All the other orders that composed the procession advanced in the reverse of their order of march from the President's Square, to the south east corner of the Capitol, and the artillery filed off to a destined ground to display their manœuvres and discharge their cannon. The President of the United States, the Grand Master P. T. and the Worshipful Master of No. 22 took their stands to the east of a huge stone, and all the craft forming in a circle westward stood a short time in silent awful order.

" The artillery discharged a volley. The Grand Marshal delivered the commissioners a large silver plate with an inscription thereon, which the commissioners ordered to be read, and was as follows:

" ' This southeast corner-stone of the Capitol of the United States of America in the city of Washington was laid on the 18th day of September, 1793, in the 13th year of American Independence, in the first year of the second term of the Presidency of George Washington, whose virtues in the civil administration of his country have been as conspicuous and beneficial as his military valor and prudence have been useful in establishing her liberties, and in the year of Masonry 5793, by the President of the United States in concert with the Grand Lodge of Maryland, several lodges under its jurisdiction, and Lodge No. 22, from Alexandria, Virginia.

" ' Thomas Johnson, ⎫
" ' David Stuart,   ⎬ *Commissioners.*
" ' Daniel Carroll, ⎭
" ' Joseph Clark, *R. W. G. M. P. T.*
" ' James Hoban,   ⎫ *Architects.*
" ' Stephen Hallate, ⎭
" ' Collen Williamson, *M. Mason.*'

" The artillery discharged a volley. The plate was then delivered to the President, who, attended by the Grand Master P. T. and three most worshipful masters, descended to the caisson trench and deposited the plate, and laid on it the corner-stone of the Capitol of the United States of America, on which was deposited corn, wine, and oil. Then the whole congregation joined in prayer, which was succeeded by Masonic chanting honors and a volley from the artillery. The President of the United States and his attendant brethren ascended from the caisson to the east of the corner-stone and there the Grand Master P. T. elevated on a triple rostrum delivered an oration, after which there was more Masonic chanting and a 15th volley from the artillery.

"The whole company retired to an extensive booth where an ox of 500 lbs. was barbacued, of which the company generally partook, with every abundance of other recreation. The festival concluded with 15 successive volleys from the artillery, and before dark the whole company departed with joyful hopes of the production of their labor."

Stephen Hallate never forgot that he had been deprived of the honor of designing the Capitol, and upon every occasion took particular pains to annoy and insult the commissioners. They bore this a while, and, when patience had ceased to be a virtue, dismissed the cantankerous Frenchman, and appointed George Hatfield, a resident of Washington, to finish the construction of the north wing of the Capitol. He was also full of "quarrel and offence," and remained only a few months at the work, and James Hoban was finally compelled to carry it on alone. He completed the north wing in time for Congress to occupy it in November, 1800. Two years afterwards the commissioners secured a very capable English architect named Benjamin Henry Latrobe, and gave him full power to complete the Capitol after his own plan. Latrobe had been a pupil of Cockrell, the greatest London architect of his day, had travelled extensively in Europe, was the master of seven languages, and a man of rare inventive genius. He had come to America in 1796, and had made a fine reputation by architectural work in Southern cities. The first thing he did was to demolish the greater part of the north wing of the Capitol, which had been very badly constructed, and then he began to build upon a better plan. He secured variegated marble from Virginia for columns and capitals, employed a number of Italian sculptors to make artistic ornaments, and used brains and method in his work. He finished both wings in 1811, and connected them by a wooden bridge. No attempt was made to construct the central part of the Capitol, as Congress was not inclined to appropriate sufficient money for the purpose.

After the British had burned the Capitol in 1814, Congress wrangled a long time over the matter of rebuilding, and, Latrobe, fretting at the delay, left Washington and went to Pittsburg to build a steamboat for

STATUE OF WAR IN MAIN ENTRANCE OF THE CAPITOL.

Robert Fulton. It was not long before he was invited to return, and was informed that if he would undertake the reconstruction of the Capitol he would be furnished with ample means. He accepted the invitation, and began the work with the determination to make the Capitol rise from its ashes grander than before. Congress leased a building in which to hold its sessions during the reconstruction.

Latrobe was the real architect of the old Capitol,—the central or original building as it now stands. Thornton's plan was not followed by him in the slightest particular, and the small amount of finished work he found when he first took charge he pulled to pieces and rebuilt after his own ideas. All of the exterior of the building is his work save, perhaps,

STATUE OF PEACE IN MAIN ENTRANCE OF THE CAPITOL.

the walls of the north wing, and the interior was either constructed or designed by him. He fashioned the old Senate chamber and the old Hall of Representatives,—two remarkable specimens of classical grace and symmetry. From 1815 to 1817 he was busily engaged in restoring the Capitol, but resigned before the work was completed, and Charles Bulfinch, a Boston architect, took his place. Bulfinch used Latrobe's plans during the ten years he labored, and in 1827 he reported the building finished.

The Capitol at that time had cost $2,433,814. It was three hundred and fifty-two feet four inches long and one hundred and twenty-one feet six inches wide, exclusive of the projections or steps, which on the east side were sixty-five feet in width and on the west eighty-three feet.

The wings were seventy feet high to the top of the balustrade, and the central dome, which was constructed of wood with a covering of copper, was seventy-five feet high.

NATIONAL BOTANICAL GARDEN.

Until 1851 nothing of consequence was done to the exterior of the Capitol, but its architect, Robert Mills, made some slight improvements to the interior. Congress decided to build greater wings or extensions north and south, in which both houses might be better accommodated, and accordingly, on the 4th of July, 1851, the corner-stone of the south extension was laid with Masonic rites. President Fillmore participated in the ceremony, and Secretary of State Daniel Webster delivered an oration. A tablet, inscribed as follows, was placed under the corner-stone:

"On the morning of the first day of the seventy-sixth year of the Independence of the United States of America, in the city of Washington, being the 4th day of July, 1851, this stone, designated as the corner-stone of the Extension of the Capitol, according to a plan approved by the President, in pursuance of an act of Congress, was laid by Millard Fillmore, President of the United States, assisted by the Grand Master of the Masonic Lodges, in the presence of many members of Congress; of officers of the Executive and Judiciary Departments, National, State, and District; of officers of the Army and Navy; the corporate authorities of this and neighboring cities; many associations, civil, military, and Masonic; officers of the Smithsonian Institution and National Institute; professors of colleges and teachers of schools of the District of Columbia, with their students and pupils; and a vast concourse of people from places near and remote, including a few surviving gentlemen who witnessed the laying of the corner-stone of the Capitol by President Washington, on the 18th day of September, 1793. If, therefore, it shall be hereafter the will of God that this structure shall fall from its base, that its foundations be upturned, and this deposit brought to the eyes of men, be it known that on this day the Union of the United States of America stands firm; that their Constitution still exists unimpaired, and with all its original usefulness and glory, growing every day stronger and stronger in the affections of the great body of the American people, and attracting more and more the admiration of the world. And all here assembled, whether belonging to public life or to private life, with hearts devoutly thankful to Almighty God for the preservation of the liberty and happiness of the country, unite in sincere and fervent prayers that this deposit, and the walls and arches, the domes and towers, the columns and entablatures, now to be erected over it, may endure forever! God save the United States of America.

"DANIEL WEBSTER,
" Secretary of State of the United States."

The architect of the extensions was Thomas U. Walter, of Philadelphia, who had designed Girard College and other important structures. He prepared plans not only for the extensions, but for the present dome. Sixteen years were required to complete this reconstruction of the Capitol, and very nearly ten million dollars were expended. All of the work was done in a thoroughly excellent manner under the supervision of General M. C. Meigs. The great and imposing building has been very little changed since 1867, the year the extensions were finished.

WEST FRONT OF THE CAPITOL

CHAPTER VIII.

NO building in America has the majestic appearance of the Capitol, and few in the world can be compared to it in grandeur and massiveness. It stands on the brow of a hill ninety feet above the level of the Potomac river, and its huge white dome glittering in the sunlight can be seen for many miles. It is 751 feet four inches long, and, including the projections, 324 feet wide, and covers nearly four acres. Around it is a beautiful park forty-six acres in extent. The central building, or what is known as the original Capitol, is of Virginia sandstone painted white, and the two extensions, or Senate and House wings, are of fine white marble from quarries at Lee, Massachusetts. There is a rustic basement upon which rests the principal story, and above this is the attic story, surmounted by the entablature and balustrade. A series of columns and pilasters go entirely around the building. The central part is 352 feet four inches long and 121 feet six inches wide, and the extensions are each 142 feet eight inches long and 238 feet ten inches wide. The corridors which connect the extensions with the centre are each forty-four feet long and fifty-six feet wide.

The Capitol faces to the east, and its rear or western front overlooks the populous part of Washington. It was originally located in this way because it was believed that the city would grow almost entirely to the east over the broad, level plateau which constitutes Capitol Hill, and the Capitol would then face the most prominent section. This was not the case, however, as the city developed on its northwestern side, and the eastern section for many years was but sparsely settled, and even to-day does not contain one-tenth part of the population of the city. The Capitol, therefore, stands with its "front door on the back side" like the Irishman's shanty, but it is likely that, before many years, the western front

DOME OF THE CAPITOL

will be made like the eastern, so that the building will then have two "front doors" precisely alike.

The central portico at the main entrance on the eastern front of the Capitol has twenty-four ponderous columns of sandstone, which were erected in 1825. They are thirty feet high, and each is composed of a single stone. On the tympanum of the portico is an allegorical group, designated as the "Genius of America," which was sculptured in sandstone by Persico, a distinguished Roman sculptor. The design was drawn by John Quincy Adams when Secretary of State. The central figure represents America with a shield and spear. The shield has on it the letters U. S. A., and rests on a low altar decorated with a wreath of oak leaves encircling the date, July 4. 1776. At the feet of America sits a large eagle, and on the right and left

STATUE OF FREEDOM ON CAPITOL DOME.

are figures representing Justice and Hope. Justice holds in her right hand an open scroll inscribed "Constitution of the United States," and in her left perfectly-balanced scales. Hope rests upon an anchor, and is addressing America, who points to Justice. The group "suggests

ALLEGORICAL GROUP ON PORTICO OF THE CAPITOL, DESIGNED BY JOHN QUINCY ADAMS.

that, however hope may flatter, all prosperity should be founded in public right and the preservation of the Constitution."

In niches at the main entrance door are two massive statues of pure Italian marble to represent War and Peace. They are the work of Persico, and cost $6000 each. Over the door is

MARBLE GROUP, "THE DISCOVERY OF AMERICA,"
ON PORTICO OF THE CAPITOL.

a basso-rilievo of Washington being crowned with a laurel wreath by
Fame and Peace. It was cut in sandstone, in 1827, by Capellano.

The portico, which is 160 feet in length, has broad stone steps flanked
by large buttresses. On one buttress is a marble group representing
" The Discovery of America." It was executed by Persico, in 1846, at a
cost of $24,000. Columbus is represented holding aloft a small globe
inscribed " America," while at his side crouches an Indian maiden. The
figure of the great navigator is encased in armor, which is stated to be a
correct copy " to a rivet" of the armor he wore. On the opposite buttress
is a marble group executed by Horatio Greenough, and which represents
" Civilization, or the first settlement of America." This has figures of a
pioneer and Indian engaged in deadly conflict, and on one side is the
pioneer's wife clasping a babe to her breast, while she watches the conflict
with anxious interest. Greenough was twelve years executing this group,
and its cost was nearly $25,000.

MARBLE GROUP, "CIVILIZATION," ON PORTICO
OF THE CAPITOL.

The door of the main entrance to the Capitol is of bronze, and on it are designs in high relief illustrative of the career of Columbus. It is one of the finest pieces of bronze work in the world, and was modelled at Rome, in 1858, by Randolph Rogers, the American sculptor, and cast at Munich, in 1860. With the casing the door is nineteen feet in height and nine feet in width, and weighs 20,000 pounds. Its cost was $28,000. The casing is covered with emblematic designs, and on the top of the arch is a bust of Columbus. There are eight panels on the door, and also a transom panel, and on them are finely represented the following scenes: "The examination of Columbus before the Council of Salamanca;" "Departure of Columbus from the Convent of La Rabida for the Spanish court;" "Columbus before the court of Ferdinand and Isabella;" "Departure of Columbus from Palos on his first voyage of discovery;" "Columbus landing at San Salvador;" "First encounter of Columbus with the Indians;" "Triumphal entry of Columbus into Barcelona;" "Columbus in chains;" "Death-bed of Columbus." The scenes begin from the bottom panel on the left side of the door, as shown in the illustration, and go up to the transom panel and then down the right side. Around the door and between the panels are statues of prominent contemporaries of the navigator and busts of the historians of his voyages.

The famous Crawford bronze door is in the entrance to the Senate extension. It was modelled by Thomas Crawford, and cast at Chicopee, Massachusetts. It is fourteen and one-half feet high, and nine and one-half feet wide, and weighs 14,000 pounds. It cost nearly $57,000, and was placed in position in 1868. On its eight panels are scenes in high relief illustrative of American history, beginning with the "Battle of Bunker Hill and Death of General Warren, June, 1775," and following with the "Battle of Monmouth, June, 1778, and rebuke of General Charles Lee, the traitor;" the "Battle of Yorktown, 1781;" a "Hessian soldier in death-struggle with an American;" an allegory of the "Blessings of Peace;" the "Ovation to Washington at Trenton, 1789;" the "Inauguration of Washington as First President of the United States;" and the "Laying of the corner-stone of the Capitol of the United States." The scenes begin at the top of the right side of the door, as shown in the illustration, and go downward and then up the left side. The frame is ornamented with designs of the acanthus, grape, maize, and cotton-boll.

On the tympanum of the portico of the Senate extension there is a marble group sculptured by Thomas Crawford, which represents "American Civilization and the Decadence of the Indian Races." The figures portray America, War, Commerce, Education, the Mechanical Arts, Pioneers, and Indians. The cost of this work was $50,000.

The porticoes of the Senate and House extensions have massive monolithic columns of marble with beautiful capitals, and similar columns are placed on the north and south projections and west front. On the grand central portico of the Capitol the Presidents of the United States take the oath of office on inauguration day.

The great dome which rises from the centre of the Capitol is of grand, symmetrical proportions, and has no equal in the world for classical beauty. It was constructed under the direction of Charles F. Thomas after designs by Thomas U. Walter, and cost $1,250,000. Eight years were required to build it, and so carefully and thoroughly was the work done that it is believed it will never need to be repaired. It was made of the strongest cast iron, and nearly four thousand tons were used. Over a series of ribs large sheets of iron were securely bolted, and all the mechanism was arranged to move together during atmospheric changes "like the folding and unfolding of a lily." The dome is thickly covered with

THE ROGERS BRONZE DOOR IN MAIN ENTRANCE OF THE CAPITOL.

white paint every year, to prevent it from rusting, and, as the builder
says, will doubtless stand for a thousand years impervious to wind and
weather.

At the base there is a peristyle composed of thirty-six iron columns
and surmounted by a wide balustrade. Above the peristyle is an attic
story, and above this begins the domical covering. From the top of the
dome rises a "lantern" fifty feet high and fifteen feet in diameter. It is
surrounded by a peristyle, and contains a large reflecting lamp, which is
lighted whenever Congress has a night session. This light can be seen
from all parts of the city. The shell of the dome has numerous windows
to admit light to the rotunda. Every part of the huge sphere is of iron.

On the top of the lantern stands a bronze statue of Freedom, designed
by Thomas Crawford, and cast in the foundry of Clark Mills, at Bladensburg, Maryland. The statue is nineteen and one-half feet high, weighs
14,985 pounds, and cost nearly $24,000. It rests upon a globe which is
inscribed "*E Pluribus Unum.*" The figure is that of the Goddess of
Liberty, and its head is crowned with a helmet surrounded by a circlet
of stars and topped with a bunch of feathers. When the design was
made, in 1855, it was submitted to Jefferson Davis, who was then Secretary of War. Crawford had placed a "liberty cap" on the figure, but Mr.
Davis objected to this cap on the ground that it suggested that Americans
had been slaves, and therefore Crawford removed the cap and substituted
the bunch of feathers. The statue was placed on its lofty pedestal December 2, 1863. When the work of erecting it was finished, the emblem
of liberty was saluted with thirty-four guns by a park of artillery stationed
on the eastern grounds of the Capitol, and to this salute the guns of all
the forts around Washington responded.

The low wooden dome, which stood where the great iron dome is
now, was removed in 1856. It was seventy-five feet high. The present
dome stands 218 feet above the balustrade on the top of the Capitol.
The total height from the base-line of the eastern front of the building to
the crest of the statue of Freedom is 307½ feet. The diameter of the
dome is 135½ feet. Persons are allowed to ascend the dome to the
gallery directly under the lantern. The view of Washington and the surrounding country from this high place is magnificent.

The celebrated statue of Washington, by Horatio Greenough, occupies a position on the eastern grounds of the Capitol, facing the grand portico. Congress ordered the work in 1832, with the intention of placing
it over the vaulted tomb of Washington, which was to be constructed
in the crypt of the Capitol, with an opening through the floor of the
rotunda, but as the heirs of Washington declined to allow his remains to

THE CRAWFORD BRONZE DOOR IN SENATE EXTENSION OF THE CAPITOL.

be removed from Mount Vernon, the tomb was not constructed. The statue was received from Italy in 1840, and for a time was placed in the rotunda. It is a colossal sitting figure of Carrara marble, on a granite pedestal, and cost $45,000. The figure, which is partially nude, is seated in a chair of Roman design, on which are small statues of Columbus and an Indian chief, and also lions' heads and acanthus leaves. Representations of Hercules strangling the serpent and Apollo driving the chariot of the sun around the world are on the sides of the chair, and on the back is the Latin inscription, "*Simulacrum istud ad magnum Libertatus exemplum, nec sine ipsa duraturum*," which can be freely translated, "This statue is for a great example of liberty, nor without liberty will the example endure." Washington is represented with his right hand pointing toward heaven and with his left holding a sheathed sword. The pedestal is inscribed, "First in war, first in peace, first in the hearts of his countrymen."

On the western grounds of the Capitol, near the steps which lead to the upper terrace, is a large bronze statue of John Marshall, Chief Justice of the Supreme Court of the United States from 1801 to 1835. It is the

GREENOUGH'S STATUE OF WASHINGTON IN EASTERN
PARK OF THE CAPITOL.

STATUE OF CHIEF JUSTICE MARSHALL IN WESTERN PARK
OF THE CAPITOL.

work of William W. Story, was executed at Rome, and unveiled May 10, 1884. The Chief Justice is represented as seated in the chair he used in the court-room. He wears his official robe, and extends one hand as if delivering a judicial opinion. The figure rests on a pedestal of drab Italian marble, which bears on its front the inscription, "John Marshall, Chief Justice of the United States. Erected by the Bar and the Congress of the United States, A.D. 1884." On the rear of the pedestal is a wreath of oak and laurel, and on the sides are two panels containing large basso-rilievo entitled "Minerva dictating the constitution to Young America," and "Victory leading Young America to swear fidelity on the altar of the Union." There are eight figures in each panel, two feet in height. The

8

statue and pedestal cost $40,000. The features of the Chief Justice are clearly portrayed, and the likeness is pronounced very accurate.

Soon after the death of Marshall, in 1835, an association was organized in Philadelphia to raise a fund to erect a statue to his memory. Contributions were received from lawyers in different parts of the country, but as only about $4000 were obtained, the fund was invested in the city bonds of Philadelphia, and as the interest accrued it was reinvested. In 1882 the fund had increased by careful management to $20,000, and the trustees appeared before Congress with the proposition that they would convey the sum to the United States if Congress would appropriate a similar amount and order the statue to be constructed, it having been estimated that it would cost $40,000. The proposition was accepted, and the contract for the statue was given to Mr. Story, who has produced a satisfactory work.

The grounds around the Capitol have been laid out in a very attractive manner during the past ten years, and now form an admirable setting to the magnificent building. Large numbers of fine trees, shrubs, and flowering plants are growing in various parts of the grounds, and there are lawns, fountains, well-paved walks and drives. The entire park of forty-six acres is enclosed by a low granite wall with ornamental entrances.

Adjacent to the western grounds of the Capitol is located the National Botanical Garden of ten acres. It was established about fifty years ago, but its greatest development has been within the past fifteen years. It contains a great conservatory filled with the choicest foreign plants, and also a number of small conservatories. Around the garden are extensive collections of trees and shrubs, which are cultivated in a scientific manner. Here are grown a large portion of the plants set out each spring in the parks, squares, and circles of the city. The garden is under the control of Congress, and the members of both houses obtain from it each session at least two thousand bouquets, besides many "botanical specimens" which they take to their homes all over the United States.

On Pennsylvania avenue, near the main entrance to the western grounds of the Capitol, stands the Naval Monument, which is inscribed. "In memory of the officers, seamen, and marines of the United States Navy who fell in defence of the Union and liberty of their country, 1861–1865." It was designed by Admiral David D. Porter, and executed by Franklin Simmons at Rome. It is of pure Carrara marble, and encircling its base is an elaborate granite foundation designed by Edward Clark, the present architect of the Capitol. Two figures, America and History, stand on the top of the monument. America is sorrowfully narrating the loss of her defenders, while History records on her tablet, "They died that their country might live." Below these figures, on the front of the monument, is a figure of Victory holding aloft a laurel wreath, and on the back is a figure of Peace offering the olive branch. The monument is forty-four feet in height, and the figures on it are six feet. It was erected in 1877 from contributions received from members of the navy, and the granite foundation was furnished by Congress. The cost was $21,000 for the monument and $20,000 for the foundation.

THE NAVAL MONUMENT.

CHAPTER IX.

THE principal story of the Capitol contains the great Rotunda, the National Statuary Hall, formerly used by the House of Representatives, the Library of Congress, the Supreme Court-Room, formerly used by the Senate, and the halls of the Houses of Congress. It has also numerous rooms for the officials of the Capitol and of Congress. The Rotunda is in the centre of the old or original Capitol. It is ninety-five feet six inches in diameter, three hundred feet in circumference, and one hundred and eighty feet in height. It has a sandstone floor, which is supported by ponderous brick arches, which rest on columns arranged in peristyles. Above the walls of the Capitol the Rotunda is entirely of iron, as it is the interior of the great dome. Light is admitted to it by the thirty-six windows of the peristyle of the dome. At its extreme height is an opening called "the eye," and suspended over this is a gigantic canopy, on which is an allegorical painting by Constantino Brumidi, entitled "The Apotheosis of Washington." The canopy is a circular sheet of iron covered with stucco, and is sixty-five feet in diameter and two hundred and five feet in circumference. It covers an area of 4664 feet. Brumidi's painting is a very elaborate work, executed with great skill, and even from the floor of the Rotunda has a fine, artistic effect. The central figure is Washington, with Freedom and Victory at his right and left, and around them are female figures to represent the original states of the Union. The border of the canopy contains six groups of emblematic figures, representing the Fall of Tyranny, Agriculture, Mechanics, Commerce, the Marine, and the Arts and Sciences. The painting is glowing with color, and every portion of it is finished in a very careful manner. All the figures are large and admirably delineated. Brumidi gave several years to this work, which was an exceedingly ardu-

117

ous one on account of the peculiar position of the canopy. The painting cost nearly $50,000.

Above the architrave of the Rotunda, on the frieze ten feet wide which encircles the walls, are frescos of the important events in the history of America. They are executed in *chiaro-oscuro* (light and shade), and were begun by Brumidi in 1878. After his death, in 1880, the work was undertaken by Castigini, his pupil, who has since carried it on. The series will not probably be completed for several years.

On the walls of the Rotunda are arabesque designs and panels with medallions of Columbus, Raleigh, Cabot, and La Salle, which were executed in 1827, by Caucici and Capellano, Italian sculptors, who were pupils of Canova. In oblong panels over the entrance doors are *alto-rilievi* of the "Landing of the Pilgrims," "Pocahontas saving the life of Captain John Smith," "William Penn holding a conference with the Indians," and "Daniel Boone in conflict with the Indians." These are also the work of Caucici and Capellano.

The Rotunda contains eight mammoth paintings set in panels round the walls. Four of them represent scenes of the discovery and settlement of America, and the others are devoted to the Revolutionary period. They are all by American artists and were painted many years ago.

The first of the early historical paintings represents the "Landing of Columbus at San Salvador," and is by John Vanderlyn, who received $10,000 for it. Columbus is represented in the act of proclaiming possession in the name of Spain of the land he had discovered, October 14, 1492.

The second painting represents "The Discovery of the Mississippi by De Soto, May, 1541." It is by William H. Powell, and cost $12,000. The central figure is De Soto mounted on a spirited horse. The painting is not considered historically correct.

The third painting represents "The Baptism of Pocahontas, 1613," and is by John G. Chapman. He received $10,000 for the work. The Indian princess, her husband, John Rolfe, John and Ann Laydon, Sir Thomas Dale, Alexander Whitaker, several Indian chiefs, and prominent people of the Virginia colony are represented.

The fourth painting represents "The Embarkation of the Pilgrims from Delft Haven, Holland, July 21, 1620." It is by Robert W. Weir, and cost $10,000. It represents the prayer on board of the little ship just before it sailed for America with the band of pilgrims who were seeking a land of religious liberty.

The other paintings are known as the Trumbull series, and represent events connected with the Revolutionary war. The artist was John Trumbull, who was born in 1756 and died in 1843. He was a son of

THE ROTUNDA OF THE CAPITOL.

Jonathan Trumbull, governor of Connecticut during the Revolution, and for a year or so was an officer on Washington's staff. He spent five years in Europe in the study of art, and for more than twenty years was engaged in gathering the material and preparing himself to paint the scenes of the struggle for American independence. It is stated that "the Trumbull series of pictures are especially valuable, because each of the many faces painted in them are actual likenesses, for which many of the subjects sat to the artist, and when this was not the case, copies of portraits at the time in the possession of the respective families were introduced." Congress gave the order for the paintings in 1817, and in 1824 they were completed, and the artist received $32,000 for them.

The first of the series is entitled "Signing of the Declaration of Independence, 1776." The hall of the Continental Congress is exactly reproduced, and the members of the Congress are painted in an accurate manner. John Hancock, President of the Congress, is represented seated at a table on which is the Declaration of Independence, and in front of the table are Thomas Jefferson, John Adams, Benjamin Franklin, Roger Sherman, and Robert L. Livingston, the committee who had charge of the document. Trumbull obtained the information as to the disposition of the persons represented in the painting from Jefferson, Adams, and others who were present when the Declaration was signed.

The second Trumbull painting is entitled "Surrender of General Burgoyne, Saratoga, October 17, 1777." The artist was present at the surrender, and made a sketch of it at the time. The painting is thus described: "General Burgoyne, attended by General Phillips and followed by other officers, has arrived near the marque of General Gates. General Gates has advanced a few steps to meet his prisoner, who, with General Phillips, has dismounted, and is in the act of offering his sword, which General Gates declines to receive, and invites them to enter and partake of refreshments. A number of the principal officers of the American army are assembled near their General."

The third painting is entitled "Surrender of Lord Cornwallis at Yorktown, October 19, 1781." Lord Cornwallis and the officers of the defeated British army, conducted by General Lincoln, are represented as entering the lines of the American and French troops. A writer says, "When General Lincoln had surrendered to the British at Charleston some time before, Lord Cornwallis refused to permit the Americans to march out with flying colors, as was usual. When Cornwallis surrendered, General Washington appointed General Lincoln to oversee the manner in which the British should submit, which was with arms shouldered and colors lowered."

CANOPY OF THE ROTUNDA.

NATIONAL STATUARY HALL, SHOWING
THE HISTORICAL CLOCK.

The fourth painting is entitled "Resignation of General Washington at Annapolis, December 23, 1783." After bidding farewell in New York to his companions in arms, Washington, attended by only two of his aides, journeyed to Annapolis, where Congress was sitting in the old State House, and resigned his commission as Commander-in-Chief of the Continental Army. Martha Washington met her husband at Annapolis, and after the resignation accompanied him to Mount Vernon. Trumbull has painted her in the gallery of the State House prominent among the spectators of the resignation.

The hall formerly occupied by the House of Representatives is now known as the National Statuary Hall. It was designed by Latrobe in 1803, and when he reconstructed the Capitol after the British invaders had burned it, in 1814, he improved and extended the original design, adding marble columns and various works of art. The hall is fashioned somewhat after the ancient theatre at Athens, and is considered an almost perfect example of classic symmetry. It is semicircular in form, ninety-five feet in length, and to the top of the domed ceiling fifty-seven feet in height. The ceiling is beautifully painted. On one side of the hall is a high, wide arch supported by marble pillars, and on the other side a colonnade of twenty-six tall columns of variegated marble, with capitals of pure white marble, sculptured in Italy. The floor is of marble with mosaic tiling. On the arch is a plaster statue of Liberty, and also a large sandstone eagle with outspread wings. The old marble clock used by the Representatives is standing over the entrance door from the Rotunda. It was executed by Charles Franzoni, in 1819, and is a notable work of art. The Genius of History is represented as recording on a tablet the events of the nation. She stands gracefully on a winged car, which is rolling over the globe. The wheel of the car is the face of the clock.

The House of Representatives used this hall from 1808 until 1814, and then from 1817 until December 16, 1857; and during that period of nearly fifty years many legislative matters of great national importance were discussed and acted upon. Here the " giants in those days"—Clay, Webster, the younger Adams, Calhoun, Randolph, Cass, Burges, Wise, Forsyth, Corwin, Wright, and many others—won reputation for states-manship, and made the walls ring with their fiery eloquence. Here were many fierce and bitter wrangles over vexed questions,—turbulent scenes, displays of sectional feeling ; and here also was much legislative action which has gone into history as wise and beneficial. Where the Congress-men of the age that is gone attended to the business of the nation often-times with a torrent of words, now stand mute "chosen sons" of the states in dignified effigies of marble and bronze. Seven years after the House of Representatives had removed to its new hall in the south extension of the Capitol, the old hall was devoted to its present use. Congress authorized the President, in 1864, to invite each state "to send the effigies of two of her chosen sons, in marble or in bronze, to be placed permanently here."

Comparatively few of the states have as yet responded to the invitation, but it is believed they will all be represented in this grand hall of statues before many years. Rhode Island was the first state to send statues, and Connecticut and New York followed. The collection at present is as follows : Rhode Island, statues of Roger Williams and General Nathaniel Greene ; Connecticut, statues of Governor Jonathan Trumbull and Roger Sherman ; New York, statues of Vice-President George Clinton and Chancellor Robert R. Livingston; Massachusetts, statues of Governor John Winthrop and Samuel Adams; Vermont, statues of Colonel Ethan Allen and Jacob Collamer ; Maine, statue of Governor William King ; Pennsylvania, statues of Robert Fulton and William Muhlenberg. Eleven of the statues are of marble and two are of bronze. They are all excellent in design and execution.

The hall also contains a number of statues, busts, and portraits, furnished by the government. In the collection is a plaster copy of Houdon's statue of Washington, and the marble statue of Lincoln, sculptured by Vinnie Ream Hoxie in 1870, and for which she received $15,000. There is also Horatio Stone's marble statue of Hamilton, which cost $10,000; and a bronze statue of Jefferson by D'Angers, which formerly stood on the lawn in front of the White House. There are busts of Lincoln, Kosciusko, and Thomas Crawford; and portraits of Washington, Jefferson, Lincoln, Charles Carroll of Carrollton, Gunning Bedford, Benjamin West, and Joshua R. Giddings.

In the basement story of the Capitol are the post-offices of Congress, the document and folding rooms, and numerous committee rooms. A great quantity of mail matter is handled daily in the post-offices during a session of Congress, and a number of clerks and carriers are employed. In the document and folding rooms the books and pamphlets printed by the government are stored until they are distributed by Congressmen to their constituents. The government publishes every year about three hundred different books, some of them very large and costly, and each Congressman is entitled to a certain number. The books are reports of the various departments, special reports ordered by Congress, Acts of Congress, Public Statutes, etc. Over 300,000 copies of the bulky report of the Department of Agriculture are annually distributed. To illustrate this work usually costs about $30,000, and some of the other reports are illustrated at a large expense. Dozens of men are employed in the document and folding rooms in packing books to be sent over the country, and enough printed matter to fill three hundred mail-cars is forwarded every year. All the books and pamphlets are printed and bound at the Government Printing-Office.

STATUE OF FULTON IN STATUARY HALL.

HOUDON'S STATUE OF WASHINGTON IN STATUARY HALL.

In the sub-basement is located the apparatus by which the halls of Congress and all parts of the Capitol are heated and ventilated. The apparatus consists of four engines and eight boilers, and three enormous revolving fans, which draw the air from the outside of the building into the ducts which convey it to the halls and rooms. The air is heated after it comes from the outside. There is a very ingenious appliance for ascertaining whether the air in the halls of Congress is too dry or too moist, and it is regulated by a single human hair six inches long. Perfectly dry air is marked at 0; air with all the moisture it will hold is marked at 100. A dial with a pointer indicates the different degrees from 0 to 100. The hair rapidly absorbs the moisture in the air and becomes shorter when wet, and the difference in its length when dry and when wet is indicated on the dial by the pointer, which moves back and forth as the moisture of the hair varies. If the air is too dry, more steam is turned on ; if too moist, less steam is used ; and thus by means of the hair the atmosphere for the nation's legislators is kept at a healthful point.

Below the basement are many dark, gloomy chambers and corridors filled with old models, plaster casts of statues, and refuse of all sorts. The subterranean story is a perfect labyrinth of crooks and crannies, cells and mysterious recesses, which are dimly lighted by a few gas-jets placed at long intervals. In these dismal vaults and passages one could easily be lost and wander for days without finding the way out. The young wife of a Congressman was lost here some years ago. Curiosity had led her to explore the vaults alone, and becoming bewildered by the dark, winding passages, she was unable to retrace her steps, and was compelled to remain in the silent and desolate region all night. The night was one of horror to her, and when she was discovered by her husband the next morning it was found that her brown hair had changed to snowy white, and that her reason had fled. She recovered her reason, but for many years suffered from excessive fear and nervousness.

The attic story of the Capitol is mainly devoted to the committee rooms of Congress. These rooms are handsomely painted and furnished and have considerable ornamentation. In the attic are stored great quantities of government records. Here are all the records of the early Congresses, and many other ancient documents of historical value.

The Capitol is open every week-day to visitors, and all parts of it can be freely inspected. It is in charge of the official known as the Architect of the Capitol, and has a large force of policemen, engineers, firemen, and laborers. Many thousands of dollars are expended annually in caring for the huge structure.

How much has the Capitol cost? is often asked. This is a very difficult question to answer. Upon the work of construction it is known there had been expended up to June 30, 1883, the sum of $15,599,656; but what the expenditure has been for statues, paintings, frescos, improving and adorning the grounds, etc., it is almost impossible to ascertain. The expenditure outside of the construction must have been several millions; and it is even declared that at least thirty millions in all have been expended on the nation's building during the nearly one hundred years that have passed since the laying of its corner-stone.

7

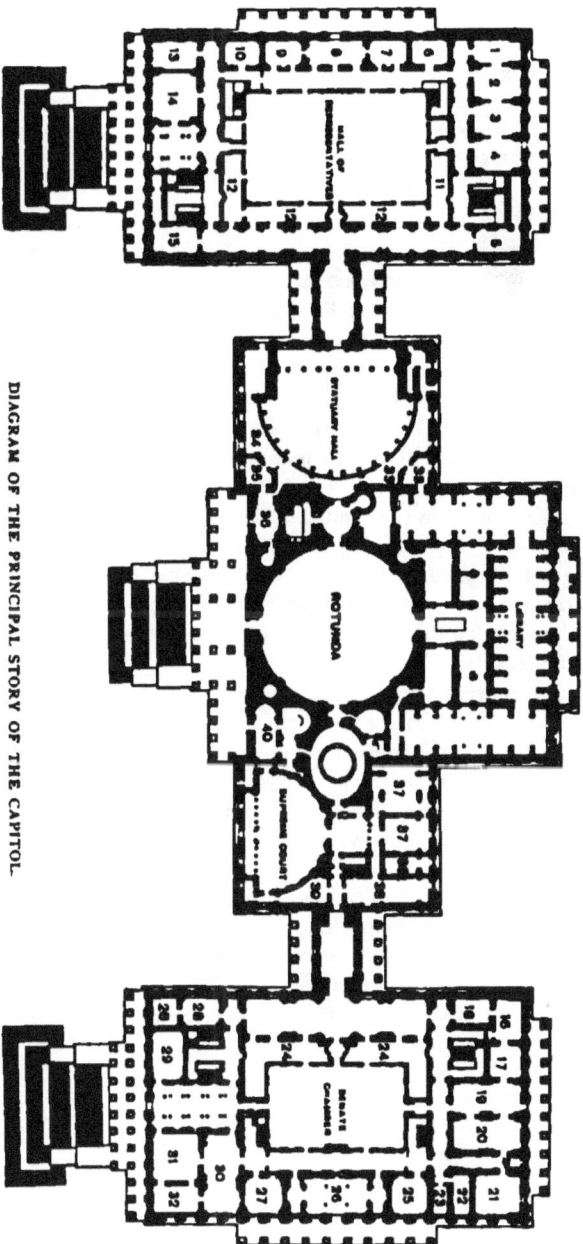

DIAGRAM OF THE PRINCIPAL STORY OF THE CAPITOL.

HOUSE WING.

1. Office of the Speaker.
2. Office of the Sergeant-at-Arms.
3. Engrossing Clerks of the House.
4. Journal and Printing Clerks of the House.
5. Office of the Clerk of the House.
6, 8, 9. Members' Retiring Room.
10. Lobby.
11. Hall Folding-Room.
12. Cloak-Room.
13. Committee on Appropriations.
14. Committee on Ways and Means.
15. Committee on Military Affairs.

MAIN BUILDING.

32. House Document-Room.
34. House Stationery-Room.
35, 36. House Committee on Banking and Currency.
37. Office of the Clerk of the Supreme Court.
38. Robing-Room of the Supreme Court.
39. Withdrawing-Room of the Supreme Ct.
40. Office of the Marshal of the Supreme Ct.

Supreme Court Chamber:
Old Hall of the House of Representatives (now Statuary Hall).
The Congressional Library.

SENATE WING.

16. Office of the Secretary of the Senate.
17. Executive Clerk of the Senate.
18. Financial Clerk of the Senate.
19. Chief Clerk of the Senate.
20. Engrossing and Enrolling Clerks of the Senate.
21. Committee on Appropriations.
23. Committee on Enrolled Bills.
24. Cloak-Room.
25. The President of the United States' Room.
27. The Senators' Withdrawing-Room.
28. The Vice-President's Room.
29. Committee on Finance.
30. Official Reporters of Debates.
31. Reception-Room.
32. Committee-Room.
33. Office of the Sergeant-at-Arms of the Senate.

CHAPTER X.

N the central projection of the western front of the Capitol is the great Library of Congress, which contains 545,000 books and 185,000 pamphlets, and which ranks as fifth among the prominent libraries of the world. It was originally established as a library of reference for Congress and the high officials of the government, but as it grew large and valuable its scope was extended, and now it can be properly called the National Public Library, as every one is allowed to freely use its rare and extensive collections, and daily its rooms are filled with men and women from all parts of the country consulting the books which they can find nowhere else. There is no other library in the United States one-half as large and complete as this one, and in some of its departments it is fully the equal of any of the great libraries of Europe. Its historical collections have a wide, ample range, and are particularly comprehensive in everything which pertains to America, and in general literature its collections are remarkably full and serviceable.

Congress founded the library in 1802, with some 3000 books carefully selected in London, and John Beckley, of Virginia, then clerk of the House of Representatives, was the first librarian. One of its earliest friends and supporters was John Randolph, and the eccentric statesman always took special pains to secure liberal appropriations for it, and had a good deal to do with the selection of its books. When the British soldiers invaded the Capitol in 1814 they used the books and papers of the library to kindle the fire which destroyed the building. The library was stripped of everything it contained, and a large quantity of government records stored in it were burned. Thomas Jefferson had a fine library at his mountain home in Virginia, which he had collected during his long residence in Europe, and, as he was at that time in financial

128

LIBRARY OF CONGRESS.

difficulty, he offered to sell his books to the government as a nucleus for a new Library of Congress. He made the proposition in September, 1814, and after considerable discussion of the matter the library was purchased by Congress for $23.950. There were 6000 volumes, including some rare works of history and philosophy, and also "many Bibles and religious works." When the library left Monticello for Washington it is said that Jefferson shed tears. He had greatly enjoyed the companionship of these books, and nothing but the poverty of his old age would have induced him to part with them.

In 1824 the present main hall of the Library of Congress was finished and occupied. It was constructed by Charles Bulfinch after designs by Latrobe, and for the first time the library was suitably housed. Previous to the completion of the hall, the library had occupied the room now the office of the clerk of the Supreme Court of the United States. George Watterson, of Washington, was the librarian, and he held the position fourteen years. The library developed rapidly in its new quarters, and in

9

1851 it had nearly 60,000 books. Its pleasant hall, with windows over-looking the city, became a favorite resort, and was daily filled with ladies and gentlemen of the highest society discussing literary matters and social events. On December 24, 1851, a fire, caused by a defective flue, swept through the library hall and destroyed over 30,000 books, and also some valuable paintings. The hall was reconstructed in 1852 by Thomas U. Walter, and two other halls added, nearly $300,000 being expended to make the accommodations for the library ample, convenient, and elegant. Congress made liberal appropriations from year to year, and the three great halls were soon well stocked with books. In 1866 the scientific works of the Smithsonian Institution, amounting to 40,000 volumes, were deposited in the Library of Congress, which has since continued to be the depository of all the publications received by the Smithsonian Institution from learned societies throughout the world. In 1867 Congress purchased for $100,000 the collection of rare historical books and pamphlets, files of newspapers, maps, engravings, etc., accumulated by Peter Force, of Wash-ington, during thirty years of antiquarian research. The Force collection now forms a very valuable department of the Library of Congress. From 1829 to 1861 the librarian was John S. Meehan, of New York, and from 1861 to 1864, John G. Stephenson, of Indiana. In 1864, President Lincoln appointed as librarian Ainsworth R. Spofford, of Ohio, and he has con-tinued in the position to the present time. In 1876 the library contained 293,000 volumes, and in 1879 more than 352,000. Since then the yearly increase has been large, and the library halls are now so crowded that a number of rooms in the basement of the Capitol have to be used to store the books. It is likely that within a short time a magnificent new build-ing, with shelf-room for a million and a half volumes, will be erected, at a cost of $3,000,000, expressly for the use of this inestimable library.

The law library of the government is a part of the Library of Congress. It contains 60,000 volumes, and is the largest of its kind in the United States. Since 1859 it has occupied the old chamber of the Supreme Court in the basement of the Capitol.

The halls of the Library of Congress are constructed of iron and glass, and are prettily ornamented in gold and delicate colors. The main hall is ninety-one feet long, thirty-four feet wide, and thirty-eight feet high; and the two other halls are of nearly the same size. The library is in charge of an official with the title of "Librarian of Congress." He is an officer of Congress, and has charge of the copyright business of the government. His salary is $4000 per year, and he has two assistants with salaries of $2500, two assistants with salaries of $1800, and nineteen assistants and employés with salaries ranging from $1400 to $480. The entire salary list is $38,320. The library is open daily from 9 A.M. to 4 P.M. Members of Congress and certain officials of the government have the right to take books out of the library, and other persons can secure the privilege by depositing the money value of the books. Every one has the right to use the library freely within the halls.

There are about five thousand books out of the library all the time, and most of them are in the possession of members of Congress. Senators read a great many books relating to treaties and commercial relations with foreign nations, and books upon finance, political economy, and social questions are constantly demanded by the members of both houses. Some Congressmen are very fond of fiction and poetry, and read all the latest works; others are all the time seeking historical information, and reading of the views and actions of the great men of the country in the early days. Many of the wives of Senators and Representatives, notwithstanding the demands made upon them during the social season, read a large number of books, and some of the wives earnestly study historical and political questions expressly for the purpose of aiding their husbands in their public duties; and even young ladies aid their fathers in this way. The families of Congressmen read all the popular books upon art and household decoration, and upon social customs at home and abroad, and there is also a great deal of novel reading in these circles. The American and English poets are extensively read, and not a few of the nation's legislators and their women folk are careful readers and ardent admirers of the classic poets.

Almost any day one can see in the library a number of men of national reputation busily reading at tables covered with books. There is no restriction in this library as to the number of books one can obtain at a time. The attendants are courteous and ready, and will bring to a reader all the works on a subject that have been published for a hundred years, if they are wanted; for it is a remarkable fact that upon many subjects this library has every book that has ever come from a press for a century,—books in twenty languages; books good, bad, and indifferent. On these crowded shelves the works of great and little authors jostle each other,—productions which have long been the admiration of the world and those of brief life and remembrance.

AINSWORTH R. SPOFFORD, LIBRARIAN
OF CONGRESS.

Congress annually appropriates about $54,000 for the expenses of the library. From 40,000 to 50,000 books and pamphlets are added each year by purchase, gift, and exchange, and by the operation of the copyright laws. Many publications are purchased at the sales of private libraries, and many publications are donated by patriotic citizens. Files of the leading American, English, French, and German newspapers and periodicals are preserved. The collection of ancient periodicals is very large and valuable.

In the library all the records of the copyright office are preserved. The copyright business was transferred from the Patent Office to the Library of Congress in 1870. The following is a summary of the laws of copyright under the revised acts of Congress, as prepared by the Librarian of Congress expressly for public use:

A *printed* copy of the title of the book, map, chart, dramatic or musical composition, engraving, cut, print, photograph, or a description of the painting, drawing, chromo, statue, statuary, or model or design for a work of the fine arts, for which copyright is desired, must be sent by mail or otherwise, *prepaid*, addressed Librarian of Congress, Washington, D. C. This must be done before publication of the book or other article. The *printed title* required may be a copy of the title-page of such publications as have title-pages. In other cases, the title must be printed expressly for copyright entry, with name of claimant of copyright. The style of type is immaterial, and the print of a type-writer will be accepted. But a separate title is required for *each* entry, and *each* title must be printed on paper as large as commercial note. A fee of fifty cents, for recording the title of each book or other article, must be enclosed with the title as above, and fifty cents in addition (or one dollar in all) for each certificate of copyright under seal of the Librarian of Congress, which will be transmitted by early mail. Within ten days after publication of each book or other article, two complete copies of the best edition issued must be sent, to perfect the copyright, with the address Librarian of Congress, Washington, D. C. The postage must be prepaid, or else the publications enclosed in parcels covered by printed Penalty Labels, furnished by the Librarian, in which case they will come free by mail, according to rulings of the Post-Office Department. Without the deposit of copies above required the copyright is void, and a penalty of $25 is incurred. No copy is required to be deposited elsewhere.

No copyright is valid unless notice is given by inserting in every copy published, on the title-page or the page following, if it be a book; or, if a map, chart, musical composition, print, cut, engraving, photograph, painting, drawing, chromo, statue, statuary, or model or design intended

STATUE OF GENERAL RAWLINS.

to be perfected as a work of the fine arts, by inscribing upon some portion
thereof, or on the substance on which the same is mounted, the following
words, viz.: "*Entered according to act of Congress, in the year ——, by
——, in the office of the Librarian of Congress at Washington,*" or at the
option of the person entering the copyright, the words, "*Copyright, 18—,
by ——.*" The law imposes a penalty of $100 upon any person who
has not obtained copyright who shall insert the notice, "*Entered according
to act of Congress,*" or "*Copyright,*" etc., or words of the same import, in

or upon any book or other article. Any author may reserve the right to translate or to dramatize his own work. In this case notice should be given by printing the words, "*Right of translation reserved*," or "*All rights reserved*," below the notice of copyright entry, and notifying the Librarian of Congress of such reservation, to be entered upon the record.

The original term of copyright runs for twenty-eight years. *Within six months before* the end of that time the author or designer, or his widow or children, may secure a renewal for the further term of fourteen years, making forty-two years in all. Applications for renewal must be accompanied by explicit statement of ownership, in the case of the author, or of relationship, in the case of his heirs, and must state definitely the date and place of entry of the original copyright.

The time within which any work entered for copyright may be issued from the press is not limited by any law or regulation, but depends upon

STATUE OF ADMIRAL DUPONT.

the discretion of the proprietor. A copyright may be secured for a projected work as well as for a completed one.

A copyright is assignable in law by any instrument of writing, but such assignment must be recorded in the office of the Librarian of Congress within sixty days from its date. The fee for this record and certificate is one dollar, and for a certified copy of any record of assignment, one dollar. A copy of the record (or duplicate certificate) of any copyright entry will be furnished, under seal, at the rate of fifty cents each.

In the case of books published in more than one volume, or of periodicals published in numbers, or of engravings, photographs, or other articles published with variations, a copyright is to be entered for each volume or part of a book, or number of a periodical, or variety, as to style, title, or inscription of any other article.

To secure a copyright for a painting, statue, or model or design intended to be perfected as a work of the fine arts, so as to prevent infringement by copying, engraving, or vending such design, a definite description must accompany the application for copyright, and a photograph of the same, at least as large as " cabinet size," should be mailed to the Librarian of Congress within ten days from the completion of the work or design. Copyrights cannot be granted upon trade-marks, nor upon mere names of companies or articles, nor upon prints or labels intended to be used with any article of manufacture. If protection for such names or labels is desired, application must be made to the Patent Office, where they are registered at a fee of $5 for labels and $25 for trade-marks.

Citizens or residents of the United States only are entitled to copyright. Every applicant for a copyright should state distinctly the full name and residence of the claimant, and whether the right is claimed as author, designer, or proprietor. No affidavit or formal application is required.

CHAPTER XI.

THE SUPREME COURT OF THE UNITED STATES—THE COURT-CHAMBER—MEMBERS OF THE COURT—ANCIENT OFFICIAL COSTUME—THE COURT IN SESSION—LIST OF CHIEF JUSTICES FROM THE ESTABLISHMENT OF THE COURT TO THE PRESENT TIME.

THE Supreme Court of the United States holds its sessions in the chamber of the Capitol originally constructed for the use of the Senate. The chamber was designed by Latrobe, and is a fine testimonial of his skill and taste. It is a pure example of classic architecture, and has been declared the most beautiful small court-chamber in the world. It is semicircular in form, and its greatest length is seventy-five feet, and its greatest width and height forty-five feet. The ceiling is a portion of the interior of a low dome. There is a wide arch over the judicial bench, and back of the bench is a series of columns of variegated marble with white marble capitals. The walls are supported by marble pilasters, and on the walls are marble busts of the six deceased Chief Justices. The central part of the chamber is arranged for the use of lawyers attending the court, and has mahogany chairs and tables, some of which were used by eminent Senators half a century ago. At the sides of the chamber are seats upholstered in red velvet for visitors. The Senate first occupied this chamber in November, 1800, and, with the exception of the time during which the Capitol was being reconstructed after the British invasion, continued in occupancy until December, 1859, when the new Senate chamber was taken possession of. The Supreme Court began its sessions here in 1860.

The court is in session from the second Monday in October to the early part of May of each year, and usually sits five days in the week, Saturday being reserved for consultation about cases. The Chief Justice has a salary of $10,500 per year, and the eight Associate Justices have salaries of $10,000. All the justices are appointed by the President and confirmed by the Senate, and hold their positions for life, or, as the Constitution of the United States says, " during good behavior." When a justice has reached the age of seventy, if he has been on the bench for ten years, he may retire, and his full salary is paid to him during the remainder of his life. The court hears all cases appealed from the United States circuit and district courts, and gives the final decision upon them. It also decides finally all constitutional questions. The court at present consists of Chief Justice Morrison R. Waite, of Ohio, who was appointed by President Grant in January, 1874; and Associate Justices Samuel F. Miller, of Iowa; Stephen J. Field, of California; Joseph P. Bradley, of New Jersey; John M. Harlan, of Kentucky; William B. Woods, of Georgia; Stanley Matthews, of Ohio; Horace Gray, of Massachusetts; and Samuel Blatchford, of New York.

Justices Miller and Field are the senior justices, and they sit on the bench at the right and left of the Chief Justice. They were appointed by President Lincoln in 1862 and 1863, respectively. Justice Bradley was appointed by President Grant in 1870, and Justices Harlan and Woods by President Hayes in 1877 and 1880, respectively. Justice Matthews was originally appointed by President Hayes, but the Senate failed to confirm his appointment, and he was afterwards reappointed by President Garfield in 1881. Justices Gray and Blatchford were appointed by President Arthur in 1881 and 1882, respectively.

When the court was first established the justices wore long black silk gowns, knee-breeches, silk stockings, and low shoes adorned with great silver buckles. They also donned white wigs of the "pig-tail" style. This official costume was continued for many years, or until the time of Chief Justice Taney, who is said to have been the first justice to give "a decision in pantaloons." At the present time the justices wear black suits covered with the time-honored silk gowns. The formal court customs which prevailed in the first part of the century have been also laid aside with the wigs and small-clothes and silver buckles, and the customs of to-day are very simple.

The clerk of the court is James H. McKenney, of the District of Columbia. He was appointed in 1880, and has a salary of $6000 per year. The marshal is John G. Nicolay, of Illinois. He was the private secretary of President Lincoln, and was appointed to his present position in 1872. His salary is $3000. The court reporter is J. C. Bancroft Davis, of New York. He was appointed in 1883, and has a salary of $5700.

COURT SEAL.

Each day's session of the court begins promptly at noon and continues without intermission until four o'clock. When the nine justices enter the court-chamber from the robing-room the marshal

JUSTICES OF THE SUPREME COURT.

1. Justice Gray.   4. Justice Miller.   7. Justice Woods
2. Justice Harlan.   5. Chief Justice Waite.   8. Justice Bradley.
3. Justice Matthews.   6. Justice Field.   9. Justice Matchford.

requests all persons present to rise, and then makes this announcement:
" The Honorable the Chief Justice and Associate Justices of the Supreme
Court of the United States." The justices range themselves on the bench
in the order of their appointment, with the Chief Justice in the centre.
They salute those present very politely and then seat themselves. The
ancient formula is then uttered by the court-crier, " Oyez! Oyez! Oyez!
All persons having business before the honorable Supreme Court of the
United States are admonished to draw near and give their attention, for
the court is now sitting. God save the United States and this honorable
court."

The court business begins immediately after the crier has made his
announcement. If there is no decision to be read by any of the justices,
the first case on the docket of the day is taken up, and the justices sit back
in their comfortable chairs to listen to the arguments of the lawyers. As
a case progresses questions are asked by the Chief Justice or the other
members of the court, books are consulted, and the pages of briefs turned
over. Patient attention is paid to the arguments, and all the members of
this high tribunal are very courteous and pleasant in their intercourse with
the lawyers. As soon as the hands of the clock over the long judicial
bench point to four the court is adjourned for the day, and the justices
march out to the robing-room, where colored attendants remove their
silken robes. Every Saturday the justices meet in the consultation room
to consider the cases submitted to them. The cases are all considered by
the full bench, but when a decision is reached one justice is designated to
put it in form to be publicly announced. At each annual session of the
court there are more than one thousand cases on the dockets, and about
four hundred are added yearly.

On the day the court begins its annual session the justices make a
ceremonious call upon the President, and also pay their respects to him
on New Year's day. In the latter part of the winter the President gives
a grand dinner at the White House to the members of the court and
their wives.

Congress created the Supreme Court by act of September 24, 1789,
and the court assembled in February, 1790. President Washington appointed as the first Chief Justice the famous statesman, John Jay, of New
York, who was then but forty-four years old. There were five Associate
Justices, as follows: John Rutledge, of South Carolina; William Cushing,
of Massachusetts; James Wilson, of Pennsylvania; John Blair, of Virginia; and James Iredell, of North Carolina. The official seal adopted
was " the arms of the United States engraven on a circular piece of steel
of the size of a dollar, with these words on the margin, ' Seal of the

Supreme Court of the United States.'" During the first twenty years of
the court it had very little business. From 1820 to 1840 the cases submitted to it averaged only about fifty-five a year. After 1860 the court
dockets became crowded, and now suitors have to wait a long time for a
hearing. Most of the new cases entered are not likely to be heard under
four or five years.

Chief Justice Jay was on the bench until 1795. John Rutledge, of
South Carolina, was appointed to succeed him, and presided during one
term of the court, but was not confirmed by the Senate. Washington
then appointed William Cushing, who was the senior Associate Justice,
but Cushing only retained his commission a few days, and never acted
as Chief Justice. His name, therefore, is not placed in the list of Chief
Justices. In 1796, Oliver Ellsworth, of Connecticut, was appointed, and
remained as Chief Justice until 1801, when he resigned, and John Marshall, of Virginia, became the head of the Supreme Court. Marshall had
been a soldier in the Revolution, a Representative in Congress, Minister
to France, and Secretary of State during the last year of President John
Adams' administration. When he became Chief Justice he was forty-six
years old. From 1801 until 1835 he presided over the court, and it has
been said that "it was he who established the power of the Supreme
Court as we recognize it at the present day. It was he who, more than
any other man of his time, carried forward the work of the Constitution
in welding the loose league of states into a compact, powerful nationality."
His decisions, contained in thirty-two volumes of the court reports, gave
him a prominent place among the great jurists of the world.

Chief Justice Marshall was tall and awkward, and had homely features
and a small head. He had little, twinkling eyes which often had a merry
look, and he dearly loved a hearty laugh. He was gentle in speech and
engaging in manner, and entirely free from pride of office. He was very
careless in dress, and his clothes usually looked as if they had come
"from the wardrobe of some antiquated slop-shop." When he attended
the circuit courts he rode in a one-horse gig without an attendant, and
few who saw the shabby-looking traveller would have believed he was
"the great Chief Justice," as he was called. He daily visited the Center
Market when in Washington to purchase his household supplies, and it is
related by Justice Story that "one morning while doing his marketing he
came across a young Virginia blood who was swearing loudly because he
could hire no one to take home his turkey. Marshall stepped up and,
ascertaining of him where he lived, replied, 'That is in my way, and I
will take it for you.' When he arrived at the dwelling the young man
inquired, 'What shall I pay you?' 'Oh, nothing,' was the rejoinder;

'you are welcome. It was in my way, and no trouble.' ' Who was that polite old gentleman who brought home my turkey for me?' inquired the other of a bystander, as Marshall stepped away. ' That,' replied he, ' is John Marshall, Chief Justice of the United States.' "

After the death of Marshall, in 1835, President Jackson nominated Roger B. Taney, of Maryland, to be Chief Justice. The nomination was confirmed at once by the Senate, and Chief Justice Taney sat on the bench for twenty-eight years. He had been the leading lawyer of the Maryland bar, and was a man of great ability. He died in 1864, and Salmon P. Chase, of Ohio, became Chief Justice, but only remained in office a little more than nine years. Chase died in 1873, and a few months after his death the present Chief Justice was appointed.

During the existence of the court there have been forty-three Associate Justices. The eminent jurist, Joseph Story, was a member of the court thirty-four years, and Bushrod Washington, a nephew of President Washington, was a member thirty-one years. John Catron served twenty-eight years; John McLean and James M. Wayne, thirty-two years; Samuel Nelson, twenty-seven years; Robert C. Grier and Nathan Clifford, twenty-three years; Noah H. Swayne, twenty years; and David Davis, fifteen years.

CHAPTER XII.

ONGRESS occupies the extensions of the Capitol, or the north
and south wings. In these wings the two halls of legislation
are arranged in the form of squares, with capacious lobbies
and galleries extending entirely around them. The Senate
chamber is in the north wing, and the hall of the House of Representatives is in the south wing. Both wings are constructed of marble and iron,
and have rich and tasteful ornamentation. The Senate chamber is one
hundred and twelve feet long, eighty-two feet wide, and thirty feet high.
It has a ceiling of iron girders and cross-pieces with glass panels, on which
are painted various national emblems. The walls have pilasters, niches, and
wide panels, and are finely painted and decorated in gold and buff. The
floor is covered with a costly carpet, and arranged in concentric semi-
circles on the floor are the desks and chairs of the Senators. All the
desks are of the finest mahogany, and some of them were used in the old
Senate chamber by the famous Senators of by-gone days. Each desk
has on its front a silver plate inscribed with the name of the occupant.
The chairs are of various styles and material to suit the fancy of the
Senators. The President of the Senate sits on a small platform or dais,
and in front of his chair is a wide desk. At his right sits the sergeant-
at-arms, and at his left sits the assistant door-keeper. The desk of the
Senate clerks and the tables of the official reporters are in front of the
desk of the presiding officer. The chamber has large galleries which
will seat upwards of 1000 persons. There is a gallery reserved for the
members of the foreign legations residing in Washington, and galleries
for the families and friends of the Senators. There is also a gallery for
the reporters of the press, which is directly over the chair of the presiding
officer, and galleries for the public. When an important debate is going
on the galleries will be crowded, but on ordinary occasions there is plenty

of room for spectators. The chamber has a magnificent appearance, but in size it does not compare with the hall of the House of Representatives, which is the largest legislative hall in the world. The Senate first occupied the chamber on January 4, 1859.

A lobby extends along the back of the chamber, and leading from it is the "marble room" where Senators receive visitors, and where consultations are held. Every part of the room is of marble. The rooms of the President and Vice-President of the United States are near the marble

THE SENATE MARBLE ROOM.

10

room. The President's room is richly decorated, and on the walls are finely-executed frescos of President Washington and the members of his first Cabinet. The room is used by the President on the closing day of each session of Congress for the purpose of examining and signing the bills that are passed. The Vice-President's room is handsomely furnished. Here is the celebrated painting of Washington, by Rembrandt Peale, which the government purchased in 1832 for $25,000.

The eastern and western grand staircases, which lead to the Senate galleries from the main floor, are very beautiful. They are of fine polished marble, and have ponderous pillars and balustrades. A marble statue of Benjamin Franklin, by Hiram Powers, stands at the foot of the eastern staircase, and on the wall, over the first landing, is a mammoth painting of "Perry's Victory on Lake Erie," by W. H. Powell. The painting cost $25,000, and is one of the finest in the Capitol. It gives a spirited delineation of Commodore Perry's heroic act of transferring his flag from the disabled ship, the "Lawrence," to the "Niagara." The boat containing Perry and his little brother and a brave crew was exposed to a furious cannonading by the British fleet during the fifteen minutes required for the perilous voyage, but Perry succeeded in hoisting his flag on the "Niagara." This act inspired the Americans with fresh courage, and by a prompt movement they scattered the British fleet and won the victory.

There is a marble statue of John Hancock, by Horatio Stone, at the foot of the western staircase. On the wall of the landing is James Walker's painting of "The Storming of Chapultepec by General Scott's troops."

The hall of the House of Representatives is one hundred and thirty-nine feet long, ninety-three feet wide, and thirty-six feet high. It has a ceiling similar to that of the Senate chamber, but on the glass panels are the coats of arms of the states. The great size of the hall and its elegant ornamentation give it a grand appearance. When there is a night session of the House the hall is beautifully illuminated by 1500 gas-jets, placed back of the ceiling. The desks and chairs of the Representatives fill the greater part of the floor. The Speaker of the House sits behind a white marble table, on a platform elevated about four feet from the floor, and at his right hand, on a marble pedestal, is his symbol of authority, the time-honored mace. The mace was adopted by the House in the First Congress, and has been in use ever since. When it is placed on its pedestal it signifies that the House is in session and under the Speaker's authority; when it is placed on the floor, that the House is in committee of the whole. The mace is a bundle of black rods fastened with transverse

THE SENATE LOBBY.

bands of silver, like the Roman *fasces*. On its top is a silver globe surmounted by a silver eagle. When the sergeant-at-arms is executing the
commands of the Speaker he is required to bear aloft the mace in his
hands.

In front of the Speaker's table are marble desks for the House clerks
and reporters. On the wall to the right and left of the Speaker's table are
large paintings by Bierstadt, representing the "Settlement of California,"
and the "Discovery of the Hudson River;" and there are also paintings
of Washington and Lafayette by Vanderlyn and Ary Scheffer respectively.
A fresco of "Washington at Yorktown," by Brumidi, also adorns the
walls. Above the Speaker's table is the gallery for the press reporters.
There are other galleries with accommodations for 1300 persons. The
House first occupied this hall on December 16, 1857.

At the rear of the hall is the members' lobby, on the walls of which
are portraits of past Speakers. Opening from the lobby is the retiring-
room, which is large and handsomely furnished. Rooms for the various
officials of the House open from the main corridor.

Leading from the corridor are grand staircases similar to those of the
Senate. There is a marble statue of Jefferson, by Hiram Powers, at the
foot of the eastern staircase, and on the wall of the landing hangs the

GRAND STAIRCASE IN SENATE EXTENSION OF THE CAPITOL.

painting, by Frank B. Carpenter, of " President Lincoln signing the Proclamation of Emancipation." The painting was sold by the artist for $25,000 to Mary E. Thompson, who presented it to the government February 12, 1878.

The wall of the western staircase is ornamented with a huge chromosilica, which represents a party of emigrants crossing the Rocky Mountains. It was painted by Emanuel Leutze, and cost $20,000. Below this chromo is one by Bierstadt, representing the entrance to the harbor of San Francisco. A bronze bust of a chief of the Chippewa Indians stands on a marble pedestal at the foot of the staircase.

The Congress of the United States has met annually at Washington since the 17th of November, 1800. On that day the second session of the Sixth Congress was begun in the partly finished Capitol, and on the

22d of November the building was formally dedicated to national legislation. Previous to 1800 the sessions of Congress had been held at New
York and Philadelphia. When the Capitol was first occupied it was a
poorly constructed, inconvenient building, and it was not until 1808 that
Congress had suitable accommodations. In that year what is now the
central part of the Capitol (with the exception of the rotunda and its projections) was completed, and the House of Representatives, which had
met for several sessions in small apartments,—one of which was facetiously
designated as "the oven,"—was enabled to occupy the beautiful hall
especially constructed for it. The Senate had occupied its chamber from
the first, but the chamber was altered and improved from year to year.
Until the British troops invaded the Capitol in the summer of 1814 and
fired the "harbor of Yankee Democracy," Congress continued its sessions
in the building. The fire only destroyed the interior of the Capitol, very
little damage being done to the walls and foundations. While Latrobe
was engaged in the work of reconstruction, from 1815 to 1817, Congress
met in Blodget's "Great Hotel" for one session, and afterwards in a brick
building, erected by citizens of Washington, adjacent to the eastern grounds
of the Capitol. This building was called the "Old Capitol," and during
the Civil War was known as the "Old Capitol Prison," as it was used as
a place of confinement for Confederates. The picture of the building
which is presented in this chapter was drawn from a photograph taken by

PAINTING, "PERRY'S VICTORY ON LAKE ERIE," IN SENATE EXTENSION.

the War Department in 1864. The building is at present used for residences, having been considerably reconstructed.

After the original halls of Congress were restored they were used for legislative purposes for some forty years, or until the present halls in the extensions of the Capitol were completed. The old Senate chamber, now used by the Supreme Court, can thus be described : On a small platform in the centre of the screen of marble columns at the back of the chamber was the chair of the President of the Senate, and in front of his chair were the desks of the Senate officials. Above the screen of columns was a small gallery, and another gallery, supported by large iron columns and with a gilded iron balustrade, extended around the chamber. Over the gallery on the east was a great painting of Washington, by Charles Wilson Peale, which was set in a deep gilt frame and handsomely draped. The fine mahogany desks and chairs of the Senators filled the central part of the chamber, and were arranged in concentric circles. Outside of the railing which enclosed the desks were large, comfortable sofas for distinguished visitors. At night a large chandelier gave brilliant illumination. In this chamber Daniel Webster, Henry Clay, John C. Calhoun, Lewis Cass, Thomas Hart Benton, and other famous Senators of the first part of the century performed their legislative work and made many of their most celebrated speeches.

The old hall of the House of Representatives, now the National Statuary Hall, appeared as follows in the latter years of its use by the House : The Speaker's chair and table stood on a rostrum four feet from the floor, and back of the rostrum were crimson curtains, hanging in folds from the capitals of the ponderous marble columns which supported the great arch of the hall. The clerk's desk stood below the rostrum, and between the columns were sofas and tables for the reporters. The Representatives were provided with mahogany desks and wide arm-chairs, which were arranged in concentric circles. The hall could accommodate two hundred and fifty members. A bronzed iron railing with curtains enclosed the outer row of desks, and this constituted the bar of the House. Beyond the railing was the members' lobby, and above the lobby were galleries seating about five hundred persons. One of the galleries was reserved for ladies, and in two of its panels were paintings of Washington and Lafayette, which now hang in the present hall of the House. Under the paintings were large copies of the Declaration of Independence in frames ornamented with national emblems. The hall was lighted by a chandelier, which hung from the centre of the domed ceiling.

Congress at present has four hundred and nine members. The Senate is composed of seventy-six Senators, two from each state ; and the House

of Representatives is composed of three hundred and twenty-five Representatives. Eight Delegates who represent the eight territories are also allowed seats in the House, but cannot vote. They receive the same compensation as the other members of Congress. The Senators are elected by the state legislatures for a term of six years, and the Representatives and Delegates are elected by the people for two years. Each Congress is designated by a number, and has a legislative existence of two years, during which time there are two regular sessions, termed the "long session" and the "short session." The long session is held in the first year of each Congress, and usually continues six months or more, as may be desired; the short session is held in the second year, and by law expires at noon on the 4th of March. Congress meets annually on the first Monday in December. There have been forty-eight Congresses from March 4, 1789, when the First Congress of the United States met at New York, to March 4, 1885.

The states are entitled to representation in Congress according to their population. At present the ratio of representation, under the tenth census, is one Representative for each 154,325 people. Until the eleventh census is taken, in 1890, the apportionment of Representatives will be as follows: Alabama, eight; Arkansas, five; California, six; Colorado, one; Connecticut, four; Delaware, one; Florida, two; Georgia, ten; Illinois, twenty; Indiana, thirteen; Iowa, eleven; Kansas, seven; Kentucky, eleven; Louisiana, six; Maine, four; Maryland, six; Massachusetts, twelve; Michigan, eleven; Minnesota, five; Mississippi, seven; Missouri, fourteen; Nebraska, three; Nevada, one; New Hampshire, two; New Jersey, seven; New York, thirty-four; North Carolina, nine; Ohio, twenty-one; Oregon, one; Pennsylvania, twenty-eight;

THE SPEAKER · MACE

REPRESENTATIVES' RETIRING-ROOM.

Rhode Island, two; South Carolina, seven; Tennessee, ten; Texas, eleven; Vermont, two; Virginia, ten; West Virginia, four; Wisconsin, nine.

Each member of Congress has a salary of $5000 per year, payable monthly. The President *pro tempore* of the Senate and the Speaker of the House of Representatives have extra salaries of $3000, or $8000 in all. The members are allowed mileage of twenty cents per mile to and from Washington each annual session, and also have an allowance of $125 per year for newspapers and stationery. The amount expended yearly for the salaries of Senators is $380,000; for Representatives and Delegates, $1,665,000. The amount expended for mileage is $143,624, and for newspapers and stationery, about $70,000. There are many high salaried officials connected with Congress, and the miscellaneous expenses are large. The cost of an annual session is nearly three million dollars.

The Vice-President of the United States is empowered by the Constitution to act as President of the Senate, "but shall have no vote unless they are equally divided." The Senate is empowered to choose a President *pro tempore*, who presides in the absence of the Vice-President. The other principal officers of the Senate are as follows: Chaplain with a yearly salary of $900; secretary, with $4896; chief clerk and financial clerk, with $3000 each; executive clerk, principal clerk, minute and

journal clerk, and enrolling clerk, with $2592 each; sergeant-at-arms and
door-keeper, with $4320; two assistant door-keepers, with $2592 each;
principal book-keeper, with $4320, and two assistant book-keepers, with
$2592 each; postmaster, with $2250; librarian, with $2220; keeper of
stationery, with $2102; and superintendents of folding-room and docu-
ment-room, with $2160 each.   There are also numerous clerks, door-
keepers, messengers, pages, and other employés, all of whom have large
salaries.

The proceedings of the Senate are reported in short hand, at an
expense of $25,000 per year.   The full amount is paid to the chief
official reporter, who contracts to perform the work.   He employs four
assistants and a number of copyists.   The present system of verbatim
reporting was begun in 1848, and has been continued at each session
since that year.

The House of Representatives elects its Speaker at the beginning of
each Congress, and he holds the office during the legislative period of the
Congress.   The Speaker is provided with a private secretary, who has a
salary of $1800, and there are also a Speaker's clerk and a clerk to the
Speaker's table, whose salaries are $1600 and $1400 respectively.   The
House has a chaplain with a salary of $900, a principal clerk with $4500,

OLD CAPITOL PRISON IN 1864.

and nine other clerks with salaries ranging from $3000 to $2240. There are also ten assistant clerks with from $2000 to $1440. The sergeant-at-arms and his deputy have salaries of $4000 and $2000 respectively. There is a principal door-keeper with $2500, and there are numerous other door-keepers with from $2000 to $1200. The force of messengers, pages, committee clerks, etc., is large and well paid.

There are five official reporters of the House. The chief reporter has a salary of $6000, and the others $5000 each. Verbatim reporting was first introduced in the House in 1850. It is an exceedingly difficult task. At first sight one would hardly believe the most expert reporters could catch all the rapid speeches that are made during an important debate and all the proceedings in the great hall during a day of intense excitement, but the work is done day after day with remarkable accuracy. The reports of both the Senate and House are printed in the official publication called *The Congressional Record*, which is issued every morning from the Government Printing-Office during the session of Congress, and supplied to the members of both houses. The annual cost of this publication is nearly $200,000.

Congress assembles daily at noon. Each house is opened with prayer by the chaplain, and then follows what is called "the morning hour," when bills, petitions, and reports are presented. After the morning hour bills are taken from the regular or special calendars and discussed. The House has many complicated rules and practices which often greatly retard its business. Usually the day's session closes about five o'clock. During the latter part of an annual session there are frequent meetings in the evening.

CHAPTER XIII.

THE plain, classic building in which all the Presidents of the United States, except Washington, have resided during their official terms, is always an object of interest. The Executive Mansion, or, as every one calls it, the White House, was the first public building erected at the national capital, and when the seat of government was transferred from Philadelphia to Washington, in October, 1800, President John Adams was able to set up his lares and penates very comfortably in the new official home. To be sure, Mrs. Adams complained that there were no bells in the great house to summon the servants, and that it required many blazing fires to keep off the dampness, but she was well pleased with the spacious, elegant apartments, and diligently set to work, good housewife that she was, to make everything as pleasant as possible.

The White House was designed and constructed by James Hoban, a talented young architect who had come to the United States from Ireland at the close of the American Revolution, and had resided for a while at Charleston, South Carolina, before going to Washington. In March, 1792, the commissioners who had charge of the new capital city advertised in the New York and Philadelphia newspapers for a plan "for a President's House, to be erected in the city of Washington," offering for the most approved plan "a premium of $500, or a medal of that value, at the option of the party." This liberal premium, for $500 was a goodly sum in the last century, brought out a dozen or more of plans for the President's House, but the plan submitted by James Hoban was the favored one. In fact, the commissioners were so greatly attracted toward the bright young Irishman, that they not only accepted his plan and awarded him the premium (he took the money and not the medal), but they gave him full and absolute authority to construct the house at a

large salary. Hoban's plan was
not original in its main features.
He closely copied the plan of the
palace of the Duke of Leinster,
at Dublin; and the White House,
as it stands to-day, is almost a
counterpart of that palace.

SOUTH VIEW OF THE WHITE HOUSE.

On the 13th of October, 1792,
the corner-stone of the White House
was laid with Masonic ceremony.
Hoban went to work at once. He
secured all the sandstone required
for the walls of the building from a
quarry in Virginia (they didn't know
anything about marble in those days,
although the hills of Virginia and
Maryland, adjacent to the District
of Columbia, were full of this better
building material, as was discovered some years later), obtained good
mechanics from New York and elsewhere, and for a time made satisfactory progress. President Washington frequently inspected the work
and exerted himself to obtain the necessary funds to carry it on. The
commissioners permitted Hoban to have his own way, and he enjoyed
the rare privilege of doing as he thought best without interference.
But there came a time when the money gave out. Congress, sitting at
Philadelphia, rather sullen and displeased because the capital city was
to be established on the banks of the Potomac simply for the reason that

the Southern States had desired it, and had consummated a legislative bargain to obtain their desire, flatly refused to make further appropriations for the White House. In consequence of this refusal the building operations were suspended for nearly two years. Hoban went to New York, where there was a demand for good architects, and declared he would never return. The commissioners, who were doing gratuitous and thankless work in looking after the interests of the new national city, were indignant, and one of them resigned, washed his hands of the whole matter, and began to erect a fine mansion. At last President Washington's influence prevailed in Congress, and a sufficient sum was appropriated to finish the White House. Hoban again took charge of the construction, and in the latter part of 1799 the building was ready for occupancy.

Up to the time President Adams entered into possession of the White House its cost had been about $250,000. There is good reason to believe that Washington selected the site of the building and that he always had an ardent interest in its construction. He had resided in small, inconvenient houses at New York and Philadelphia while President, and he desired that his successor and the long line of Presidents to come after should be well housed. He believed some of Hoban's ideas of construction and decoration were rather extravagant, but he gave way to them, and permitted him to complete unmolested what the satirists of that period called " The President's Palace."

EAST ROOM OF THE WHITE HOUSE.

James Hoban, whose name will be forever connected with this building, and also with the Capitol as one of its architects, became a permanent resident of the city of Washington, and followed his profession for many years with distinguished success. He designed and constructed a number of the finest mansions and business buildings, and became a very wealthy man. He was social and hospitable, went in the best society, and possessed in a high degree the esteem and confidence of all who knew him. He died December 8, 1831, aged seventy-three, and was buried in one of the city cemeteries.

When John Adams and his family first occupied the White House only six of its rooms were furnished. In the great East Room, the largest in the house, were piles of lumber and scaffolding, and here where so many magnificent fêtes have been held during the past seventy-five years, Mrs. Adams had the family linen spread out to dry on wash-days. The grounds around the house were in a wild, rough state, and continued so for many years. When Jefferson became President the East Room was completed, and during his administration the house was otherwise improved.

In the middle of President Madison's second term the British troops invaded the city and fired the White House. After the battle of Bladensburg, August 24, 1814, the President left Washington for a place of safety in Maryland, but his wife, Dolly Paine Madison, remained in the White House. She had invited some friends to a dinner-party that night, and, not believing that the enemy would reach the city before the next day, she went on with her preparations for the party. The guests were seated at the table, when a servant rushed in and gave the startling intelligence that the British were on Capitol Hill, only a mile and a half away. Then there was a panic. Men and women left the house without a minute's delay. Mrs. Madison gathered a few articles of clothing, had the horses harnessed to the family carriage, and with her favorite serving-woman was driven across the Potomac to a farm-house in Virginia. The British soldiers arrived at the White House about half an hour after its inmates had departed. On a long table in the East Room they found a bountiful dinner set out. There were meats and rich viands, fruits, ices, and wines, and the soldiers had a merry feast before they applied the torch to the house

The fire did little serious damage, as it was speedily extinguished by a heavy rain, which began soon after the soldiers had marched away and continued all that night. Some of the rooms were partially burned, and others were discolored by smoke, but the walls of the house were very little injured.

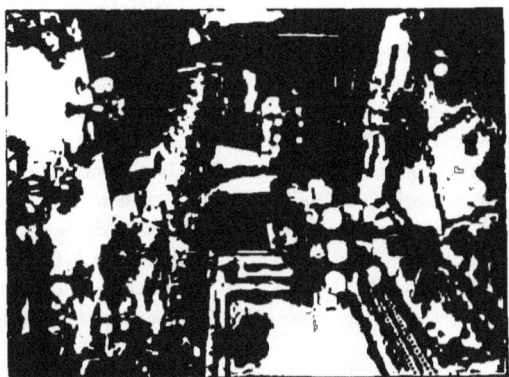

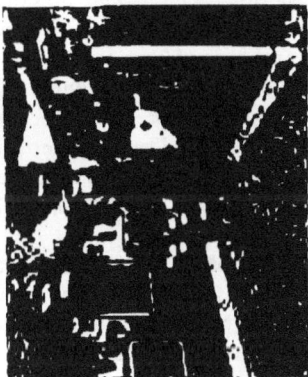

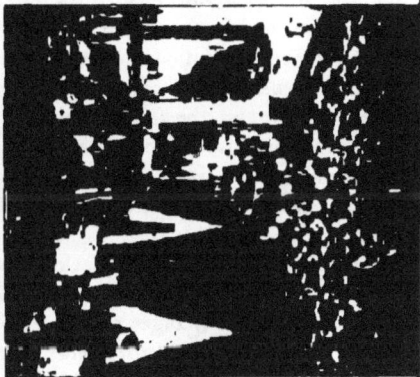

• State Dining Room   • Blue Room   Red Room   • Green Room

When the invading army had sailed down the Potomac the President and Mrs. Madison returned to the city, taking up their residence in the large brick mansion known as the Octagon House, at the corner of Eighteenth street and New York avenue, which was erected by Colonel John Tayloe in 1798, and is now standing in a good state of preservation. Here they lived until Madison's term as President had expired, and here his successor, President Monroe, also lived until the winter of 1817, when the White House was fully restored and refurnished, the work of restoration having been done by Hoban. In the Octagon House the treaty of Ghent was signed, and numerous official gatherings and brilliant receptions were held.

On New Year's day, 1818, President Monroe gave a public reception, and the *National Intelligencer* the next morning said, "The President's House for the first time since its restoration was thrown open yesterday for the general reception of visitors. It was thronged from 12 to 3 o'clock by an immensely large concourse of ladies and gentlemen, among whom were to be found the foreign ministers, heads of departments, Senators and Representatives, and others of our distinguished citizens, residents, and strangers. It was gratifying to be able to salute the President of the United States with the compliments of the season in his appropriate residence."

In 1829, when General Jackson was President, the grand portico with tall Ionic columns was placed on the front of the White House, but since then few changes of importance have been made to the exterior of the building. Its history since Jackson's time has been simply the history of its occupants. Presidents have come and gone; there have been scenes of gayety and scenes of gloom,—weddings, brilliant festivals, and all the pomp and circumstance of high official life; and intermingled with the joyful notes and glowing colors have been the dark shades and dismal tones of pain and anguish and death.

Up to the present time very nearly $800,000 have been expended upon the house in its construction and ornamentation. It has a fine location on the western part of Pennsylvania avenue, directly opposite the beautiful Lafayette Park. It stands some distance from the avenue in an enclosure of many acres. Around the house is a grove of tall, luxuriant sycamores, oaks, and poplars, many of which have given grateful shade to nearly all the Presidents. On one side is the great Treasury building, and on the other the imposing and magnificent State, War, and Navy building. All these structures are situated on the government reservation designated as "The President's Grounds," which extends to the Potomac river, and is laid out in an attractive manner. When the harbor improve-

ROOMS OF THE WHITE HOUSE.

1. Cabinet-Room.   2. President's Room

ments are com-
pleted there will
be fine walks and
drives all through
this section, which
will then be the
great pleasure re-
sort of the people
of Washington.

The White
House is built of
sandstone, and to
prevent this soft, porous stone from crumbling and wearing away, it is
covered every year with thick coats of white paint. The house is one
hundred and seventy feet from east to west, and eighty-six feet from
north to south. It has two stories and a basement, the latter, however,
not showing from the front, and a broad balustrade surmounts it. A
large portico is at the main entrance, and a circular colonnade is on the

south side. From Pennsylvania avenue there are two spacious drive-
ways, bordered with trees and ornamented with tropical plants. The
grounds contain fountains, beautiful beds of flowers, and luxuriant lawns,
and they are open to the public all through the day. Plenty of comfortable seats are provided, and every one can enjoy the pleasant sylvan
tract. From the south grounds can be obtained charming views of the
Potomac and the adjacent hills of Maryland and Virginia.

What are called the state parlors of the White House are on the first
floor. They consist of the East Room, the Green Room, the Blue
Room, and the Red Room. The East Room is eighty feet long and
forty feet wide, but the other parlors are much smaller. Until 1837 all
the state dinners were given in the East Room, and the official receptions
were held there. The room is arranged somewhat after the ancient Greek
style, and has a very rich and elegant appearance. The ceiling consists
of three large exquisitely decorated panels, in each of which is a splendid
glass chandelier. Around the room are eight white mantels adorned with
carvings in gold and surmounted by long mirrors. A thick Axminster
carpet covers the floor, and the furniture is of ebony upholstered in plush
of old-gold color. At the doors and windows are hangings to match the
upholstery of the furniture. On the walls are paintings of President
Washington and Martha Washington.

CONSERVATORY OF THE WHITE HOUSE.

The Green Room has its walls covered with paper of Nile-green color, with sprays of gold, and its furniture is upholstered in green satin. The Blue Room, where the President holds his state receptions, is oval in shape, and its color is that designated as " robin's-egg blue." The furniture is of gilt and blue silk. When the President has a reception the guests enter this room from the cloak-rooms, and are presented by the Marshal of the District of Columbia. After paying their respects to the President they retire to the other state parlors. The Red Room has its walls painted in Pompeiian red, and the ceiling is decorated with bronze and copper stars. At the windows are crimson plush curtains, and the furniture is upholstered with the same material. The room is used as a family sitting-room at night, and has a very cheerful appearance. Visitors to the White House in the daytime are allowed to enter the East Room at pleasure, but the other parlors are closed, except when an usher escorts a party through them at certain intervals during the morning hours. When the President entertains, all the parlors are profusely embellished with flowers and luxuriant plants from the White House conservatory, the East Room in particular having great masses of tropical plants. The parlors open into a long private corridor, which is separated from the public vestibule by a screen of jewelled glass. The walls of the corridor are hung with portraits of the Presidents.

Leading from the corridor is the grand dining-room in which the state dinners are given,—the dinners to the members of the Cabinet, the Justices of the Supreme Court, Senators and Representatives, foreign ministers, and other distinguished persons. These dinners take place once or twice a week during the winter, and are given by the President at his own expense, no allowance being made by Congress for them, although they are a necessary part of the social life of the White House. All the table service, the china, silver, and linen, is provided by the government, but the food and wines are furnished by the President, and the expenditure for the dinners is very large, as each dinner will cost the greater part of $1000. Usually there are twelve courses served, and as many as fifty-four guests can sit at the table when it is fully extended, although generally there are only from thirty-six to forty persons invited. The state dining-room is richly furnished, and when it is lighted at night by many gas-jets and wax candles has a splendid appearance, with its table covered with the state china and silver, beautiful floral designs, and delicious viands.

The second story of the White House contains the business offices of the President and his private apartments. The library-room, where the President receives his callers during the day, and the Cabinet-room, where the members of the Cabinet consult with the President every Tuesday and Friday, are the principal public rooms. The library-room was furnished much as it is at present during the administration of President Fillmore, and it is stated that Mrs. Fillmore selected most of the books which fill the cases. It is a large oval room, with two long windows looking out upon the south grounds, and contains mahogany furniture upholstered in red leather. There are numerous bookcases around the room, and on the walls are paintings of the early Presidents. The President uses a massive desk constructed of oak timber taken from the ship "Resolute," which was sent to the Arctic regions in 1852 by the English government to search for Sir John Franklin. The desk was presented to the United States by England in 1881, for use in the White House.

The Cabinet-room has a long table, around which the heads of the executive departments of the government sit when they meet for consultation with the President. At the head of the table the President sits, and at his right hand sits the Secretary of State, and at his left the Secretary of the Treasury.

It takes no small sum to "run" the White House. Yearly the expenses are very nearly $100,000, exclusive of the President's salary of $50,000. The private secretary to the President has a salary of $3250, and the assistant secretary $2250. Two executive clerks are employed at salaries of $2000, and there are six other clerks who receive from $1800 to $1200. A short-hand writer with a salary of $1800 attends to the President's correspondence. The steward of the house has $1800, and two day ushers have $1400 and $1200. Besides this force there are five messengers, two door-keepers, and one night usher, whose salaries are $1200. Then there is a watchman at $900 and a fireman at $864. The government furnishes all these employés. The cooks and dining-room and kitchen servants are paid by the President. For the contingent expenses of the business offices, such as stationery, record books, furniture and carpets, telegrams, care of a horse and carriage, etc., the sum of $8000 is annually appropriated. It costs $15,000 per year to light the White House and its grounds. The greenhouses are maintained at an expense of $6000. And with all these expenses there are others which call for the expenditure of about $20,000 more. So it will be seen that Uncle Sam's family mansion is quite a costly institution.

STATE, WAR, AND NAVY BUILDING

CHAPTER XIV.

OCATED in the city of Washington are the seven executive departments of the government, as follows: The Department of State, the Treasury Department, the War Department, the Navy Department, the Post-Office Department, the Department of the Interior, and the Department of Justice. The heads of these departments constitute the President's Cabinet, and have the title of Secretary, with the exception of the heads of the Post-Office Department and the Department of Justice, whose titles are Postmaster-General and Attorney-General. The compensation of each member of the Cabinet is $8000 per year. Besides the regular executive departments there are government bureaus or institutions, such as the Department of Agriculture, the Smithsonian Institution and National Museum, the Government Printing-Office, and others, which are managed by commissioners or superintendents, but are not directly responsible to any of the executive departments.

The State, War, and Navy Departments occupy the great and magnificent building on Pennsylvania avenue west of the White House. The erection of this building was begun in 1871, and it is not yet entirely finished. Up to the present time it has cost $8,000,000, and it is likely that two or three millions will be expended to complete it. The design is a modification of the Italian renaissance order of architecture. The architect was A. B. Mullett. The building is four hundred and seventy-one feet long and two hundred and fifty-three feet wide, and is constructed of granite from Maine and Virginia quarries. When completed it will have four façades precisely alike. There will be a grand entrance on each façade. The building has four stories resting on a rustic basement, and an imposing mansard roof crowns the whole. The interior is fashioned in a very handsome manner. The Department of State has apart-

168

FOREIGN LEGATION BUILDINGS.

1. Russian Legation.   2. English Legation.   3. Spanish Legation.

ments in the south front, the War Department in the north front, and the Navy Department in the east front.

The Department of State has the supervision of all matters which arise in the intercourse of the United States with foreign governments, and also with the States of the Union. It was created by the First Congress in 1789, and for many years directed the affairs of the territories, and had charge of the patent and copyright business. At present it attends to the publication and preservation of all the acts of Congress, supervises the diplomatic and consular service, and performs other special work. Besides the Secretary of State, who is the leading member of the President's Cabinet, the officials of the department include three assistant secretaries, a chief clerk, and six chiefs of bureaus. The first assistant secretary has a salary of $4500, and the other secretaries $3500 each. The chief clerk who directs the sixty or more clerks and employés of the department has a salary of $2750, and the chiefs of bureaus have salaries of $2100. There are six bureaus, viz, Diplomatic Bureau, Consular Bureau, Bureau of Indexes and Archives, Bureau of Accounts, Bureau of Statistics, and Bureau of Rolls. The annual appropriation for the department is about $1,400,000, of which sum about $1,200,000 are expended for the maintenance of the diplomatic and consular service. Every portion of the state business is regarded as confidential, and the greatest pains is taken to prevent disclosures of the many affairs constantly under consideration. When the volumes of consular reports are prepared for publication, all passages are omitted which might prove embarrassing to the government or to the consuls. The consular reports are very popular with members of Congress, and they send thousands of copies to their constituents, particularly to persons interested in educational matters. The reports contain a large amount of information concerning foreign countries.

The "foreign intercourse," as it is officially styled, is maintained by means of thirty-five legations and about three hundred consulates in all parts of the world. Twenty-five foreign governments have legations in Washington. The ministers who represent the United States at what are called the first-class missions, such as those at London, Paris, Berlin, and St. Petersburg, have salaries of $17,500 per year. At the other missions the salaries range from $12,000 to $5000. The consuls have salaries from $6000 to $1000.

All the rooms of the Department of State are elegantly decorated and furnished. In the department are to be found many valuable archives of the government extending back to the past century. Every document received by the department is preserved, and can be referred to when

THE TREASURY BUILDING.

wanted. The accumulation of papers is enormous, but the rooms of the department are spacious enough to contain all that may be received for a hundred years.

The War Department occupies numerous large and handsome rooms in the State, War, and Navy building. This department was established in 1789, and has charge of all the military affairs of the government. Besides this work it has the supervision of all the improvements made to the rivers and harbors of the United States, and has also the charge of the weather service, the military asylums and cemeteries, and many public works. It also supervises the government surveys and explorations. A vast business is done and a vast sum, expended. Nearly thirty millions of dollars are disbursed every year for the army and its adjuncts, and nearly as much more for other purposes. The department has the following divisions: Office of the Secretary of War, the Headquarters of the Army, the departments of the Adjutant-General, Inspector-General, Quartermaster-General, Commissary-General, Surgeon-General, and Paymaster-General; the Corps of Engineers, the Ordnance Department, the Bureau of Military Justice, the Signal Office or Weather Bureau, the Bureau of War Records, and sundry other divisions. All the sub-departments are directed by army officers of high rank, and have many clerks and employés. In the office of the Secretary of War there are a chief clerk with a salary of $2500, a disbursing clerk with $2000, three chiefs of divisions with $2000 each, and about seventy clerks. The Adjutant-General, Inspector-General, Quartermaster-General, Paymaster-General, Commissary-General, Judge-Advocate-General, the Chief of Engineers, the Chief Signal Officer, and the Chief of Ordnance have salaries of $5500. The Surgeon-General has $4500.

The army of the United States consists of ten cavalry regiments, five artillery regiments, and twenty-five infantry regiments. There are also several detached forces employed in the signal service, hospital duty, etc. The entire military force amounts to 2143 officers and 23,335 enlisted men. The troops are stationed in three military divisions, as follows: Division of the Missouri, under the command of Major-General John Pope, with headquarters in Chicago; Division of the Atlantic, under the command of Major-General Winfield S. Hancock, with headquarters in New York; Division of the Pacific, under the command of Major-General John M. Schofield, with headquarters in San Francisco. Each division is divided into departments commanded by brigadier-generals. By law the number of major-generals is limited to three, and the number of brigadier-generals to six. The brigadier-generals are Oliver O. Howard, Alfred H. Terry, Christopher C. Augur, George Crook, Nelson A. Miles, and Ronald

NAVAL OBSERVATORY, SHOWING THE GREAT
EQUATORIAL TELESCOPE.

S. Mackenzie. There are sixty-six colonels, eighty-five lieutenant-colonels, two hundred and forty-three majors, and six hundred and three captains.

The general in command of the army is Lieutenant-General Philip H. Sheridan, who assumed command November 1, 1883, upon the retirement of General William T. Sherman. His pay is $13.500 per year for the first five years, after which it is increased. The army headquarters are in the State, War, and Navy building.

For the first five years of service the major-generals are paid $7500 per year; brigadier-generals, $5500; colonels, $3500; lieutenant-colonels, $3000; majors, $2500; captains, from $1800 to $2000; and lieutenants, from $1400 to $1600. After five years the pay of all officers is increased from ten to forty per cent., according to the length of service. Retired officers have three-quarters pay. Private soldiers are paid $13 per month.

The Navy Department has very elegant suites of rooms. All the affairs pertaining to the navy are directed by this department. About fifteen million dollars are expended yearly for the naval force, ships of war, etc. In the office of the Secretary of the Navy there are many clerks and employés. The department has the following bureaus: Bureau of Yards and Docks, Bureau of Navigation, Bureau of Ordnance, Bureau of Provisions and Clothing, Bureau of Medicine and Surgery, Bureau of Construction and Repairs, Bureau of Equipment and Recruiting, and Bureau of Steam-Engineering. All the bureaus are directed by naval officers.

At present the naval force consists of 1948 officers and 7500 enlisted men. There are also 750 boys or apprentices. The marine corps attached to the navy consists of 2028 officers and men. There are forty-five steam-vessels, fourteen wooden sailing-vessels, nineteen iron-clads, two torpedo-rams, and sixteen tugs. Steel ships of the best quality are in process of construction.

The admiral in command of the navy is Admiral David D. Porter, who assumed the position October 17, 1870. His pay is $13,000 per year. The office of the admiral is in the State, War, and Navy building.

There is a vice-admiral, whose pay is $9000 per year when at sea, and $8000 when on shore duty. Seven rear-admirals and twenty-one commodores are on the active list. Rear-admirals receive $6000 and commodores $5000 when at sea, and $1000 less when on shore. Captains are paid $4500, commanders $3500, and lieutenant-commanders $3000.

The Treasury Department occupies an immense freestone and granite building situated on Pennsylvania avenue at Fifteenth street. The building is four hundred and sixty feet long and two hundred and sixty-four feet wide. Very nearly $8,000,000 have been expended upon its construction. The main building was completed in 1841, Robert Mills being the architect. In 1869 the extensions, designed by Thomas U. Walter, were completed. The Treasury Department has charge of the financial affairs of the government, and has other duties. It was established in 1789 by the First Congress. The various divisions of the department are as follows: Office of the Secretary of the Treasury; offices of the First Comptroller, the Second Comptroller, the Commissioner of Customs, the Commissioner of Internal Revenue, the Treasurer of the United States, the Register of the Treasury, the Comptroller of the Currency, the Director of the Mint, the Auditors, the Supervising Architect of Public Buildings, the Light-House Board, the Bureau of Statistics, the Bureau of Engraving and Printing, the Life-Saving Service, the Coast and Geodetic Survey, the Secret Service, the Revenue Cutter and Marine Hospital Service, etc. Each division has a large force of officials and clerks, and the total salary list of the department amounts

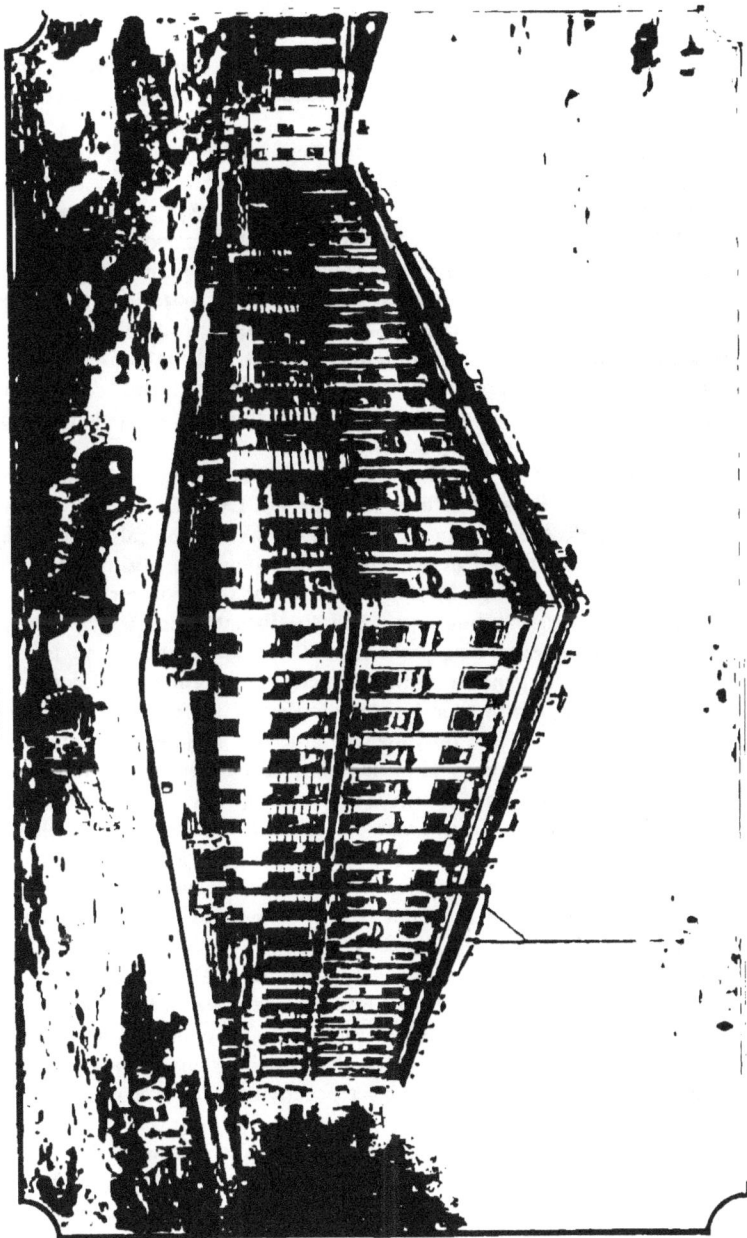

to $3,000,000 per year. In the Treasury building there are nearly 3000 persons employed, and several of the divisions, with many employés, are located elsewhere in Washington.

The Post-Office Department has its offices in a marble building, which covers an entire square, bounded by Seventh, Eighth, E, and F streets. The building was erected in 1839, and extended in 1855. The architects were Robert Mills and Thomas U. Walter. Over $2,000,000 were expended in the construction. The Postmaster-General supervises the postal service and appoints the postmasters whose salaries are not more than $1000 per year. Postmasters whose salaries exceed $1000 are appointed by the President. Three assistant postmasters-general with salaries of $4000 have charge of the various divisions of the department. There are 51,000 post-offices in the United States, and the yearly expenditure for the postal service is over $50,000,000.

The Department of the Interior has the following divisions: The Patent Office, the Pension Office, the General Land Office, the Bureau of Indian Affairs, the Bureau of Education, the Geological Survey, the Census Office, and the office of the Commissioner of Railroads. The department was established in 1849. Several of the divisions occupy the large marble and granite building called the Patent Office, which is situated on the square extending from Seventh to Ninth street, and from F to G street. The Pension Office, which now occupies buildings on Pennsylvania avenue, will soon have possession of the capacious building in process of erection for it on Judiciary Square. The Department of the Interior has charge of many important interests of the government, and a large force of officials and clerks is required to carry on its business.

The Department of Justice was established in 1870. It has charge of all the United States courts and all the law business of the government. The offices of the department are in a brownstone building on Pennsylvania avenue near Fifteenth street. The first story of the building is occupied by the Court of Claims.

In the various branches of the public service in Washington there are 15,000 persons employed. Of this number there are nearly 6000 clerks who are included within the civil service law. The officials and certain employés of the government, such as short-hand writers, translators, confidential clerks, cashiers, and persons occupying positions of trust, are not within the law.

The civil service commissioners have a suite of rooms in the second story of a small brick building adjacent to that occupied by the Department of Agriculture. There are three commissioners, who receive salaries of $3500, and are also allowed their expenses when travelling on business.

The office force consists of a chief examiner with a salary of $3000, a secretary with $1600, and several clerks. There are ten examiners for the general service in the executive departments, and eleven special examiners, all of whom are selected from the department officials in Washington, and receive no extra compensation. There are, besides, examining boards at the various post-offices and custom-houses in the United States. The yearly expense of this new branch of the public service is about $24,000.

The civil service act went into practical operation July 16, 1883. By it all appointments to clerkships in the seven executive departments in Washington where the salary is not less than $900 nor more than $1800 per year, and to subordinate places in the postal and customs service throughout the country, under certain limitations, are made as the result of a system of examinations intended to ascertain the fitness of those persons who seek to be employed by the government. Any citizen of the United States who is within the limit as to age can app.y for a position in the departmental service or in the postal or customs service, go before the civil service commission for examination, and, if he passes the examination, is eligible to office. Not the slightest "influence" is needed ; no solicitation on the part of any one has any weight or is of any advantage. Every applicant has to work his own way, so to speak, and, although there is a little "luck" in the matter, as will be described farther on, if he is meritorious he has a fair chance of obtaining what he desires. So very little is known of the method employed in carrying out the civil service act, that it may be of interest and value to describe in detail the process by which a person is enabled to enter that "fertile field" (in popular estimation) known as government service.

Whenever a man or woman desires to obtain a place in the departmental service of the government, the first thing to be done is to send to the civil service commission for an application paper. Only this and nothing more. It is not necessary, as many seem to think, to write a long letter giving a minute description of qualifications for the service, and stating that they have had this and that experience, and can give this and that reference. A few lines on a postal card are enough. By return mail an application paper will be sent, and this paper will give full information of the course of procedure. Persons not under eighteen nor over forty-five years of age are eligible for the departmental service, but limitations of age do not apply to "persons honorably discharged from the military or naval service of the country, who are otherwise qualified." The application paper contains blanks in which are to be written the name, age, residence, and occupation of the applicant, and sundry other facts of consequence. The statements have to be sworn to before an official qualified to administer

THE NEW PENSION BUILDING.

an oath, and confirmed by the vouchers of three persons. No recommendations outside of these vouchers as to character and capacity are allowed. When the applicant has properly filled out the application paper, it should be mailed to the commission at Washington. If the commission finds the paper to be proper in form, the applicant's name is entered upon the record, and his paper is filed. A short time before an examination is to be held the applicant will receive an official notice to be present at any of the places designated. Armed with this notice, and with the consciousness that he " knows something," the applicant can present himself to the examining board at the place he has chosen and meet his fate.

Examinations are held in Washington and in various other cities of the country at such times as the commissioners may think proper. There are three kinds of examinations,—limited, general, and special. For ordinary clerkships and subordinate positions in the departments the limited and general examinations apply; for positions requiring technical knowledge and skill special examinations only are held. The limited examination, which is intended mainly for copyists, messengers, and other subordinate employés, is very simple. Two subjects only are used. The applicant has to copy a few sentences from dictation and a few sentences from a printed form, in order to show his penmanship and orthography; then he is required to work out several examples in addition, subtraction, multiplication, and division, none of which are much beyond the capacity of a ten-year old child. The general examination has five subjects, with from three to five questions to a subject. The first subject is similar to that of the limited examination; the second subject embraces examples in the fundamental principles of arithmetic, fractions, and percentage; and the third subject, examples in interest, discount, and elements of book-keeping and of accounts. The two other subjects include questions of grammar and of the history, geography, and government of the United States. This examination is the one taken by the majority of applicants for government service, as success in it makes a person eligible to a $1200 clerkship, from which may come promotion to places worth $1400, $1600, or $1800 a year.

In this examination questions like the following have to be answered: " Divide three-fourths of eight-ninths by one-seventh of three-fifths, and subtract one-seventh from the quotient." " Divide one thousand and eight and three one-thousandths by three and eight one-hundredths, expressing the process in decimal fractions." " A note for $2647.34 is payable eleven months from date with interest at 3½ per cent. What will be the amount due on the note at maturity? Give all the figures in the operation." " A disbursing agent failed, owing the government one item of $308.45, another of $2901.02. The government agrees to make a discount of 13 per cent. on the first item and 11¼ per cent. on the second. How much was payable under the agreement?" " The compensation of a clerk, beginning June 30, was $133.33 a calendar month. On the 1st of October his salary was increased 15 per cent., and so remained until June 1, when it was increased a further amount of 3 per cent. on the original salary. What was the whole amount payable to the clerk for the year?" " Give a definition of a verb, a noun, an adverb, an adjective, a preposition, a conjunction, and of the phrase, ' the grammar of the English language.' " " Which states extend to or border on the sea or tide-water? What is the capital of each of said states?" " What is meant in our history by the colonial period? by the Continental Congress? by the Declaration of Independence? by the emancipation proclamation?" The questions are different at each examination, but they always follow the grade established. Each question is printed at the head of the examination paper, and only one subject at a time is given out by the examiners. The candidates sit at small desks, and are allowed not more than five hours to solve the problems. The examination-room in Washington has all the appearance of a school-room. The desks and chairs are plain and simple, and there is accommodation for a " class" of seventy-five or eighty persons.

GOVERNMENT HOSPITAL
FOR THE INSANE.

The technical or special examinations embrace a wide range of subjects. Applicants for the position of pension examiner are examined in orthography, penmanship, letter-writing, arithmetic, geography and history, the pension laws, rules of evidence, and competency of witnesses, and in anatomy and hygiene. Applicants for positions as examiners in the patent office are examined in mathematics to trigonometry, and in chemistry, physics, technics, the interpretation of mechanical drawings, and French and German. Each applicant receives a drawing of an invention, and is required to fully describe it. French and German patent specifications have to be translated. The examination in mathematics, physics, and chemistry bears directly upon the practical work of a patent examiner. The questions in physics touch those principles of physics necessary to explain patents. Those examined for the position of mechanical draughtsman have a model from the patent office placed before them, and are required to make a complete drawing of it, and then to describe it in detail and explain its mode of operation and the class of machines to which it belongs. Afterwards they are required to describe technical drawings, methods of shading to represent different surfaces, principles of perspective, and what are known as mechanical devices. Those who desire to become copyists of drawings have to make a tracing of a drawing shaded in India ink, to illustrate the methods of shading concave and convex surfaces, and to describe the views in the drawings used. Those examined for the position of assistant in the scientific library of the patent office, whose duty it is to search foreign patent records and scientific publications in order to ascertain whether or not a patent applied for here has been previously patented or described in any other country, have to translate French and German patent records, abridge and index patent specifications, classify patents according to the arts, perform some exercises to illustrate the use of the card catalogue, etc.

At the close of each examination, limited, general or special, the examiners take all the papers, look them over carefully, and determine the standing of each applicant in the subjects. The examination papers of each applicant are marked only with a number, and his name is not known to the examiners, thus preventing any favoritism. Every applicant must have an average standing of 65 per cent. in the subjects in which he is examined to become eligible to appointment. Those fortunate enough to reach this grade are notified by the commissioners, and their names are recorded in the list of "eligibles;" the others have their labor for their pains. The commissioners prepare the rules and regulations and all the questions used in the examinations, and have general charge of all matters arising from the civil service business. They do not conduct the examinations or mark the grade of persons examined, but they revise and finally decide as to the work of all the examiners.

Whenever the head of a department wishes to fill a vacancy in his clerical force, he sends a letter to the commissioners informing them of the fact, and the commissioners immediately send to that department four names taken from those having the highest grade on the list of eligibles. The names are taken according to a just apportionment to the various states and territories, the idea being not to allow one section of the country to have more appointments than it is entitled to by reason of its population. With the names are sent the examination papers of each applicant, in order that the appointing officer of the department may examine them before he takes his choice of the four names. The right of selection is possessed by the appointing officer, and he can take any name from those furnished, or he can reject them all and call for more if he chooses. If the examination papers of an eligible are especially neat and correct; if they show he has a good practical way of doing things, he may be selected at once, even if his grade is not as high as the others. If an appointing officer takes an unaccountable "fancy" to a certain name, he may select it. Sometimes the last name of the four will be selected instead of the first, or the second, or the third. The civil service commissioners have nothing to do with this. All that they can do is to send the names to the department for the choice to be made. When the appointing officer has made his choice, he notifies the commissioners, and the fact is entered in the record book. The department sends a notice to the person selected that he has been appointed to a certain clerkship, and that he must report for duty. The new clerk goes on probation for six months, and at the expiration of that time, if he has given satisfaction, his appointment is confirmed, and he can remain in the government service as long as he gives no cause for dismissal.

Each eligible can be certified twice to each department for appointment, but no more; and often names will go the rounds of the departments before they are selected, and sometimes they are not selected at all. Some men are so "lucky" that they step at once into good places, while others have to possess their souls in patience and wait and wait, and even then are not rewarded. The rule is to keep the names of those persons who are eligible for appointment on the record of the commission for two years, during which time there will be a constant chance of appointment. When four names are sent to the head of a department, and one is selected, the other three do not fall back, but they keep their rank at the front and are sent up again at the next call.

The question is often asked if the commissioners invariably select four names from those having the highest standing on the record of examinations. This is not possible under the law of apportionment to the various states and territories. For instance, if the quota of New York is full, no more names can be taken from that state, and the com-

GOVERNMENT PRINTING-OFFICE.

missioners are compelled to take the names of persons from other states who may not be graded so high as those from New York. Sometimes an eligible will make complaint that, although he was graded at 90 per cent., another person who was graded at only 70 per cent. has been appointed before him. The reason is because of the apportionment law, and the law often causes a good deal of trouble.

BUREAU OF ENGRAVING AND PRINTING.

CHAPTER XV.

ALL the paper money issued by the government is printed at the Bureau of Engraving and Printing, which is part of the Treasury Department and under the supervision of the Secretary of the Treasury. Up to 1880 the government money was printed in the Treasury, but, in order to relieve the over-crowded condition of that institution, Congress authorized the erection of the large brick building in which the Bureau of Engraving and Printing is now located. The building is situated at the southern end of Fourteenth street, and is finely arranged for the purposes of the business. It was erected at a cost of $367,000. Here the plates for the notes, bonds, and internal revenue stamps of the United States, and the plates for the national bank-notes are engraved in the finest and most accurate manner by a force of skilful engravers, some of whom have been engaged in this special work for well nigh half a century; and here also all the national currency is printed and prepared for use. The building is filled with busy employés, men and women, there being about twelve hundred in all, and a great amount of work is done every day in all the divisions of the bureau.

In one recent year the bureau completed and delivered nearly nine million sheets of notes and securities, with a face value of two hundred and sixty-eight millions of dollars. There were also completed twenty-one million sheets of stamps, containing 480,506,878 stamps, and a large amount of miscellaneous work, such as checks, drafts, etc. The bureau expends about one million dollars a year for labor and material, and of this amount over $800,000 are expended for labor alone. Every day notes of the value of $250,000 are completed. The notes, and in fact all the valuable sheets of paper, are counted thirty-five or forty times, at

DEPARTMENT OF AGRICULTURE.

different stages of the work, before they are allowed to leave the bureau, and if there is an error it can be traced in a very few minutes. Every person who handles a sheet of notes puts a private mark on it. After the notes are completed they are sent to the Treasury building in iron wagons closely guarded. When they are received by the Treasury officials they are again counted before being deposited in the great money vaults. Every precaution is taken, and it is rarely that there is an error made in handling the millions of dollars printed in the bureau. When the bureau is closed for the night, all the engraving plates and rolls, and all the sheets of notes, stamps, and securities, are carefully counted and verified and safely deposited in the vaults before any of the employés are permitted to leave the building.

All the specially prepared fibre paper used in the printing of notes and bonds comes from the Treasury upon requisition, and the purpose for which the paper is required has to be clearly stated before it is delivered by the Treasury officials. When the paper is received at the bureau, the sheets are carefully counted by ladies employed solely for this purpose. If the sheets are found to be correct, a receipt is given for the face value of them after they have been turned into money. They are then given into the hands of the plate-printers, who print the notes four on a sheet. After the printing the notes are lettered and numbered by machines, and then the seal of the government is stamped on them in red ink. The sheets are then cut and trimmed, the notes are again counted, and then they are made up in packages to be sent to the Treasury.

The portraits, vignettes, and other engraved work used upon the notes and bonds are executed in the highest style of the engraving art. The bureau has the best engravers in their several specialties of letter, ornamental, and portrait work to be found in the country. They receive large pay and retain their positions for years. No portraits of living persons are placed on the notes or bonds.

The bureau has in its possession about 40,000 pieces of engraved steel used in printing notes and bonds. They are deposited in two immense vaults, which are in charge of officials specially appointed by the Secretary of the Treasury to have the custody of this valuable stock. The vaults are made of steel, and are burglar- and fire-proof. The doors have combination and time locks. Each piece of stock taken from the vaults to be used for any purpose is charged to the division using it, and must be returned before night. The engravers are carefully supervised by special officers, and in fact in every portion of the bureau all means that human ingenuity can devise are employed to prevent unlawful use of the dies and plates, and loss in handling the vast amount of money yearly printed.

The national bank redemption division of the Treasury Department has some interesting features. The employés, some sixty in number, are mostly ladies, who count and sort the worn-out bank-notes sent to the Treasury for redemption. From sixty millions to two hundred and forty millions of dollars are handled every year in this division, and during the past ten years notes of the value of $1,391,494,237 have been redeemed. After the notes are carefully counted and examined, those that are unfit for further service are destroyed by maceration in the basement of the Treasury in the presence of a committee of officials. The paper pulp remaining is afterwards used in the manufacture of a coarse grade of paper. Formerly it was the practice to burn the notes in a great furnace, but the maceration process was found to be the most efficient. Very often national banks send more money than they mark on the outside of the packages, and nearly as often they send less. In ten years the " overs" amounted to $170,800, and the "shorts" to $135,843. Whenever there is an "over" or a "short," the bank sending the package is promptly notified and the mistake is corrected.

Money partially destroyed by fire is often sent for redemption. It is examined by lady experts, who will take a charred package of notes and, by skilfully inserting a long, thin knife, chip off the outer layer, which will expose either the face or back of the next note. The whole package will thus be carefully examined, and by certain distinguishing marks the experts are enabled to obtain the knowledge of the value of the notes.

The Soldiers' Home, which is in charge of a board of army officers of high rank, is situated a few miles from Washington, in the northern part of the District of Columbia. It was established by act of Congress in 1851 at the suggestion of General Winfield Scott, who labored earnestly for its interests. At this institution the soldiers of the army of the United States who have performed service for twenty years can reside without cost during the remainder of their lives. Those disabled in service are also entitled to a residence. A tax of twelve cents a month is assessed on each soldier during his time of service in the army to aid in paying the expenses of the institution. There are usually about five hundred residents of this beautiful estate. The main building is of white marble, and there are several other buildings of the same material. The grounds are five hundred acres in extent, and are laid out in an attractive manner and covered with groves of oak-trees. A bronze statue of General Scott, by Launt Thompson, stands in a conspicuous place on the grounds. Adjacent

THE SMITHSONIAN INSTITUTION.

STATUE OF PROF. JOSEPH HENRY, ON SMITHSONIAN
GROUNDS.

to the main building there is a pretty cottage set apart as a summer residence for the Presidents of the United States.   The estate is open to the
public and is a favorite place of resort in the vernal season.   The home
has a fund of over a million dollars, and a large yearly income from
various sources.

The Naval Observatory is situated in the westerly part of Washington,
on a government reservation which extends to the Potomac river.   It is
under the supervision of a rear-admiral of the navy, and is famous all
over the world for its astronomical work, which is performed by a corps
of distinguished astronomers.   The observatory has a great equatorial
telescope, which cost nearly $50,000.   Its object glass is twenty-six
inches clear aperture, and its focal length thirty-two and one-half feet.
The instrument is placed in a large iron dome.

The Department of Agriculture occupies many acres of the mall, and
has a large brick building and gardens for the growing of plants.   It is
not one of the regular executive departments of the government, but is a

bureau in charge of a commissioner with a salary of $4500. It has a large force of specialists, who devote themselves to investigations of agricultural matters, and the information gained is diffused throughout the country by means of reports. The department building was erected in 1868, at a cost of about $200,000. Adjacent to it are large plant-houses in which rare tropical plants are grown. The seed division of the department employs nearly two hundred men and women, at certain seasons, in assorting and packing bushels of seeds of various sorts, which are sent out to the farming regions all over the country. Great quantities of seeds are raised by the department, and great quantities are purchased. Farmers are supplied with seeds for corn, wheat, cotton, tobacco, hemp, flax, and jute, and with seeds for garden vegetables and flowers. Many rare foreign seeds are also supplied. The department issues annually a voluminous report in book form, with many illustrations, which is circulated to the extent of 300,000 copies. The beautiful gardens and lawns of the department, filled with rare flowers and aromatic plants, are very attractive.

The Signal Office is located in a brick building on G street. The "weather service" is the special work of this bureau. Throughout the country there are stationed nearly three hundred men, who are members of the signal corps of the army. Their duty is to make precise and accurate observations of the weather in their districts three times each day, and to send the record of the observations to the bureau at Washington. The facts thus obtained are charted upon a specially prepared map, and this map becomes a perfect photograph of the condition of the weather at a certain time all over the United States. The map is carefully studied by an officer at the Signal Office, and the predictions as to the weather are made up as the result of this study. The weather observations are taken at all the stations in the country at precisely the same minute of Washington time,—at 7 A.M., 3 P.M., and 11 P.M. The government owns and operates several thousand miles of telegraph lines, which are used by the weather observers to send their reports. The bureau was created

PROF. SPENCER F. BAIRD, SECRETARY OF THE SMITHSONIAN INSTITUTION.

in 1870, but it was not until 1874 that the weather service was performed upon an extended scale.

The dead-letter office of the Post-Office Department has been called "a monument to the carelessness and stupidity of the American people." It is a curious institution. It occupies a spacious apartment of the post-office building, and has over one hundred employés, who are busily engaged day by day in opening letters and packages which have gone astray in the mails. About 15,000 "dead" letters are received every day from the post-offices of the country, and these letters contain all sorts of things. Many thousands of dollars are discovered in the letters each year. If an address is found, the letters and packages are forwarded at once to their owners, but a good portion of the dead mail finds its way to the depository for waste paper, is cut into shreds, and sold to paper mills.

The patent office as it is at present was established in 1836. Previous to that year only about 10,000 patents had been issued in this country, but since then there have been over 300,000 issued. The office yearly issues about 21,000 patents, and usually has a surplus fund of over $100 000 after all the expenses are paid. There is at present in the Treasury of the United States a balance on account of the patent fund of $2,782,000. The model museum of the patent office contains many thousands of patent models, embracing mechanical devices of every description. There are four great halls devoted to the models.

The pension office is the most important bureau of the Department of the Interior. There are at present on the rolls of the office 322,756 pensioners, classified as follows: 218,956 army invalids, 75,836 army widows, minor children, and dependent relatives; 2616 navy invalids, 1938 navy widows, minor children, and dependent relatives; 3898 survivors of the war of 1812, and 19,512 widows of those who served in that war. The average value of each pension is $106.75, and the aggregate value of all pensions is $34,456,600. Every year sixty millions of dollars are paid for pensions. This amount is greater than the aggregate value of all pensions, because it includes first payments, known as arrears of pensions, which in some cases amount to several thousand dollars to a pensioner. During 1884 over twenty-seven million dollars were paid to new pensioners. Since 1861 there have been filed 927,922 claims for pensions, and nearly 550,000 claims have been allowed. There has been disbursed to pensioners since 1861 the immense sum of $680,000,000.

In the Treasury of the United States there is a fund of $703,000, which is held in trust for the Smithsonian Institution. This fund was bequeathed to the United States by James Smithson, an English gentleman, "to found at Washington, under the name of the Smithsonian In-

THE NATIONAL MUSEUM.

stitution, an establishment for the increase and diffusion of knowledge among men." The bequest was received in 1838, and in 1856 the building known as the Smithsonian Institution was finished. It stands on a portion of the mall designated as "the Smithsonian grounds," and is of red sandstone. It is four hundred and fifty feet long and one hundred and forty feet wide, and has nine towers. The style of architecture is the ancient Norman. The building contains offices for the employés of the institution, and also a large museum of natural history. On the grounds near the building is a bronze statue of Professor Joseph Henry, by W. W. Story, which was erected by the government, at a cost of $15,000, and unveiled on April 19, 1883. Professor Henry was the first secretary of the institution. The yearly receipts of the institution from interest on its fund and other sources are about $45,000. The income is expended in scientific investigations, which are embodied in reports published in volumes entitled "The Smithsonian Contributions to Knowledge." These volumes are sent to the leading scientific societies throughout the world.

In connection with the Smithsonian Institution is the National Museum, which contains large collections of industrial products, historical relics, and ethnological objects. The museum was established by the government in 1876, and is rapidly becoming one of the greatest exhibitions in

the world. The build-
ing which it occupies is
situated near the Smith-
sonian Institution, and

THE SIGNAL OFFICE OR WEATHER BUREAU.

is constructed of bricks, profusely decorated with various enamelled colors.
There are many spacious halls for exhibition purposes within the building.
Liberal appropriations are made by Congress for the museum, and in the
course of a few years it will be worth a journey across the continent to
inspect this gigantic "world's fair." The secretary of the Smithsonian
Institution is Professor Spencer F. Baird, and he is also the director of the
National Museum.

The Government Printing-Office is located in a large brick building on
North Capitol street. About 2500 persons are employed in this office in
printing and binding the various publications of the government, and
yearly over $2,000,000 are expended for the work. The office is supplied
with the best material, and much of its work is of a high order. The
establishment is in charge of an official whose title is Public Printer.

CHAPTER XVI.

HISTORIC ARLINGTON—THE LARGEST OF THE NATIONAL MILITARY CEMETERIES—
EARLY HISTORY OF THE BEAUTIFUL ESTATE—JOHN CUSTIS AND HIS DESCEND-
ANTS—GEORGE WASHINGTON PARKE CUSTIS—GENERAL ROBERT E LEE'S LIFE
AT ARLINGTON—THE CUSTIS MANSION—THE GREAT BURIAL-FIELDS—O'HARA'S
POEM, "THE BIVOUAC OF THE DEAD."

EW Southern people who visit the city of Washington fail to
go to historic Arlington, where General Robert E. Lee and
his interesting family passed so many happy years before
grim-visaged war made them exiles from the beautiful estate.
People from all parts of the South seem to revere this home of the great
Confederate soldier, and they love to walk through the rooms of his
quaint old mansion, and to sit in the shade of the noble oaks which cover
the grounds. And thousands of people from the East and West, of all
classes and conditions, year by year go to this place with reverent feeling,
for it is indeed hallowed ground,—it is the last resting-place of a mighty
host who laid down their lives for their country. Arlington contains the
largest and most important of the eighty-two military cemeteries established throughout the United States by the government, and the graves
of over 16,000 soldiers of the Civil War are in its enclosure. The cemetery is in charge of a gallant veteran of the war, and a considerable force
of laborers is constantly employed in adorning and improving the grounds,
—in making these sacred burial-fields as beautiful and attractive as the
highest skill and a lavish expenditure can accomplish. The estate is
situated directly opposite Washington, on the Virginia bank of the
Potomac, and the Lee mansion, surrounded by luxuriant groves, is on
an elevation of two hundred feet, so that it can be plainly seen from many
parts of the city. On a bright, clear day the huge portico of the mansion,
with its eight classic columns, stands out very distinctly, and one would
hardly think there was a mile of water between the mansion and the city.
The estate comprises 1160 acres, mostly good arable land, and it is part
of a grant of 6000 acres which was made by Sir William Berkeley, one
of the royal governors of Virginia, to Robert Howson during the reign

ARLINGTON MANSION.

of George II. Howson is credited with
having afterward disposed of the entire
grant for six hogsheads of tobacco. The
present Arlington estate was purchased for £11,000 by John Custis, the
great-grandfather of George Washington Parke Custis, in the early part
of the eighteenth century, and continued in the possession of his descendants until it was acquired by the government. About two hundred
acres are used for the military cemetery; the remainder is used for the
Fort Myer signal station, and for a sort of desultory farming by negro
squatters.

John Custis, who first gave the name of Arlington to this fine estate,
was a member of one of the first families of the Old Dominion. He was
a planter of many broad acres in addition to this property, and, according
to tradition, a rather obstinate, choleric worthy, given to great admiration
for his own opinions and little tolerant of the opinions or desires of others.
He married the daughter of Colonel Daniel Parke, a distinguished Vir-
ginian. She was a haughty beauty with a very bad temper, and John
was warned that she was not the proper mate for him; but, lover-like,

ardent with affection and desire, he paid no attention to the warning, and declared that to possess her was heaven enough. But the beauty having, it is likely, much the same disposition as his own, gave him no taste of paradise in his married life. He was an unhappy husband, and, when his wife died at Arlington, he could scarcely repress his joy long enough to go through with the customary forms of grief. She left a son and daughter, and they caused the father a good deal of trouble. The daughter fell in love with an officer in the English army, and secretly married him, much to the father's disgust; and the son, a handsome, gallant fellow, refused to look at a high-born girl with great expectations who had been selected for his bride, and instead paid court to Martha

BURIAL-FIELD AT ARLINGTON—TOMB OF UNKNOWN SOLDIERS.

. Dandridge, the acknowledged belle of the little town of Williamsburg, Virginia, where the royal governors resided.

Daniel Parke Custis was the name of the young man who appreciated the grace and comeliness of the Williamsburg belle, who was destined to fill a prominent place in the history of the country, and he was courageous enough to declare to his father that he should marry her if she would have him. The daughter's choice had disgusted John Custis, but the choice made by his son infuriated him. In his passion he declared that his son should not have one acre of the many hundreds he possessed, and he made a will leaving his entire estate to a negro servant, and cutting off his son with the traditional shilling. One day Martha Dandridge met old Custis at a social gathering, and fairly captivated him by her conversation, full of sense and wit, by her tact and gracious manner, by her modesty and sweetness. From that moment he withdrew his opposition, and even went so far as to say that if Daniel didn't marry her he should, for such a charming woman mustn't go out of the family.

Daniel Parke Custis and Martha Dandridge were married, and John Custis gave them a good farm on the Pamunkey river, in Virginia, to live on. When he died, it was found that he had left a will, bequeathing the Arlington estate to his son Daniel, and also the Pamunkey estate, called the " White House farm," and several other properties. In his will he directed his son, under penalty of disinheritance, to have his body placed in a white marble tomb, which should bear an inscription he had written with the intention of permanently recording his unhappy married life. The tomb was built and inscribed as he had directed. The inscription is so unique that it may be well to give it here. It is as follows:

Under This Marble Tomb Lies The Body
of the Hon. John Custis, Esq.,
Of the City of Williamsburg
And Parish of Bruton,
Formerly of Hungar's Parish On The
Eastern Shore
Of Virginia, and County of Northampton,
Aged 71 years, and yet lived but seven years, which
was the space of time he kept
A Bachelor's Home At Arlington.

The rear of the tomb is inscribed: This inscription put on his tomb was by his own positive orders.

Daniel and Martha Custis lived happily on the White House farm

GRAVE OF JOHN HOWARD PAYNE AT OAK HILL CEMETERY.

until the death of old Custis, and then they took up their residence at Arlington, living in a plain wooden house, which was removed when the present mansion was erected. Daniel was a lover of gay company, and entertained liberally. He was an enthusiastic sportsman, followed the hounds every season, and thoroughly enjoyed all the pleasures of the field. He was a worthy gentleman, a devoted husband and father. His estate was large and profitable, and he was ranked among the most opulent planters of eastern Virginia. He died before he was thirty-five, leaving two children, a boy and a girl, to the care of his young widow. Arlington was left by will to the boy, John Parke Custis, and the White House estate to the girl, Eleanor Custis. The remainder of Daniel's property, valued at about $100,000, was bequeathed to his widow for her sole use and benefit.

The widow Custis was the guardian of her children's property, and she was considered the richest widow in that section of the state. She was plump and pretty, still in the flush of youth, of a lively nature, and very popular in society. After her period of mourning, she opened her house to company, and also visited a good deal at the houses of the Virginia gentry. At one of these houses she was introduced one day to a young officer who had achieved considerable distinction in the campaigns of General Braddock. This was Colonel George Washington. He was scarcely thirty, and a very impressionable young man, having had one or two love-affairs which had not "run smooth." When he met the widow Custis it was a clear case of love at first sight. He made haste to woo and win her, and for once in his life he forgot the call of duty when by her side. They had a blithesome wedding at the White House farm, and passed their honeymoon there, going to Washington's Mount Vernon estate some months after to reside permanently. The two Custis children lived at Mount Vernon, and their estates were cared for by Washington. The Arlington estate was especially cared for, as it was regarded as a fine property, and one that in time would be of very great value. The Arlington slaves, a goodly number, were retained on it, and set to work in the cultivation of wheat, Indian corn, and tobacco, and large crops of these staples were raised. Washington was often on the estate directing the agricultural operations, and Martha Washington, who had a warm affection for the lovely place, had a small summer-house erected on the high bank overlooking what is now the capital city, where she was accustomed to sit on pleasant afternoons when she visited Arlington. This summer-house is said to have been located directly on the spot where now the great staff bearing the flag of the United States is placed.

On many an afternoon Washington and his wife have sat on this bank, elevated two hundred feet above the river, looking at the charming view, a view that Lafayette once said was the finest he had ever seen. Below the long, sloping bank with its luxuriant emerald covering, the placid Potomac widens until it is a mile in breadth, and then it gracefully curves to the southward, glistening in the sunshine. Great stretches of thickly-wooded hills border a wide, undulating plain, on which the capital city rests, and as far as the eye can reach is a panorama of rare loveliness. Conspicuous on the farther bank of the river is the tall, massive shaft of marble which has been raised to the memory of Washington, and two miles away the magnificent Capitol shows clearly on its hill-top.

John Parke Custis grew to manhood, but his sister Eleanor died when but seventeen. The boy was petted and almost spoiled by his mother, and his illustrious stepfather gave him as much attention as he would have given his own son. He married a member of the Calvert family of Maryland, and at the battle of Yorktown was an aide-de-camp to Washington. Shortly after the battle he died of fever, and Washington then adopted regularly and formally his two infant children,—George Washington Parke Custis and Nelly Custis, but had them retain their family name. They became the children of Mount Vernon, and for many years gladdened and brightened the home of Washington. Their grand-mother idolized them, and he who was destined to have no child of his own—the Father of his Country—loved them with a deep, strong affection. Nelly Custis grew to be a most beautiful woman, and is said to have been a perfect image of her grandmother, " the belle of Williams-burg," as she was in her youth. She married Major Lawrence Lewis, and from this union came the distinguished Lewis family of Virginia. George Washington Parke Custis remained at Mount Vernon until he reached his majority, when he took possession of his inheritance,—the Arlington estate. At the death of Martha Washington he also inherited the White House farm on the Pamunkey river.

When Custis came into possession of Arlington he immediately began the erection of a grand mansion on the brow of the hill. He made the designs for it, and expended a good deal of money in its construction. Its portico was fashioned in imitation of that of a famous temple near Naples. Custis occupied the mansion early in 1803, when he was a little more than twenty-one years old. He kept bachelor's hall for a year or so, and then married Mary Lee Fitzhugh, whose mother was a Randolph. Four children were born to him, all girls, but only one survived infancy. Custis was always known as the " child of Mount Vernon," and was held in special regard and even reverence on account of his intimate connection with Washington as his adopted child. His life at Arlington extended to 1857, when he died, the last male of his family. His wife died in 1853, and the graves of the couple, side by side, can be seen in the southerly part of the Arlington grounds.

George Washington Parke Custis is well remembered by many resi-dents of the District of Columbia. He was a finely-formed man, of medium height, and had a bright, intelligent, rather handsome face, and a clear, florid complexion. His forehead was high and broad, his eyes blue and sparkling, and he was always attired with scrupulous care and neatness. Genial and courteous, yet not familiar, he was at times a little aristocratic in manner. From childhood he had lived in high and dis-tinguished society, and at Arlington he entertained some of the foremost

men of the day. In 1824 Lafayette visited him, and he had seen the
great Frenchman at Mount Vernon as far back as 1784. He was a poet
and a painter, wrote plays for the amusement of his friends, and had
considerable gift as an orator. He lacked the spur of necessity to develop
his literary and artistic talent. For years he was engaged in painting a
series of battle scenes portraying the military life of Washington,—a series
which would have been very valuable in a historical sense, as he had
had such rare opportunities to gather accurate material; but the paintings
were never finished, and came to naught. He had a royal income from
his landed property, and lived the easy, comfortable life of a rich Virginia
planter, enjoying his beautiful home and taking pleasure in his social
circle.

At one time Custis developed much enthusiasm for sheep-raising,
obtained a flock of blooded merinos, and sought to arouse interest among
the planters of his neighborhood in the subject. He offered prizes for
the best sheep, and appointed a day for an annual exhibition at Arlington.
This exhibition was called the "Arlington sheep-shearing," and was held
on the lawn, near what is known as the "Custis spring." After the prizes
were distributed, a dinner, chiefly composed of fish caught in the Potomac,
was served in a large tent, used by Washington during the Revolution.
Custis' interest in sheep died out after a few years, and the flock of
merinos dwindled to two, and these were allowed to run over the hills as
they pleased.

His only child, Mary Randolph Custis, was a buxom lass, with a
handsome face something like his own. In childhood her favorite play-
fellow was the youngest son of Governor Henry Lee, who lived at Strat-
ford house, in Westmoreland county, Virginia. Governor Lee had been
an intimate friend of Washington, had served in the Revolutionary war
with him, and at the Congressional funeral ceremony delivered the
oration, in which were those famous words, "First in war, first in peace,
first in the hearts of his countrymen." The boy and girl friendship
ripened into love, and when young Robert Edward Lee went to West
Point in 1825 for a military education, at the expense of the State of
Virginia, he left behind him at Arlington a sweetheart who was eventually to be his wife. In 1832, Lieutenant Lee was married to Mary
Custis. When her father died he left her the Arlington estate for life.
After her, it was to descend to her eldest son.

The life of the Lee family at the Arlington home was an exceedingly
pleasant one. For years before Custis died, his soldier son-in-law, wife,
and children lived in the old mansion by his request. Lee was frequently
away upon military duty, but at every opportunity hastened back to

VIEWS AT THE SOLDIERS' HOME.

Arlington and his growing family, for he was domestic in his tastes, and dearly loved those who were bound to him by the ties of affection, and he also loved the fair and fertile acres washed by the Potomac. He was simple in all his habits, liked to live quietly and plainly, enjoyed romping with his children, and they often said, " Father is as good as a boy to play with." The rigorous artificial customs of army life never seemed to change his disposition, and he was always a singularly pure, unaffected, sincere man. He had the best of health, was never sick, never used liquor or tobacco, and enjoyed life in a hearty, wholesome way. He was tall, and his rather grave face was lighted by clear blue eyes, which would show a good deal of roguish fun at times. He had black hair, a close-cut beard and moustache, which afterward turned to snowy white. He had a gentle, but firmly persuasive manner, and few could resist him. One of his sons has said that his father liked to have his own way, and generally had it, but he was never obstinate, never in a passion, and always was kind and courteous in enforcing his orders. He managed the Arlington estate admirably, and took great delight in agricultural operations. Few men could drive a mule as well as he could, and it was no uncommon thing for him to be out all day with a mule team working in the field.

Mrs. Lee was an excellent wife. She understood her husband perfectly, and fully believed in him, and their companionship was of the truest and best kind all through their married life. She was very amiable,—a chatty, bright, lively woman, finely educated, a great reader, and an earnest worker for the welfare of her family. There were six children, three boys and three girls, and they helped to make up a home circle that for a long time was as delightful as any in Virginia, and one that was undisturbed by rude shocks and cares. Colonel Lee, for that was his military title then, had a marked religious proclivity, and in his family and in all his daily walks endeavored to carry out Christian principles by an exact measure. The Bible was closely studied, family worship was always maintained, and he was careful to impress upon the minds of his children the need and importance of a true Christian life. Mrs. Lee for a number of years was earnest in aiding church enterprises, and did a great deal toward sustaining several churches in the section in which they lived and also in the city of Washington. Sunday was strictly observed on the estate. No work was ever allowed to be done, and on many a Sunday afternoon Colonel Lee, Bible in hand, discoursed earnestly and thoughtfully upon the truths of religion to his negro servants and others gathered in a grove on the grounds. The servants adored their good master and mistress, for they always had kind treatment, and were sure of sympathy, of patient attention in the time of sickness and trouble.

Some of these servants are still living on and around the Arlington property, and they tell many stories of " Massa Lee" and " Missy Lee," of their kindnesses, gentle forbearance, and tender spirit. " Dey was de best folks in ole Virginny," said one negro ; " dey treated de po' ole slaves like as if dey was as good as dey was. Massa Lee, he would put his han' on my head an' say, 'Sam, do yer duty an' be a good man.'" " I worked on de Lee place," said another negro whose head was covered with snow-white curly locks, " an' I wish I was dere now. Dere was plenty to eat an' drink, an' I nebber have had such a good time since."

STATUE OF GENERAL SCOTT AT THE SOLDIERS' HOME.

The mansion which Custis erected is a two-story brick building, one hundred and forty feet long. There is a central structure with a wide, deep portico, which has eight ponderous columns, and there are two wings. The mansion is covered with plaster and painted a yellowish brown. It is located on the highest eastern bank of the estate, and from its portico and windows the view is superb. It is a fine specimen of the old mansions of Virginia, and is something like Jefferson's mansion at Monticello. From the portico a large door opens into a wide hall-way, which extends to the rear of the house. There are two parlors and a conservatory on the left of the hall, and on the right is a spacious dining-room, with an arch and pillars in the centre of it, and there are small rooms leading from it. The upper story has a number of good-sized rooms. The mansion is well preserved; it bears no appearance of decay, and is likely to last for many more years with proper care. The upper story is occupied by the official in charge of the military cemetery, and the rooms of the first story contain a few chairs and desks. On the walls are hung plans and pictures of the cemetery. Adjacent to the mansion are several small brick structures used by the house-servants of the Lee family.

Up to the time of Lee's departure from Arlington for Richmond to enter the Confederate service, the mansion contained a large collection of Washington relics which Custis had brought from Mount Vernon. In the parlors were a number of ancient paintings which had formerly hung on the walls of Washington's home, and among these were the portraits of Washington and his wife, painted soon after their marriage. The parlors also contained many pieces of furniture from Mount Vernon. There were Washington's bookcase, the china dining-set presented to him by the Society of the Cincinnati, the china tea-set presented to Martha Washington by Lafayette and the French officers of the Revolution, curtains and a fire-screen embroidered by her, brass and silver candlesticks, a clock, fire-tongs, the mahogany chairs and tables that were in the state parlor at Mount Vernon, and other articles of historical value. In one of the other rooms was the mahogany bedstead on which Washington lay when he died, and in the stable was the clumsy old yellow coach which Washington used all the time he was President. All these articles were bequeathed to Custis by his grandmother, and were sacredly cherished by him.

When Arlington was deserted by the Lee family in the spring of 1861, they had a few of the relics removed to a place of safety, but they had so little belief that there would be "much of a war" that they were content to leave the estate and the greater part of its historic treasures in the keeping of a superintendent until they should return. But they never came back to beautiful Arlington, and its shady walks and the old mansion

SUMMER RESIDENCE OF PRESIDENTS OF THE UNITED
STATES AT THE SOLDIERS' HOME.

knew them no more forever. United States troops soon took possession of the estate, and the government seized the Washington relics, and they are now deposited in the National Museum. In 1869, Mrs. Lee endeavored to obtain them, but Congress refused her request. Arlington was sold at a tax sale in January, 1864, under the tax act of 1862. It could not be confiscated, as it was entailed property. Taxes were levied on it, and, as they were not paid, the sale took place, and the government bought the estate for $23,000. A national military cemetery was established here in May, 1864.

Some years after the war, George Washington Custis Lee, the eldest son of General Lee, having inherited the estate at his mother's death, brought suit for its recovery. He claimed that the tax sale was invalid, because a tender of the taxes might have been made if the tax commissioners had not required the tender to be made in person. The suit went to the Supreme Court of the United States, and that court gave judgment for Mr. Lee. He at once proposed a compromise with the government, which was accepted by Congress, and, in 1884, Mr. Lee transferred all his right, title, and interest in the estate to the United States for the sum of $150,000.

That portion of Arlington set apart for the cemetery borders on the road which runs from the Aqueduct bridge, at Georgetown, to Alexandria. The cemetery extends 3500 feet on the Alexandria road, and runs back to the westward for a half-mile. The grounds are enclosed with a low rubble stone wall, and are very picturesque. They are thickly covered with tall, magnificent oaks, which have been growing for nearly two hundred years. Broad, well-made roads wind through ravines and over hills, and there are innumerable rich green lawns, studded with great beds of flowers and variegated plants.

At the main entrance gate is a high arch composed of marble columns taken from the portico of the old building in Washington, occupied by the War Department until 1873, when it was demolished. Three of the columns are inscribed with the names of Scott, Lincoln, and Stanton. The greater number of burials are in the southerly section, a short distance from the mansion. Here is an almost level field of many acres, and on this field are thousands of graves in parallel rows, stretching away almost as far as one can see. The graves are level with the sod, the mound system customary in most cemeteries having been dispensed with. There is a small marble headstone at each grave bearing the name of the soldier and the name of his state. This vast burial-field is covered with trees and carpeted with luxuriant turf. It is a peaceful resting-place. The patriot sons of every Northern state are here sleeping the last sleep. The field is scrupulously cared for day by day by the government officials. Flowers are constantly planted, the grass is cut, weeds are removed from the paths, and everything possible is done to keep it in the best condition. There are other burial-fields in the cemetery, but they are not so extensive as this one.

Near the mansion is a large granite tomb, in which repose the bodies of 2111 unknown soldiers, gathered after the war from the battle-fields of Bull Run and the route to the Rappahannock. The tomb is surrounded by cannon, and shaded by four gigantic oaks. In all there are 16,264 soldiers buried in this cemetery, nearly 1000 more than in the Gettysburg cemetery. Record books, containing the name and description of every soldier who was known, together with the locality of his grave and the date of his burial, are to be seen in the mansion.

On the borders of the burial-fields are large iron frames containing selections from a poem written by Colonel Theodore O'Hara, a heroic soldier of the Mexican war, and read by him at the dedication of the monument erected by the State of Kentucky in Frankfort cemetery to the memory of her citizens who fell in that struggle. O'Hara was a Southern poet and journalist, and for some time was the editor of *The*

Mobile Register. He died in Columbus, Georgia, in 1867. His poem was selected on account of its singular beauty and appropriateness. The selections are in large white letters, and are very conspicuous on the frames which contain them.

O'Hara's poem is entitled " The Bivouac of the Dead," and the verses displayed in the cemetery are as follows:

" The muffled drum's sad roll has beat
  The soldier's last tattoo!
No more on life's parade shall meet
  That brave and fallen few.
On fame's eternal camping-ground
  Their silent tents are spread,
And glory guards with solemn round
  The bivouac of the dead.

" No rumor of the foe's advance
  Now swells upon the wind,
Nor troubled thought at midnight haunts
  Of loved ones left behind.
No vision of the morrow's strife
  The warrior's dream alarms,
No braying horn, no screaming fife
  At dawn shall call to arms.

" The neighing troop, the flashing blade,
  The bugle's stirring blast,
The charge, the dreadful cannonade,
  The din and shout are past.
Nor war's wild notes, nor glory's peal
  Shall thrill with fierce delight
Those breasts that never more may feel
  The rapture of the fight.

" Rest on, embalmed and sainted dead!
  Dear is the blood you gave,—
No impious footsteps here shall tread
  The herbage of your grave;
Nor shall your glory be forgot
  While fame her record keeps,
Or honor points the hallowed spot
  Where valor proudly sleeps."

14

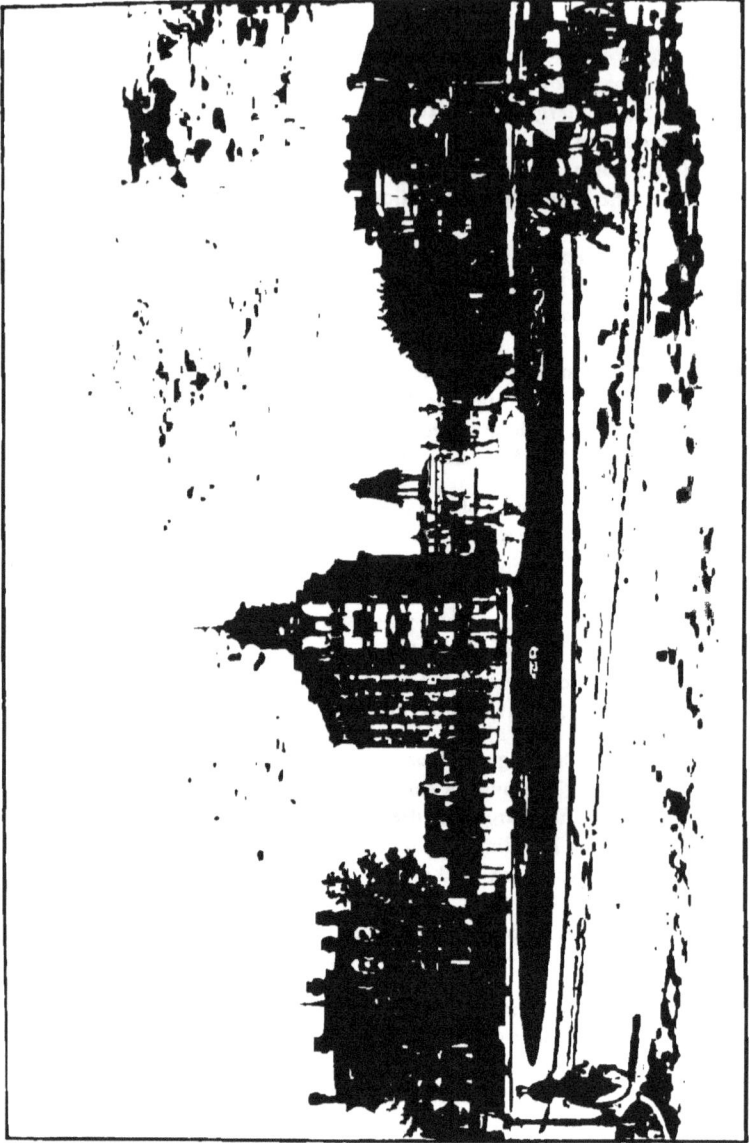

THE THOMAS CIRCLE

CHAPTER XVII.

OME twenty-five years ago Mr. William W. Corcoran, the eminent banker and philanthropist of Washington, conceived the idea of establishing a public gallery of art. He had a fine collection of paintings and statuary, valued at many thousands of dollars, which he thought would be a nucleus for such a gallery, and to this collection he proposed to add a large number of the best art-works of Europe and America. In 1859 he began the erection of a handsome and capacious building to contain the gallery, the architect being Mr. James Renwick, of New York. Before the building was completed the Civil War began, and in 1861 the government took possession of the building for the use of the Quartermaster-General, and retained it until the early part of 1869. After the government had vacated the building, Mr. Corcoran deeded it to trustees to be held forever as a gallery of art for the use and benefit of the public. The deed of trust was dated May 10, 1869, and stated that the institution was to be for "the perpetual establishment and encouragement of painting, sculpture, and the fine arts generally," and that "it should be open to visitors without charge two days in the week, and on other days at moderate and reasonable charges, to be applied to the current expenses of procuring and keeping in order the building and its contents."

The institution was granted an act of incorporation by Congress May 24, 1870, and was forever exempted from taxation. After considerable reconstruction, the building was completed in 1871, but it was not until January 19, 1874, that the gallery was opened to the public. Many fine paintings, statues, casts, bronzes, etc., had been purchased in Europe by one of the trustees, and, with Mr. Corcoran's collections which were deposited in the gallery some months before it was opened, the exhibition from the first was very extensive and interesting. Since 1874 the gallery has greatly developed. Year by year valuable art-works have been added, so that at the present time the gallery is one of the finest in the United States. It is managed by a board of nine trustees, and has a curator and assistant curator. It has an endowment fund of nearly $900,000, given by Mr. Corcoran, and its yearly income is large. The building and land cost $250,000, and the Corcoran collections of statues and pictures were valued at $100,000. The gallery is open each week-day, and is free on Tuesdays, Thursdays, and Saturdays. On other days a fee of twenty-five cents is charged. Every Monday, Wednesday, and Friday art-students are permitted to copy the paintings and to draw from the casts. The gallery always has many visitors, and on some days there are more than fifteen hundred people inspecting its treasures of art. During 1884 there were over 75,000 visitors.

The building stands on Pennsylvania avenue at Seventeenth street, and is opposite the State, War, and Navy building. It is one hundred and six feet nine inches in length, and one hundred and twenty-five feet six inches in depth, and has two stories with a mansard roof. It is constructed of brick, with facings and ornaments of brownstone. The front has an imposing effect, it being divided into recesses by a series of pilasters with

CORCORAN GALLERY OF ART.

WILLIAM W. CORCORAN.

finely sculptured Corinthian capitals. There are four niches in which are marble statues, and over the entrance door are carvings of trophies and wreaths of foliage. The Corcoran monogram is carved above the door, and over the central pediment is the inscription, "Dedicated to Art." There is a bronze medallion of Mr. Corcoran within the central pediment, and encircling it are carvings of foliage. Statues of Phidias, Raphael, Michael Angelo, and Albert Durer are in the niches on the front of the building, and statues of Titian, Da Vinci, Rubens, Rembrandt, Murillo, Canova, and Crawford are in niches on the Seventeenth street side. The statues were executed by M. Ezekiel at Rome, and are of Carrara marble.

In the first story of the building are the halls of sculpture and bronzes, and in the second story are the halls of paintings. All the halls are large, high, and well lighted, and are excellently arranged. The main hall of sculpture is nearly one hundred feet long, and about twenty-five feet wide, and the main hall of bronzes is nearly as large. The main hall of paintings is about the same size as the main hall of sculpture, and its ceiling is handsomely frescoed and decorated. There are three other halls of paintings. The gallery contains nearly two hundred casts of antique marbles, and many original works of modern sculptors. It has a large number of fine bronzes, and extensive collections of ceramic ware. There are over two hundred paintings on exhibition, representing many of the leading artists of the world. The gallery has portraits of the Presidents of the United States from Washington to Arthur, painted by distinguished artists, and many portraits of men eminent in American history. In the southwest hall is the Ogle Tayloe collection of statuary, paintings, bronzes, ceramic ware, and other articles bequeathed to the gallery by the late Mrs. B. Ogle Tayloe of Washington. In the collection are many articles of great historical interest.

Mr. William W. Corcoran, to whom the public are greatly indebted for this magnificent gallery, was born at Georgetown, December 27, 1798, and has passed his long and useful life in the District of Columbia. Thomas Corcoran, his father, was a native of Ireland. He settled in Georgetown when a youth, and for many years was a highly respected citizen of the ancient city, at one time serving a term as mayor. William began his business career as a dry-goods merchant, and subsequently entered the banking business in Washington, forming a partnership in 1839 with the late George W. Riggs, the son of a wealthy Maryland gentleman. In 1844 the firm of Riggs and Corcoran purchased the building on Pennsylvania avenue opposite the northern front of the Treasury building, which had been occupied by the historic United States Bank. Here they built up an extensive banking business, which has been continued to the present time under the firm-name of Riggs and Company. It is stated that " during the Mexican war the firm took extensive loans needed by the government, and though it proved a hazardous operation they emerged from it with safety, honor, and vast emoluments. This is considered to have been the main foundation of Mr. Corcoran's great wealth."

Mr. Corcoran was married in 1835 to Louise Morris, the daughter of Commodore Morris. She died in 1840, leaving a son and daughter. The son died shortly after his mother, but the daughter grew to womanhood, and for a number of years gracefully presided over her father's house. She became the wife of the Hon. George Eustis, a member of Congress from Louisiana. In 1867 she died of consumption at Cannes, France, leaving three children.

Since early manhood Mr. Corcoran has resided in Washington, and for many years in a fine mansion on H street. He has ever been a public-spirited citizen, and has done a great deal of beneficial work, constantly

THE LOUISE HOME.

using his wealth for the aid and advancement of worthy objects. In 1871 he founded the institution known as "The Louise Home," which was named "after his wife and daughter as a testimonial to their devoted concern for the poor and unfortunate." This noble institution is situated on Massachusetts avenue, between Fifteenth and Sixteenth streets. The building is of brick and four stories in height, and has a mansard roof. Its grounds cover an entire square. The interior of the building is arranged in a very convenient manner, and all the appointments of the home are elegant. The home is intended for women of refinement and culture who have been reduced from affluence to poverty and need assistance in their old age. At present there are forty-two inmates. The cost of the building and grounds was $200,000. The home has an endowment fund of $250,000, and is managed by a board of nine lady trustees.

The Columbian University is one of the leading educational institutions of Washington. It was originally incorporated by act of Congress,

February 9, 1821, and was then known as the Columbian College. On March 3, 1873, it was incorporated as a university. For many years the institution occupied a building on Meridian Hill, a short distance beyond the northern boundary-line of Washington, but in 1884 it took possession of a new and magnificent building especially erected for it on the southeast corner of H and Fifteenth streets. This building is four stories in height, and is constructed of fine pressed and moulded bricks. It has terra-cotta ornamentations of artistic design. It has a frontage of one hundred and twenty-one feet on Fifteenth street, and of sixty-four and one-half feet on H street. There is an annex extending back on the south one hundred and fifty-six feet. The interior of the building is arranged in a convenient manner for the purposes of the university. The president of the university is James C. Welling, and there is an able corps of professors and instructors in the collegiate departments, and in the departments of law and medicine. The medical school holds its sessions in a fine building on H street, between Thirteenth and Fourteenth streets, which was erected for the university by Mr. William W. Corcoran, at a cost of $40,000. The law school is held in the university building. There are many students in the different departments, and the university is in a very prosperous condition.

The Government Hospital for the Insane, or, as it is often called, St.

COLUMBIAN UNIVERSITY.

JAMES C. WELLING, PRESIDENT OF COLUMBIAN UNIVERSITY.

Elizabeth's Asylum, is situated on a hill which rises from the banks of the Anacostia river, near Greenleaf's Point, and is about a mile from the city of Washington.   It is intended for the insane of the army and navy, and also receives the insane of the District of Columbia.   It has high rank among institutions of this kind, and is one of the largest in the world.   The hospital building was erected in 1855, at a cost of $1,000,000, and has accommodations for nearly one thousand patients.   The grounds of the institution cover more than four hundred acres, and are laid out in an attractive manner.

Howard University is located on a hill near the northern boundary-line of Washington, and is adjacent to what is called the Seventh street road.   This famous institution, which was established for the purpose of giving a higher education to the colored race, has about three hundred students, and is in a flourishing condition.   Its principal building is large and well arranged, and it has extensive grounds, valued at many thousands of dollars.   It has schools of theology, medicine, and law, besides

HOWARD UNIVERSITY.

collegiate departments, and is well equipped for educational purposes. It was established in 1867, and was named after its first president, General Oliver O. Howard.

In the beautiful Oak Hill Cemetery at Georgetown is the grave of John Howard Payne, author of "Home, Sweet Home." His remains were removed from Tunis, in Africa, where they had been interred for many years, and brought to America through the liberality of Mr. William W. Corcoran. On the 9th of June, 1883, the remains were interred in Oak Hill with impressive ceremony.

CHAPTER XVIII.

N the beautiful tract of one hundred acres, situated just beyond the northeastern boundary-line of Washington, and known as Kendall Green, are the buildings occupied by the Columbia Institution for the Deaf and Dumb and National Deaf-Mute College. The institution was incorporated by Congress in 1857, and at first was intended for the primary education of the deaf-mute children of the District of Columbia; but, in 1864, it was authorized to establish a collegiate department, to be called the National Deaf-Mute College, which was to admit students from all parts of the United States. The originator of this excellent institution was Amos Kendall, who was Postmaster-General from 1835 to 1840. He had a residence on the green called by his name, and, becoming interested in the unfortunate children deprived of speech and hearing, he established a school for them in a small wooden house on his estate, securing as teacher Edward M. Gallaudet, a son of Dr. Thomas H. Gallaudet, of Hartford, Connecticut, the first instructor of the deaf and dumb in America. In this humble way the institution began its career, and for some time it was almost entirely supported by Mr. Kendall. In 1859 he erected a brick building for its use, and also set apart for it ten acres of his green for gardens and playgrounds. He gave freely of his limited means and labored earnestly until his death, in 1869, for the success of this noble educational work. Scholarships were endowed by prominent people in various parts of the country, and year by year the institution attracted public attention and developed steadily. In 1872 the entire Kendall Green was purchased by Congress for $80,000, for the use of the institution, and since then the government has liberally sustained these "silent schools."

No institution of the kind in the country has a higher rank and character. Its college is the only one in the world where deaf-mutes

219

COLUMBIA INSTITUTION FOR THE DEAF AND DUMB AND NATIONAL DEAF MUTE COLLEGE

can obtain a thorough collegiate education, and it has already graduated nearly three hundred young men, who have gone forth to engage in the affairs of life as well fitted for their duties as those blessed with the ability to hear and talk. Some of its graduates have attained distinguished success in the professions, and, as lawyers, teachers, editors, and writers, have reflected great credit on the institution which afforded them the opportunity to become well educated and able to compete successfully with those who were not "sent into this breathing world scarce half made up." Its students are from every quarter of the United States, and some have come from foreign lands.

EDWARD M. GALLAUDET, PRESIDENT OF THE NATIONAL DEAF-MUTE COLLEGE.

The institution has "a group of picturesque and stately buildings," the central one being of the pointed Gothic style prevailing during the fourteenth century. This building was erected in 1871, and is two hundred and sixteen feet long and seventy-six feet wide, the material being brownstone with courses of white sandstone. The roofs are of blue and red slate laid in courses. The other buildings are of good size and of pleasing architecture. The grounds are laid out in an attractive manner, and have lawns, gardens, and wooded fields. The property of the institution is valued at about $400,000.

In the primary school there are usually about fifty scholars, who are instructed in the sign-language and in articulation and lip-reading. After they are able to converse freely by these methods, they are taught the elements of an English education. The scholars are mostly young, but occasionally there will be seen in the classes matured men and women who had not been able to receive thorough instruction and training in their youth. The teachers are skilful and very patient, and, as a rule, the scholars make satisfactory progress, many of them in a very short time acquiring such proficiency in the deaf-mute system that they are able to converse and understand, to read and write, remarkably well.

The college curriculum embraces the Latin, French, and German languages, the higher mathematics, chemistry, botany, astronomy, geology, mineralogy, physiology, zoology, English philology, ancient and modern history, etc. The students have the use of an excellent museum, and a library especially valuable for its collections of rare works pertaining to the education of deaf-mutes.

What is known as the " French method" of instruction for the deaf and dumb is generally used in the Columbia institution and college, but the German and English methods are taught to some extent. The French method consists of the familiar sign-language, and was devised by the Abbé de l'Epée in 1760, and afterwards was perfected by the Abbé Sicard. It was introduced in the United States by Dr. T. H. Gallaudet in 1817. The other methods, which are practically one, teach the deaf-mutes articulation and how to interpret the motions of the lips when they are spoken to.

There are about thirty-five thousand deaf-mutes in the United States, and about one-fifth of the number are under instruction in the various institutions provided for them. The state institution in Illinois has more than five hundred scholars, and is the largest in the world.

Washington has numerous benevolent institutions, some of which receive substantial aid from the government. The City Asylum, on the banks of the Anacostia river, cares for the poor of the district. Its building was erected in 1859. The Freedman's Hospital, in the northern part of the city, was especially intended for the colored people, but of late years white patients have been received. It is amply provided with

VIEW ON SEVENTH STREET.

all necessary appliances for its work, and can accommodate about three
hundred patients. The students in the medical school of Howard
University receive practical instruction in this hospital. The Providence
Hospital, in the southeast quarter of Washington, is a large and important
institution, and is in charge of the Sisters of Charity. It has a large
medical staff and ample accommodations for patients. It was founded in
1862, and its present fine brick building was erected in 1867, partly by
the help of Congress. Every year an appropriation for the hospital is
made by Congress, and the non-resident poor who need medical or
surgical treatment can receive it here. The Garfield Memorial Hospital,
the City Orphan Asylum, the Children's Hospital, the Columbia Hospital
for Women, the St. John's Hospital, the Home for the Aged, the National
Soldiers' and Sailors' Orphan Home, the St. Ann's Infant Asylum, the St.

Joseph's Male Orphan Asylum, the St. Vincent Female Orphan Asylum, and the Epiphany Church Home are the prominent institutions of benevolence, and they accomplish a vast beneficial work.

In the Washington depot of the Baltimore and Potomac Railroad President James A. Garfield was shot by Charles J. Guiteau, on the morning of July 2, 1881. The President, accompanied by James G. Blaine, Secretary of State, had arrived at the depot to take a train east, for a visit to his wife, who was sojourning at Long Branch, and afterwards intended to visit various parts of New England. As he entered the ladies' waiting-room, Guiteau advanced towards him from the side of the room, and, quickly pulling out a pistol, fired several shots at him. The President fell to the floor, pierced by the bullets. He was removed in a few moments to another room, and afterwards carried to the White House, where he lay in intense pain and distress all through the summer, patiently bearing his suffering and uttering no word of complaint. The prayers of the whole country—ay, of the world—were for his recovery, but it was not so to be. He died on the 19th of September, 1881, at Elberon, New Jersey, whither he had been removed in the hope that the sea air would benefit him. Guiteau was arrested as he was leaving the depot after his dastardly act, tried, convicted of murder in spite of his pretence of insanity, and executed in the jail of the District of Columbia. Shortly after Garfield's death the railroad company placed a beautiful marble tablet on the wall of the room, directly over the spot where he fell, as a memorial to him.

VIEW ON F STREET.

THE MASONIC TEMPLE.

There are about three thousand Masons in the District of Columbia. Soon after the city of Washington was founded a lodge of Masons was established, and in 1816 there were two lodges. They had their meetings in a small wooden building in the southern quarter of the city, near the banks of the Potomac. The various lodges, chapters, and commanderies now occupy the Masonic Temple, which is situated on the northwest corner of F and Ninth streets. This building was erected in 1868, at an expense of nearly $200,000, and is constructed mainly of Nova Scotia freestone. The front is ornamented with Masonic emblems. All the rooms occupied by the order are handsomely furnished and adorned. In the second story of the building is a public hall used for various entertainments.

During the years that Washington had a municipal government—from 1802 to 1871—the following persons held the office of mayor: 1802, Robert Brent; 1812, Daniel Rapine; 1813, James H. Blake; 1817, Benjamin G. Orr; 1819, Samuel M. Smallwood; 1822, T. Carberry; 1824, Roger C. Weightman; 1827, Joseph Gales, Jr.; 1830, John P. Van Ness; 1834, W. A. Bradley; 1836, Peter Force; 1840, W. W. Seaton; 1850, Walter Lenox; 1852, John W. Maury; 1854, John T. Towers; 1856,

W. B. Magruder; 1858, J. G. Berrett; 1862, Richard Wallach; 1868, S. J. Bowen; 1870, M. G. Emery. In 1871 a territorial government was established, and Henry D. Cooke was the first governor, holding the office until 1873, when it was assumed by Alexander R. Shepherd. The present government, by three commissioners, was instituted in 1874.

Seventh and F streets are prominent business localities, and contain a large number of fine buildings. On Seventh street there are many retail stores. There are numerous banking-houses and real estate establishments on F street, and year by year the street is becoming the centre of important financial transactions.

The Congressional Cemetery is situated in the southeast quarter of the city, on the banks of the Anacostia, or Eastern Branch of the Potomac river. It is about fifty acres in extent, and was originally laid out by Christ Episcopal Church in 1807. Many men of prominence in the early history of the country are buried here, and in the centre of the grounds are numerous sandstone cenotaphs, which were erected in memory of deceased members of Congress. Oak Hill Cemetery has a picturesque situation on Georgetown Heights, and extends along the banks of Rock creek. It is one of the most beautiful burial-grounds in the United States. The remains of many persons of national fame are interred in it. Other prominent cemeteries are Mount Olivet Cemetery, Glenwood Cemetery, Rock Creek Cemetery, Prospect Hill Cemetery, and Graceland Cemetery.

The District Court-House is located on the south front of Judiciary Square, and is a building of Grecian architecture. It was planned by George Hadfield, and was begun in 1820, but was not completed until

THE DISTRICT COURT-HOUSE.

THE W. B. MOSES BUILDING.

1849. It is of brick, covered with stucco, is two stories in height, and has a frontage of two hundred and fifty feet. It was originally intended for the City Hall, as well as for the courts of the district, and was occupied by the municipal officers until 1871. The government purchased it in 1873. and at present it is entirely used for court purposes. Many famous cases have been tried in this building during the past fifty years.

Post Building   PENSSYLVANIA AVENUE LOOKING DOWN D STREET.   Vernon Row.

Ward's Dairy Building.

CHAPTER XIX.

DIRECTLY in front of the Lutheran Memorial Church, in the northwest quarter of Washington, stands a huge bronze statue of Martin Luther, which was erected in May, 1884, by the contributions of members of the Lutheran denomination throughout the United States. The statue fronts on Thomas Circle, and has a conspicuous position. At the unveiling ceremony there was a large assemblage, Lutherans from every portion of the country being present. Addresses were made by prominent churchmen, and Luther's battle hymn was sung by many voices. This memorial to the great Protestant reformer is a duplication of the central figure of the famous bronze group which was erected in the city of Worms during the summer of 1868, and which commemorates the entire story of the reformation. The figure is eleven and one-half feet in height, and stands upon a granite pedestal of the same height. A solid block of granite constitutes the base of the pedestal, and resting upon this are two smaller blocks, on one of which are the words, " Martin Luther," this being the only inscription on the memorial. Luther is represented as he appeared at the conclusion of his defence at the Diet of Worms, when he uttered the memorable words, " Here I stand ; I cannot do otherwise. God help me ! Amen." He wears a clerical gown, and holds a closed Bible in his left hand. His right hand, firmly clenched, rests on the sacred book. His head is thrown back in a dauntless manner, and his face expresses sturdy resolution. The figure is posed naturally and gracefully, and is suggestive of a strong, resolute personality.

The idea of having this memorial erected at the capital of the nation was first suggested by a gentleman in New York in the early part of 1883. The suggestion received the hearty endorsement of prominent clergymen of the Lutheran denomination, and a call for contributions was issued at once. There was such a prompt and liberal response to the call

STATUE OF MARTIN LUTHER.

that in April, 1883, the statue was ordered to be cast at the foundry, in Germany, where the Worms memorial was cast. When the statue was finished, it was transported from Hamburg, across the ocean, to Washington free of cost. It was thought at first that permission might be obtained to place the statue in one of the public reservations, but, as objections were made for various reasons, the Lutheran Memorial Church transferred to the statue association a part of the land on the south of the church for the location of the statue. The cost of the statue and pedestal was $9000.

The Army Medical Museum, on Tenth street, is a unique institution. It is located in Ford's old theatre, where President Lincoln was shot. After this tragic event the government closed the theatre, and finally purchased the property. The interior of the building was remodelled and adapted for the use of the Surgeon-General, and now contains a large force of clerks and officials constantly employed in examining and compiling the vast collections of records pertaining to the medical and hospital department of the army. From the records of the Civil War is gathered the information used in deciding pension claims. The museum occupies the third story of the building. It was established for the purpose of illustrating the diseases and casualties incident to armies and war, but it really includes all the prominent objects of medical and surgical study. Nothing like it is to be found elsewhere in the world. Many

years of arduous labor and a large amount of money have been expended
in developing and perfecting it, and it is now a wonderful exhibition,
and greatly instructive to those professionally interested in its range of
subjects. It has some twenty-two thousand specimens systematically
arranged in six sections. In the anatomical section there is a very large
collection of human crania arranged for the purpose of ethnological
study, and in the section of comparative anatomy there are about fifteen
hundred specimens of skeletons of American mammals. In the miscellaneous sections are the latest appliances for the treatment of diseases,
all sorts of surgical instruments, and models of ambulances, hospitals,
etc. The surgical, medical, and microscopical sections are very full and
interesting.

On the second floor of the museum building is the great medical
library of the government, which contains sixty-seven thousand books
and seventy-five thousand pamphlets relating to medicine and surgery
and the allied sciences. It is stated by competent authority that "this
library not only contains more medical literature than the British Museum

ALBAUGH'S GRAND OPERA HOUSE AND INFANTRY ARMORY.

NATIONAL RIFLES' ARMORY.

or the National Library of France, but that it covers a wider field, and is a better practical reference and working collection for medical purposes than either of these great libraries." The library was begun in 1830 by Surgeon-General Lovell, but for many years only numbered a few hundred books. In 1865 it had two thousand books, and in 1872 nearly thirteen thousand. Within a few years the increase has been very great, owing largely to the fact that physicians in various parts of the country donate to it their books and pamphlets. It has books in all the principal European languages, and some of the volumes are over two hundred years old. Physicians are permitted to use the library gratuitously. A fire-proof building is shortly to be erected on the grounds of the Smithsonian Institution, at a cost of $200,000, for the library and medical museum.

The building erected in 1884 by the Washington Light Infantry, on Fifteenth street, south of Pennsylvania avenue, is of imposing proportions, and unique and graceful in its architecture. The infantry organization occupies a part of the building, and the remainder is Albaugh's Grand Opera House, one of the largest and most magnificent theatres in the country. The National Rifles' armory on G street is a handsome brick structure, excellently arranged for military purposes.

YOUNG MEN'S CHRISTIAN ASSOCIATION BUILDING.

The Young Men's Christian Association occupies a pretty building on New York avenue. The association has a free reading-room well supplied with newspapers and periodicals, and in its special line is constantly accomplishing a very beneficial work.

At the eastern extremity of the city, on the banks of the Anacostia, is the jail of the District of Columbia. It is a stone structure, and was erected at a cost of $400,000. In this jail Guiteau was executed, and many other murderers have here paid the extreme penalty of the law.

The Washington Navy Yard has an excellent location on the Anacostia about a mile southeast of the Capitol. It is under the direction of the Bureau of Yards and Docks of the Navy Department, and its commanding officer is a commodore of the navy. It was established shortly after the government took possession of the capital city, and during the British invasion in 1814 its workshops and other buildings were destroyed. For more than half a century many of the largest and finest ships of war possessed by the United States were constructed in this yard. At present it is devoted to the manufacture of ordnance and various articles used in the equipment of naval vessels. It has great workshops and foundries, employing many men. In the naval museum attached to the yard are extensive collections of relics and other objects of interest. Near the yard are the Marine Barracks, where the marine corps of the navy has its headquarters.

The General Land Office, which is a bureau of the Department of the Interior, is charged with the care of the vast domain belonging to the government known as the public lands. It is under the supervision of a commissioner, whose salary is $4000 per year, and has about five hundred officials and clerks. The work of this bureau is very important, and requires the most competent and intelligent consideration. In the division devoted to the examination of contested homestead cases there is a great accumulation of business, and in all the other divisions the business is in arrears because it cannot possibly be disposed of promptly on account of the lack of a sufficient working force. All the work of this bureau has to be done very carefully, and it requires a long time to examine and decide the majority of the matters brought up. The public lands yet to be disposed of amount to nearly 1,900,000,000 acres, situated in nineteen states and territories. About one-half of this vast estate has been surveyed by the surveyors-general of the government, and is open for settlement. The unsurveyed lands include all the Indian reservations. Land offices are established in the districts where the public lands are situated, each office being in charge of an official designated as Register of the Land Office. In these offices all the records of the surveyed lands are kept, and all applications for lands under the homestead, pre-emption, and timber culture laws are filed.

There are two classes of the public lands. The lands of the first class are the alternate sections reserved by the government in all the grants of

THE DISTRICT JAIL.

THE CENTER MARKET.

ODD FELLOWS' BUILDING.

lands to railroad corporations. They are held at a minimum price of two dollars and a half per acre. The lands of the second class are those situated away from the lines of railroads. They are held at a minimum price of one dollar and a quarter per acre. These lands can be acquired by purchase or by settlement under the homestead laws. The right to acquire eighty acres of the first-class lands, or one hundred and sixty acres of the second-class, is given to every citizen of the United States by the homestead laws if he will take up his residence on the tract selected and actually cultivate it five years. All the payment he will have to make will be for the legal fees and commissions, which range from seven to thirty-four dollars. At the expiration of the five years of residence and cultivation a patent, or full title, to the land is issued by the land office at Washington.

One hundred and sixty acres of land in any part of the surveyed territory not previously claimed may be taken up by an actual settler under the pre-emption law, and purchased by him at the price per acre affixed to the section by the government. Before the full title is obtained certain provisions of the law have to be complied with. Under the timber culture laws, which were enacted for the purpose of promoting the growth of trees on the public domain, any settler on a homestead of one hundred and sixty acres, who has planted and cultivated for two years ten acres of trees, receives the patent for his homestead in three years instead of five. Settlers on homesteads of eighty acres, who plant and cultivate five acres of trees for two years, are also allowed the same reduction of time in the issuing of their patents. Over eighty millions of acres of the public lands have been disposed of under the homestead laws since 1870.

Another important bureau of the Department of the Interior is the Bureau of Indian Affairs. All matters concerning the nearly 250,000 Indians who are cared for by the government are in the charge of this bureau. The Commissioner of Indian Affairs has a salary of $4000 per year, and his office force consists of about one hundred officials and clerks. Upon the Indian reservations in the far west are fifty-nine agencies whose officials report to the bureau at Washington. About eight million dollars are expended for the Indian tribes every year.

The Bureau of Education, which is under the direction of the Department of the Interior, was established in 1867 for the purpose of collecting and diffusing reliable information in regard to education in the United States and in foreign countries, and for other purposes connected with educational work. The bureau is in charge of a commissioner, with a salary of $3000 per year, and has about fifty clerks. The reports of the

BANKING-HOUSE OF RIGGS & CO.
(This building was originally occupied by the historic United States Bank.)

ANCIENT ARCHITECTURE.

bureau are widely circulated, and have great value for those interested in the schools and colleges of the country.

The Ordnance Museum of the War Department is contained in Winder's building, on Seventeenth street. This museum has large collections of arms, relics of the various wars, and other military articles. The collections of relics pertaining to the Civil War are very interesting and valuable. The museum is open daily for public inspection.

In the city of Washington there are two thousand Odd Fellows, with fourteen lodges and four encampments. The order has a fine brick building on Seventh street. In the upper story of the Odd Fellows' building are the lodge and encampment rooms, all of which are elegantly furnished and adorned.

The building on the northwest corner of Pennsylvania avenue and Fifteenth street, now occupied by the banking-house of Riggs and Company, was originally occupied by the historic United States Bank. This financial institution, in which the government was a large stockholder, was bitterly opposed by President Jackson, and by his orders the deposits of government funds in it were removed. This crippled the bank, and it wound up its affairs in 1837 with the loss of its entire capital.

CHAPTER XX.

IXTEEN miles below the capital city is Mount Vernon, the venerated home of Washington. The estate is situated in Fairfax county, Virginia, and borders on the western shore of the Potomac. Originally it comprised about six thousand acres and was divided into five farms, on which large crops of wheat, corn, and tobacco were raised. It was considered one of the finest estates in that part of Virginia, and in Washington's time was carefully culti- vated and improved. What is now known as Mount Vernon is but a few acres in extent, and is a part of what was originally designated as "the mansion-house farm." It is in the possession of the Mount Vernon Association, which was incorporated in 1856 expressly for the purpose of acquiring the estate, in order that it might be forever retained for the benefit of the American people. The association purchased it in 1860 for $200,000, which sum was contributed in large and small amounts by people in all the states. It can never go out of the possession of the association, and must be carefully protected and preserved. The State of Virginia has the supervision of it, and annually a board of state officials inspect it and make a report as to its condition. The utmost care is taken of it, and it will always remain the chief of America's historic treasures.

Washington inherited Mount Vernon when he was a little over twenty-one years old. His half-brother, Lawrence Washington, received the estate at the death of his father, named it Mount Vernon in honor of Admiral Edward Vernon, of the British navy, erected the mansion and brick barn which now remain, and lived on the estate for some years. When he died his infant daughter was the heir, but she survived her father only a short time. George Washington then came into possession of the estate, and when he had closed his service with General Braddock he took up his residence on it. In 1759 he married Martha Dandridge Custis,—"the rich widow Custis," as she was called,—and thereafter for over forty years Mount Vernon was his home,—the one dear spot to which he turned for cheer and comfort, for peaceful domestic joys, whenever he was able to throw off the burdens and responsibilities of public life.

Visitors to Mount Vernon are transported from the city of Washington by the fine steamboat W. W. Corcoran, which makes daily trips down the Potomac. The steamboat is commanded by Captain L. L. Blake, who has had a long experience in navigating the river, and who is exceedingly popular with the public by reason of his unfailing courtesy and careful attention to all who make the trip to Washington's home. As has been fitly said, "Mount Vernon has become, like Jerusalem and Mecca, the resort of people of all nations who come within its vicinity." Daily, winter and summer, there are many visitors to the estate, and on some days the number is very large. During 1884 the number of visitors aggregated seventeen thousand. The estate has a superintendent, and its lands are devoted largely to the pasturage of Ayrshire cattle.

In the summer Mount Vernon is a mass of foliage to the river's edge. It has a great growth of ancient trees and luxuriant undergrowth. Like all the region in which it is located, it is thickly wooded, and from the river has an exceedingly picturesque appearance. The mansion is very nearly concealed by the trees surrounding it. There is only one place as you approach it from the north where it can be seen at all. Approaching it from the south nothing of it can be seen save a small part of the roof. From the south the river curves directly to the estate. Until you get within a short distance of it a high, jutting bank hides it from view. When the bank is passed the estate comes boldly in sight and presents a most beautiful appearance. It is located on an elevation,—the highest point on the Virginia side of the Potomac,—and from the grounds delightful views of river and shore can be obtained through openings in the groves of trees.

The mansion in which Washington lived from early manhood till his death is a wooden structure ninety-six feet long and thirty feet wide, and has two stories and an attic. A portico of panelled columns extends across its whole eastern or river front. It has a peaked roof with a cupola. On the western front is a circular driveway leading to the public road, and on the sides of the driveway are lawns and gardens and small brick houses for servants. On the eastern front is a spacious lawn sloping to the river. The interior of the mansion is plainly constructed.

MOUNT VERNON MANSION.

Most of the rooms are rather small. The state parlor, so called, is the largest room, and that is not remarkable for size. The parlor has a beautiful mantel of variegated Sienna marble, sculptured artistically. On its panels are objects of agriculture and husbandry in bas-relief. There is a spacious hallway in the centre of the mansion. On the first floor there are six rooms, furnished by the Mount Vernon Association with antique articles. There are a few pieces of furniture in the rooms which belonged to Washington, but only a few. Most of his furniture was disposed of by his heirs after the death of Martha Washington.

The second story contains a number of sleeping-rooms. The room in which Washington died is in this story. It is the largest of the rooms, and has been arranged nearly as possible as it was on the night of his death. It contains the mahogany bedstead, six feet square, on which he lay, and several other pieces of furniture he used. It has also a number of articles used by him during his military campaigns. Directly above this room, in the attic, is the room occupied by Martha Washington after her husband's death.

Some three hundred yards south of the mansion is the old family vault, "situated on the declivity of a deep dell and surrounded by trees of a large growth." For many years Washington's body remained in this vault. In 1828 a new tomb was constructed at the foot of what was called "the vineyard enclosure," a short distance from the old tomb, and the bodies of Washington and his wife and the other members of his family were deposited in it. In 1837, John Struthers, a marble mason of Philadelphia, offered to construct a marble coffin or sarcophagus for Washington's remains. The offer was accepted by Washington's heirs, and in October of that year the coffin arrived at Mount Vernon. It was thought best to place the coffin in the outer enclosure of the tomb, in order that it might be protected from dampness, and Washington's body was therefore removed from the interior of the tomb, where it was surrounded by the bodies of his relatives. One who was present during the removal says:

"The coffin containing the remains of Washington was in the extreme back part of the vault, and to remove the case containing the leaden receptacle it was found necessary to put aside the coffins that were piled up between it and the doorway. After clearing a passageway, the case, which was much decayed, was stripped off, and the lead of the lid was discovered to have sunk very considerably from head to foot; so much so, as to form a curved line of four to five inches in its whole length. This settlement of the metal had perhaps caused the soldering of the joints to give way about the upper or widest part of the coffin.

This fractured part was turned over on the lower part of the lid, exposing to view a head and breast of large dimensions, which appeared by the dim light of the candles to have suffered but little from the effects of time. The eye-sockets were large and deep, and the breadth across the temples, together with the forehead, appeared of unusual size. There was no appearance of grave-clothes; the chest was broad; the color was dark, and had the appearance of dried flesh and skin adhering to the bones. We saw no hair, nor was there any offensive odor from the body. A hand was laid upon the head and instantly removed; the lead of the lid was restored to its place; the body, raised by six men, was carried and laid in the marble coffin, and the ponderous cover being put on and set in cement, it was sealed from our sight on Saturday, the 7th of October, 1837."

The tomb extends into a bank, and is constructed of brick. It has an interior vault over which is a stone panel inscribed, " I am the Resurrection and Life; he that believeth in Me, though he were dead, yet shall he live." An enclosure of brickwork surrounds the tomb. On the front is an iron gate, above which, on a plain slab, are the words, " Within this enclosure rest the remains of General George Washington."

The marble sarcophagus containing Washington's remains is placed directly in front of the opening of the tomb, and is plainly visible through the gate. It is eight feet in length, three feet wide, and two feet high, and rests on a plinth which projects several inches round the base. It was excavated from a solid block of Pennsylvania marble, and its lid, or covering stone, is of Italian marble. On the lid are sculptured in bold relief the arms and insignia of the United States, and lower down, upon the plain field of the lid, is deeply and boldly sculptured the name, " Washington."

The remains of Mrs. Washington are deposited in a similar marble sarcophagus, which is placed a few feet from the other. Her sarcophagus is inscribed, " Martha, consort of Washington. Died May 21st, 1801, aged 71 years."

Augustine Washington, the father of George Washington, died in 1743, leaving a large landed estate. George was the eldest of five children by a second marriage. He was born February 22, 1732, in Westmoreland county, Virginia, where his father cultivated an extensive plantation. He inherited the lands his father possessed in Westmoreland county, and the " Hunting creek estate," afterwards renamed Mount Vernon, was inherited by Lawrence Washington, the eldest son by a first marriage. In his youth George Washington was engaged for several years in surveying the western lands of Lord Fairfax, and afterwards performed military duty

under General
Braddock. On
January 7, 1759,
he was married
to Martha Dan-
dridge Custis, the
widow of Daniel
Parke Custis, and
daughter of John
Dandridge, of Vir-
ginia. Mrs. Custis
was three months

TOMB OF WASHINGTON.

older than Colonel
Washington, and was
"distinguished alike
for her beauty, ac-
complishments, and
wealth." She had
two children, a son
of six years and a
daughter of four.
After their marriage
Washington and his
wife lived for three

WEST FRONT MOUNT VERNON MANSION.

months near Williamsburg, Virginia, in order that he might attend the
session of the state legislature, of which he was a member. At the close
of the session they took up their residence at Mount Vernon.

For sixteen years Washington cultivated his great farm and lived the
usual life of a Virginia planter. He raised large quantities of tobacco,
which he shipped to London direct from his own wharf at Mount Vernon.
He had no ambition for public life after his term of service in the Virginia
legislature had expired, and was content with the pursuit of agriculture
and the social pleasures of a country gentleman. He had some of the
best society in Virginia,—"the polite, wealthy, and fashionable,"—was a
profuse and liberal host, was fond of fox hunting, fishing, fowling, and
athletic sports, and was happy in his home and domestic relations. His
wife was thoroughly domestic in her tastes and habits, and a careful

housekeeper. She prided herself on her knitting and spinning, and wove many of her own dresses, and even some of her husband's clothes. The suit Washington wore when he was inaugurated as President was woven at Mount Vernon. In his early manhood Washington appeared as " a very proper young fellow, six feet tall, rather stately in carriage, and exceedingly fond of dancing and gay society."

In 1775 he became a member of the Continental Congress, and in June of that year the Congress appointed him as Commander-in-Chief of the Continental Army. All through the Revolutionary War, a period of more than eight years, he was compelled to be absent from Mount Vernon. Mrs. Washington was with him during several of the campaigns. In a letter written in 1811 by a gentleman of South Carolina, who was the captain of a company serving in the Revolution, is the following personal description of Washington as he appeared during the War :

" In the first place, you should know that Washington was not what the ladies call a pretty man. It seems that fate has destined handsome men for other purposes than heroic endeavor. But in military costume he was a splendid figure, such as would impress the memory ever afterwards. The first time I was ever brought in contact with the great hero was three days before the crossing of the Delaware. It was under the most unfavorable circumstances, as the weather was bitterly cold, and a fierce wind was blowing. Washington had a large, thick nose, and it was very red that day, giving me the impression that he was not so moderate in his use of liquors as he was supposed to be. I found afterwards that this was a peculiarity. His nose was apt to turn scarlet in a cold wind. He was standing near a small camp fire, evidently lost in thought, and making no effort to keep warm. He seemed six feet and a half in height, and was as erect as an Indian, and did not for a moment relax from a military attitude. Washington's exact height was six feet two inches in his boots. He was then a little lame from striking his knee against a tree. His eye was so gray that it looked almost white, and he had a troubled look on his colorless face. He had a piece of woolen tied around his throat, and was quite hoarse. Perhaps the throat trouble from which he died had its origin about that time. Washington's boots were enormous. They were No. 13. His ordinary walking shoes were No. 11. His hands were large in proportion, and he could not buy a glove to fit him, and had to have his gloves made to order. His mouth was his strong feature, the lips being always tightly compressed. That day they were compressed so tightly as to be painful to look at. At that time he weighed two hundred pounds, and there was no surplus flesh about him. He was tremendously muscled, and the fame of his great strength was everywhere. His huge tent when wrapped up with the poles was so heavy that it required two men to place it in the camp wagon. Washington could lift it with one hand and throw it in the wagon as easily as if it were a pair of saddle-bags. He could hold a musket with one hand and shoot with precision as easily as other men did with a horse-pistol. His lungs were his weak point, and there he was never strong. He was at that time in the prime of life. His hair was a chestnut brown, his cheeks were prominent and his head was not large, in contrast to every other part of his body, which seemed large and bony at all points. His finger joints and wrists were so large as to be genuine curiosities."

Washington resigned his commission as commander of the army at Annapolis, December 23, 1783, and immediately went to Mount Vernon. Congress had offered him $500 per month as compensation for his services during the war, but he declined to accept any compensation. He had been the saviour of his country, and he retired to private life crowned with laurels.

He immediately began to repair his fortune, which had been somewhat diminished by the war. He began a precise system of cultivation of his farm, and in various ways sought to improve his resources. He extended his mansion, built new cabins for his negroes, and labored earnestly at the occupations of his early years. At this time he wrote to General Lafayette, " I am become a private citizen on the banks of the Potomac, and, under the shadow of my own vine and fig-tree, I am solacing myself with tranquil enjoyments." To General Knox he wrote, " I feel now as I conceive a wearied traveller must do, who, after treading many a painful step with a heavy burden on his shoulders, is eased of the latter, having reached the haven to which all the former were directed."

Mount Vernon was open to all who came. He had many visitors—soldiers of the war, distinguished foreigners, artists, statesmen, men and women of the highest social rank. He entertained Lafayette, for whom he had a warm friendship; he gave balls and receptions, and was disposed to take some pleasure and recreation after the toilsome military work he had performed. For over five years he remained at Mount Vernon, busy with the care of his estate; but in 1789 he was elected as the first President of the United States, and on April 16 of that year he left his home for New York to assume the great office. He wrote in his diary the day he left home, "About ten o'clock I bade adieu to Mount Vernon, to private life, and to domestic felicity; and, with a mind oppressed with more anxious and painful sensations than I have words to express, set out for New York with the best disposition to render service to my country in obedience to its call, but with less hope of answering its expectations."

For eight years he was President, retiring from the office on the 4th of March, 1797. From this time until his death Washington never left Mount Vernon for a single night. During the short time that was left him on earth he confined himself to "putting his house in order," being seemingly aware that, as he came of a short-lived family, he had not long to live. His hair was gray, his form was slightly bent, and his chest was thin. He had lost the greater part of his old-time vigor, and was slower in his movements, less inclined to undertake new tasks, and disposed to shun the gay society he had formerly enjoyed. He superintended his farming operations, and

WASHINGTON'S BED-CHAMBER.

on every pleasant day rode over his lands. He was a rather reserved man, speaking but little, and never of himself. His adopted daughter has said, "I never heard him relate a single act of his life. I have sometimes made him laugh heartily from sympathy with my joyous and extravagant spirits." At night he liked to be surrounded by his family,—his wife and

PARLOR IN MOUNT VERNON MANSION.

adopted children, and his nieces and nephews, who frequently visited him, —and would seem to greatly enjoy their conversation and frolics. In the summer of 1799 he made his will, writing the lengthy document with his own hand and without consulting a lawyer. A little over six months from the time the will was finished he died of acute laryngitis in his sixty-eighth year.

Immediately after the death of Washington a complete account of it was written by Tobias Lear, who was his private secretary and intimate companion for many years. This account, which was the only one written, has been preserved, and, as it has been garbled and distorted in the biographies of Washington, it is herewith presented as a matter of historical reference precisely as it originally appeared. Mr. Lear dates his account " Mount Vernon, Saturday, December 14th, 1799," and says:

" This day has been marked by an event which will be memorable in the history of America, and, perhaps, of the world. I shall give a particular statement of it, to which I was an eye-witness.

" On Thursday, December 12th, the General rode out to his farms about ten o'clock, and did not return home till past three. Soon after he went out the weather became very bad, rain, hail, snow falling alternately, with a cold wind. When he came in I carried some letters to him to frank, intending to send them to the post-office in the evening. He franked the letters, but said the weather was too bad to send a servant to the office that evening. I observed to him that I was afraid he had got wet. He said no; his great-coat had kept him dry. But his neck appeared to be wet, and the snow was hanging upon his hair. He came to dinner (which had been waiting for him) without changing his dress. In the evening he appeared as well as usual.

" A heavy fall of snow took place on Friday, which prevented the General from riding out as usual. He had taken cold, undoubtedly, from being so much exposed the day before, and complained of a sore throat. He, however, went out in the afternoon into the ground between the house and the river to mark some trees which were to be cut down in the improvement of that spot. He had a hoarseness, which increased in the evening, but he made light of it.

" In the evening the papers were brought from the post-office, and he sat in the parlor with Mrs. Washington and myself reading them till about nine o'clock, when Mrs. Washington went up into Mrs. Lewis's room, who was confined, and left the General and myself reading the papers. He was very cheerful, and when he met with anything interesting or entertaining he read it aloud, as well as his hoarseness would permit. He requested me to read to him the debates of the Virginia Assembly on the election of a Senator and Governor, and, on hearing of Mr. Madison's observations respecting Mr. Monroe, he appeared much affected, and spoke with some degree of asperity on the subject, which I endeavored to moderate, as I always did on such occasions. On his retiring I observed to him that he had better take something to remove his cold. He answered, ' No ; you know I never take anything for a cold. Let it go as it came.'

" Between two and three o'clock on Saturday morning he awoke Mrs. Washington, and told her that he was very unwell, and had had an ague. She observed that he could scarcely speak, and breathed with difficulty, and would have got up to call a servant, but he would not permit her, lest she should take a cold. As soon as the day appeared the woman (Caroline) went into the room to make a fire, and Mrs. Washington sent her immediately to call me. I got up, put on my clothes as quickly as possible, and went to his chamber. Mrs. Washington was then up, and related to me his being ill, as before stated. I found the General breathing with difficulty, and hardly able to utter a word intelligibly. He desired Mr. Rawlins (one of the overseers) might be sent for to bleed him before the doctor could arrive. I despatched a servant immediately for Rawlins, and another for Dr. Craik, and returned again to the General's chamber, where I found him in the same situation as I had left him.

" A mixture of molasses, vinegar, and butter was prepared to try its effects in the throat, but he could not swallow a drop. Whenever he attempted it he appeared to be distressed, convulsed, and almost suffocated. Rawlins came in soon after sunrise, and prepared to bleed him. When the arm was ready the General, observing that Rawlins appeared to be agitated, said, as well as he could speak, ' Don't be afraid.' And when the incision was made he observed, ' The orifice is not large enough.' However, the blood ran pretty freely. Mrs. Washington, not knowing whether bleeding was proper or not in the General's situation, begged that much might not be taken from him, lest it should be injurious, and desired me to stop it ; but when I was about to untie the string the General put up his hand to prevent it, and, as soon as he could speak, he said, ' More, more.' Mrs. Washington being still very uneasy lest too much blood should be taken, it was stopped after taking about half a pint. Finding that no relief was obtained from bleeding, and that nothing would go down the throat, I proposed bathing it externally with *sal volatile*, which was done ; and in the operation, which was with the hand, and in the gentlest manner, he observed, ' It is very sore.' A piece of flannel dipped in *sal volatile* was put around his neck, and his feet bathed in warm water, but without affording any relief.

THE MOUNT VERNON STEAMBOAT.

" In the mean time, before Dr. Craik arrived, Mrs. Washington desired me to send for Dr. Brown, of Port Tobacco, whom Dr. Craik had recommended to be called, if any case should ever occur that was seriously alarming. I despatched a messenger for Dr. Brown between eight and nine o'clock. Dr. Craik came in soon after, and, upon examining the General, he put a blister of cantharides on the throat, took some more blood from him, and had a gargle of vinegar and sage tea prepared ; and ordered some vinegar and hot water for him to inhale the steam of it, which he did ; but in attempting to use the gargle he was almost suffocated. When the gargle came from the throat some phlegm followed, and he attempted to cough, which the doctor encouraged him to do as much as possible ; but he could only attempt it. About eleven o'clock Dr. Craik requested that Dr. Dick might be sent for, as he feared Dr. Brown would not come in time. A messenger was accordingly despatched for him. About this time the General was bled again. No effect, however, was produced by it, and he remained in the same state, unable to swallow anything.

" Dr. Dick came about three o'clock, and Dr. Brown arrived soon after. Upon Dr. Dick's seeing the General, and consulting a few minutes with Dr. Craik, he was bled again. The blood came very slow, was thick, and did not produce any symptoms of fainting. Dr. Brown came into the chamber soon after, and, upon feeling the General's pulse, the physicians went out together. Dr. Craik returned soon after. The General could now swallow a little. Calomel and tartar emetic were administered, but without any effect.

" About four o'clock he desired me to call Mrs. Washington to his bedside, when he requested her to go down into his room and take from his desk two wills which she would find there and bring them to him, which she did. Upon looking at them, he gave her one, which he observed was useless, as being superseded by the other, and desired her to burn it, which she did, and took the other and put it into her closet.

" After this was done I returned to his bedside and took his hand. He said to me, ' I find I am going. My breath cannot last long. I believed from the first that the disorder would prove fatal. Do you arrange and record all my late military letters and papers. Arrange my accounts and settle my books, as you know more about them than any one else, and let Mr. Rawlins finish recording my other letters which he has begun.' I told him this should be done. He then asked if I recollected anything which it was essential for him to do, as he had but a very short time to continue with us. I told him that I could recollect nothing, but that I hoped he was not so near his end. He observed, smiling, that he certainly was, and that, as it was the debt which we must all pay, he looked to the event with perfect resignation.

" In the course of the afternoon he appeared to be in great pain and distress from the difficulty of breathing, and frequently changed his posture in the bed. On these occasions I lay upon the bed and endeavored to raise him, and turn him with as much ease as possible. He appeared penetrated with gratitude for my attentions, and often said, ' I am afraid I shall fatigue you too much ;' and upon my assuring him that I could feel nothing but a wish to give him ease, he replied, ' Well, it is a debt we must pay to each other, and I hope when you want help of this kind you will find it.'

" He asked when Mr. Lewis and Washington Custis would return (they were then in New Kent). I told him about the 20th of the month.

" About five o'clock Dr. Craik came again into the room, and, upon going to the bedside, the General said to him, ' Doctor, I die hard, but I am not afraid to go. I believed from my first attack that I should not survive it. My breath cannot last long.' The doctor pressed his hand, but could not utter a word. He retired from the bedside, and sat by the fire absorbed in grief.

" Between five and six o'clock Dr. Dick and Dr. Brown came into the room, and with Dr. Craik went to the bed, when Dr. Craik asked him if he could sit up in the bed. He held out his hand, and I raised him up. He then said to the physicians, ' I feel myself going; I thank you for your attentions, but I pray you take no more trouble about me. Let me go off quietly. I cannot last long.' They found that all which had been

done was without effect. He lay down again, and all retired except Dr.
Craik. He continued in the same situation,—uneasy and restless,—but
without complaining, frequently asking what hour it was. When I helped
him to move at this time he did not speak, but looked at me with strong
expressions of gratitude.

"About eight o'clock the physicians came again into the room and
applied blisters and cataplasms of wheat bran to his legs and feet, after
which they went out, except Dr. Craik, without a ray of hope. I went
out about this time and wrote a line to Mr. Law and Mr. Peter, requesting
them to come with their wives (Mrs. Washington's granddaughters) as
soon as possible to Mount Vernon.

"About ten o'clock he made several attempts to speak to me before
he could effect it. At length he said, 'I am just going. Have me
decently buried, and do not let my body be put into the vault in less than
three days after I am dead.' I bowed assent, for I could not speak. He
then looked at me again and said, 'Do you understand me?' I replied,
'Yes.' ''Tis well,' said he.

"About ten minutes before he expired (which was between ten and
eleven o'clock) his breathing became easier. He lay quietly; he withdrew his hand from mine and felt his own pulse. I saw his countenance
change. I spoke to Dr. Craik, who sat by the fire. He came to the bedside. The General's hand fell from his wrist. I took it in mine and
pressed it to my bosom. Dr. Craik put his hands over his eyes, and he
expired without a struggle or a sigh.

"While we were fixed in silent grief, Mrs. Washington, who was
sitting at the foot of the bed, asked with a firm and collected voice, 'Is he
gone?' I could not speak, but held up my hand as a signal that he was
no more. ''Tis well,' said she in the same voice; 'all is now over; I
shall soon follow him; I have no more trials to pass through.'

"At the time of his decease Dr. Craik and myself were in the situation above mentioned. Mrs. Washington was sitting near the foot of the
bed. Christopher was standing near the bedside. Caroline, Molly, and
Charlotte were in the room, standing near the door.

"As soon as Dr. Craik could speak after the distressing scene was
closed, he desired one of the servants to ask the gentlemen below to come
up-stairs. When they came to the bedside I kissed the cold hand which
I had held to my bosom, laid it down, and went to the other end of the
room, where I was for some time lost in profound grief, until aroused by
Christopher desiring me to take care of the General's keys, and other
things, which were taken out of his pockets, and which Mrs. Washington
directed him to give to me. I wrapped them in the General's handker-

CAPT. L. L. BLAKE, OF STEAMBOAT W. W. CORCORAN.

chief, and took them to my room. About twelve o'clock the corpse was brought down-stairs and laid out in the large room.

"During his whole illness he spoke but seldom, and with great difficulty and distress, and in so low and broken a voice as at times hardly to be understood. His patience, fortitude, and resignation never forsook him for a moment. In all his distress he uttered not a sigh nor a complaint, always endeavoring, from a sense of duty as it appeared, to take what was offered him, and to do as he was desired by the physicians."

On Sunday, December 15th, Mr. Lear, by request of Mrs. Washington, sent to Alexandria to have a mahogany coffin made. On the following day he had the old family vault opened, the "rubbish about it" cleared away, and a new door to it made. Mourning was ordered for the family, domestics, and overseers. On Tuesday he says, "The coffin was brought from Alexandria. Mr. Grater accompanied it with a shroud. The body was laid in the coffin. The mahogany coffin was lined with lead, soldered at the joints, with a cover of lead to be soldered on after the body should be in the vault. The coffin was put in a case, lined and covered with black cloth."

Mr. Lear gives the following account of the funeral ceremony, which took place at Mount Vernon on Wednesday, December 18th:

"About eleven o'clock numbers of people began to assemble to attend the funeral, which was intended to have been at twelve o'clock; but as a great part of the troops expected could not get down in time, it did not take place till three. Eleven pieces of artillery were brought from Alexandria, and a schooner, belonging to Mr. Robert Hamilton, came down and lay off Mount Vernon to fire minute-guns while the body was being carried to the grave. About three o'clock the procession began to move. The pall-bearers were Colonels Little, Simms, Payne, Gilpin, Ramsey, and Marsteler. Colonel Blackburn preceded the corpse. The procession moved out through the gate at the left wing of the house, and proceeded round in front of the lawn and down to the vault on the right wing of the house. The procession was as follows:

" The Troops, horse and foot.

" The Clergy, namely,—The Reverend Messrs. Davis, Muir, Moffatt, and Addison.

" The General's horse, with his saddle, holsters, and pistols, led by two grooms, Cyrus and Wilson, in black.

" The Body, borne by the Freemasons and Officers.

  " Principal Mourners, namely,—
  " Mrs. Stuart and Mrs. Law.
  " Misses Nancy and Sally Stuart.
  " Miss Fairfax and Miss Dennison.
  " Mr. Law and Mr. Peter.
  " Mr. Lear and Dr. Craik.
  " Lord Fairfax and Fernando Fairfax.
  " Lodge No. 22.
  " Corporation of Alexandria.

" All other persons, preceded by Mr. Anderson and the Overseers.

" When the body arrived at the vault the Rev. Mr. Davis read the service, and pronounced a short address. The Masons performed their ceremonies, and the body was deposited in the vault."

The *Alexandria Times and Advertiser* of Friday, December 20, 1799, thus announced Washington's death and funeral:

" The effect of the sudden news of his death upon the inhabitants of Alexandria can better be conceived than expressed. At first a general disorder, wildness, and consternation pervaded the town. The tale appeared as an illusory dream, as the raving of a sickly imagination. But these impressions soon gave place to sensations of the most poignant sorrow and extreme regret. On Monday and Wednesday the stores were all closed and all business suspended, as if each family had lost its father. From the time of his death to the time of his interment the bells continued to toll, the shipping in the harbor wore their colors half-mast high, and every public expression of grief was observed. On Wednesday the inhabitants of the town, of the county, and the adjacent parts of Maryland proceeded to Mount Vernon to perform the last offices to the body of their illustrious neighbor. All the military within a considerable distance and three Masonic lodges were present. The concourse of people was immense. Till the time of interment the corpse was placed on the portico fronting the river, that every citizen might have an opportunity of taking a lasting farewell of the departed benefactor."

At the time of Washington's death Congress was in session at Philadelphia. When the news was received both houses immediately adjourned. It is stated that "the next morning, as soon as the House of Representatives had convened, Mr. Marshall, afterwards Chief Justice, rose in his place and addressed the Speaker in an eloquent and pathetic speech, briefly recounting the public acts of Washington. He then offered three resolutions, previously prepared by General Henry Lee, which were accepted. By these it was proposed that the House should in a body wait on the President to express their condolence; that the Speaker's chair should be shrouded in black, and the members and officers of the House be dressed in black during the session; and that a committee in conjunction with a committee from the Senate should be

HON. ROBERT C. WINTHROP, ORATOR OF THE
WASHINGTON MONUMENT.

appointed to consider the most suitable manner of paying honor to the memory of Washington. The Senate had similar proceedings. A joint committee of the two houses was appointed, who reported resolutions recommending that a marble monument should be erected to commemorate the great events in the military and political life of Washington; that an oration suited to the occasion should be pronounced in the presence of both houses of Congress; that the people of the United States should wear crape on the left arm thirty days as a badge of mourning; and that the President, in the name of Congress, should be requested to write a letter of condolence to Mrs. Washington. These resolutions were unanimously adopted. The funeral ceremonies were appropriate and solemn. A procession consisting of the members of the two houses, public officers, and a large assemblage of citizens moved from the hall of Congress to the German Lutheran Church, where a discourse was delivered by General Henry Lee, then a Representative in Congress." The funeral ceremonies took place December 26, 1799.

In General Lee's oration were these words: "First in war, first in peace, and first in the hearts of his countrymen, he was second to none in the humble and endearing scenes of private life; uniform, dignified, and commanding, his example was as edifying to all around him as were the effects of that example lasting. To his equals he was condescending; to his inferiors, kind; and to the dear object of his affections, exemplarily tender; correct throughout, vice shuddered in his presence, and virtue always felt his fostering hand; the purity of his private character gave effulgence to his public virtues. His last scene comported with the whole tenor of his life. Although in extreme pain, not a sigh, not a groan escaped him; and with undisturbed serenity he closed his well-spent life. Such was the man America has lost; such was the man for whom our nation mourns."

Washington left property valued, according to his own estimate, at $530,000. Besides his Mount Vernon estate, he had 13,000 acres of land in other parts of Virginia, over 1000 acres in Maryland, about 1200 in New York and Pennsylvania, and great tracts, amounting to over 8000 acres, in Kentucky and what was then called the "northwest territory" on the Little Miami river. He had lots in the cities of Washington, Alexandria, and Winchester. He possessed $25,000 worth of shares in the Bank of Columbia and Bank of Alexandria in Alexandria, and the Potomac Company and James River Company. His live stock at Mount Vernon was valued at $35,000. No estimate was made of his slaves, as he proposed to free them. His will is herewith given. It begins as follows:

"In the name of God, Amen. I, George Washington, of Mount Vernon, a citizen of the United States, and lately President of the same, do make, ordain, and declare this instrument, which is written with my own hand, and every page subscribed with my name, to be my last Will and Testament, revoking all others.

"*Imprimis.*—All my debts, of which there are but few, and none of magnitude, are to be punctually and speedily paid, and the legacies, hereinafter bequeathed, are to be discharged as soon as circumstances will permit, and in the manner directed.

"*Item.*—To my dearly beloved wife, *Martha Washington*, I give and bequeath the use, profit, and benefit of·my whole estate, real and personal, for the term of her natural life, except such parts thereof as are specially disposed of hereafter. My improved lot in the town of Alexandria, situated on P and Cameron streets, I give to her and her heirs forever; as I also do my household and kitchen furniture of every sort and kind, with the liquors and groceries which may be on hand at the time of my decease, to be used and disposed of as she may think proper.

"*Item.*—Upon the decease of my wife, it is my will and desire that all the slaves whom I hold *in my own right* shall receive their freedom. To emancipate them during her life would, though earnestly wished by me, be attended with such insuperable difficulties, on account of their intermixture by marriage with the dower negroes, as to excite the most painful sensations, if not disagreeable consequences to the latter, while both descriptions are in the occupancy of the same proprietor; it not being in my power, under the tenure by which the dower negroes are held, to manumit them. And whereas, among those who will receive freedom according to this devise, there may be some who, from old age or bodily infirmities, and others who, on account of their infancy, will be unable to support themselves, it is my will and desire that all who come under the first and second description shall be comfortably clothed and fed by my heirs while they live; and that such of the latter description as have no parents living, or, if living, are unable or unwilling to provide for them, shall be bound by the court until they shall arrive at the age of twenty-five years; and, in cases where no record can be produced whereby their ages can be ascertained, the judgment of the court, upon its own views of the subject, shall be adequate and final. The negroes thus bound are (by their masters or mistresses) to be taught to read and write, and to be brought up to some useful occupation, agreeably to the laws of the Commonwealth of Virginia, providing for the support of orphan or other poor children. And I do hereby expressly forbid the sale or transportation, out of the said Commonwealth, of any slave I may die possessed of,

DEPARTMENT OF JUSTICE.

under any pretence whatsoever. And I do, moreover, most pointedly and most solemnly enjoin it upon my executors hereafter named, or the survivors of them, to see that this clause respecting slaves, and every part thereof, be religiously fulfilled at the epoch at which it is directed to take place, without evasion, neglect, or delay, after the crops which may then be in the ground are harvested, particularly as it respects the aged and infirm; seeing that a regular and permanent fund be established for their support, as long as there are subjects requiring it, not trusting to the uncertain provision to be made by individuals. And to my mulatto man, *William*, calling himself *William Lee*, I give immediate freedom, or, if he should prefer it (on account of the accidents which have befallen him, and which have rendered him incapable of walking, or of any active employment), to remain in the situation he now is, it shall be optional in him to do so; in either case, however, I allow him an annuity of thirty dollars during his natural life, which shall be independent of the victuals and clothes he has been accustomed to receive, if he chooses the last alter-1 native; but in full with his freedom, if he prefers the first; and this I give him, as a testimony of my sense of his attachment to me, and for his faithful services during the Revolutionary war.

" *Item.*—To the trustees (governors, or by whatsoever other name they may be designated) of the Academy in the town of Alexandria, I give and bequeath, in trust, four thousand dollars, or in other words, twenty of the shares which I hold in the Bank of Alexandria, towards the support of a free school, established at and annexed to the said Academy, for the purpose of educating such orphan children, or the children of such other poor and indigent persons as are unable to accomplish it with their own means, and who, in the judgment of the trustees of said seminary, are best entitled to the benefit of this donation. The aforesaid twenty shares I give and bequeath in perpetuity; the dividends only of which are to be drawn for and applied, by the said trustees for the time being, for the uses above mentioned; the stock to remain entire and untouched, unless indications of failure of the said bank should be so apparent, or a discontinuance thereof should render a removal of the fund necessary. In either of these cases, the amount of stock here devised is to be vested in some other bank or public institution, whereby the interest may with regularity and certainty be drawn and applied as above. And to prevent misconception, my meaning is, and is hereby declared to be, that these twenty shares are in lieu of, and not in addition to, the thousand pounds given by a missive letter some years ago, in consequence whereof an annuity of fifty pounds has since been paid towards the support of this institution.

" *Item.*—Whereas by a law of the Commonwealth of Virginia, enacted in 1785, the Legislature thereof was pleased, as an evidence of its approbation of the services I had rendered the public during the Revolution, and partly, I believe, in consideration of my having suggested the vast advantages which the community would derive from the extension of its inland navigation under legislative patronage, to present me with one hundred shares, of one hundred dollars each, in the incorporated Company established for the purpose of extending the navigation of James River from the tide water to the mountains; and also with fifty shares, of £100 sterling each, in the corporation of another Company, likewise established for the similar purpose of opening the navigation of the River Potomac from tide water to Fort Cumberland; the acceptance of which, although the offer was highly honorable and grateful to my feelings, was refused, as inconsistent with the principle which I had adopted, and had never departed from, viz., not to receive pecuniary compensation for any services I could render my country in its arduous struggle with Great Britain for its rights, and because I had evaded similar presents from other States in the Union; adding to this refusal, however, an intimation that, if it should be the pleasure of the legislature to permit me to appropriate the said shares to *public uses*, I would receive them on those terms with due sensibility; and this it having consented to, in flattering terms, as will appear by a subsequent law, and sundry resolutions, in the most ample and honorable manner:—I proceed after this recital, for the more correct understanding of the case, to declare that, as it has always been a source of serious regret with me to see the youth of these United States sent to foreign countries for the purpose of education, often before their minds were formed, or they had imbibed any adequate ideas of the happiness of their own; contracting too frequently not only habits of dissipation and extravagance, but principles unfriendly to republican government, and to the true and genuine liberties of mankind, which thereafter are rarely overcome; for these reasons it has been my ardent wish to see a plan devised, on a liberal scale, which would have a tendency to spread systematic ideas through all parts of this rising empire, thereby to do away with local attachments and State prejudices, as far as the nature of things would, or indeed ought to admit, from our national councils. Looking anxiously forward to the accomplishment of so desirable an object as this is (in my estimation), my mind has not been able to contemplate any plan more likely to effect the measure than the establishment of a UNIVERSITY in a central part of the United States, to which the youths of fortune and talents from all parts thereof may be

FRANKLIN SCHOOL.

sent for the completion of their education in all the branches of polite literature, in arts and sciences, in acquiring knowledge in the principles of politics and good government, and, as a matter of infinite importance in my judgment, by associating with each other, and forming friendships in juvenile years, be enabled to free themselves in a proper degree from those local prejudices and habitual jealousies which have just been mentioned, and which, when carried to excess, are never-failing sources of disquietude to the public mind, and pregnant of mischievous consequences to this country. Under these impressions, so fully dilated, I give and bequeath, in perpetuity, the fifty shares which I hold in the Potomac Company (under the aforesaid acts of the Legislature of Virginia) towards the endowment of a University, to be established within the limits of the District of Columbia, under the auspices of the general government, if that government should incline to extend a fostering hand towards it; and until such seminary is established, and the funds arising on these shares shall be required for its support, my further will and desire is, that the profit accruing therefrom shall, whenever the dividends are made, be laid out in purchasing stock in the Bank of Columbia, or some other bank, at the discretion of my executors, or by the Treasurer of the United States for the time being, under the direction of Congress, provided that honorable body should patronize the measure; and the dividends proceeding from the purchase of such stock are to be vested in more stock, and so on until a sum adequate to the accomplishment of the object is obtained; of which I have not the smallest doubt before many years pass away, even if no aid or encouragement is given by the legislative authority, or from any other source.

" *Item.*—The hundred shares which I hold in the James River Company I have given, and now confirm in perpetuity, to and for the use and benefit of Liberty Hall Academy, in the County of Rockbridge, in the Commonwealth of Virginia."

Jared Sparks says in his life of Washington : " The donation to Washington College (formerly known as Liberty Hall Academy) has been productive, and the proceeds arising from it have contributed essential aid to that institution. No part of the other fund has been employed for literary purposes. The Potomac Company seems to have been merged in the Chesapeake and Ohio Canal Company. The shares appropriated by Washington's will are doubtless held in trust by the latter company for their destined object."

The will directs that the estate of his deceased brother, Samuel Washington, shall be released from the payment of money due for land, and also that the balance due from the estate of Bartholomew Dandridge shall be released. Sundry legacies were given to the nieces and nephews of Washington. His papers and library were given to his nephew, Judge Bushrod Washington, the son of his brother, John Augustine Washington. Legacies were given to friends, such as " To my companion in arms and old and intimate friend, Dr. Craik, I give my bureau (or as the cabinet-makers call it, my tambour secretary) and the circular chair, an appendage of my study." " To General de Lafayette, I give a pair of finely-wrought steel pistols, taken from the enemy in the Revolutionary war." " To Tobias Lear, I give the use of the farm which he now holds in virtue of a lease from me, free of rent during his life." He gave each of his five nephews a sword, with the injunction " not to unsheath them for the purpose of shedding blood, except it be in self-defence, or in defence of their country and its rights; and in the latter case to keep them unsheathed, and prefer falling with them in their hands to the relinquishment thereof."

To his nephew, Bushrod Washington, and his heirs, he gave a certain part of the Mount Vernon estate, with the mansion and other buildings, as, he says, " partly in consideration of an intimation to his deceased father while we were bachelors, and he had kindly undertaken to superintend my estate during my military services in the former war between Great Britain and France, that, if I should fall therein, Mount Vernon, then less extensive in domain than at present, should become his property." His estate of 2027 acres east of Little Hunting creek he gave to his nephews, George Fayette Washington and Lawrence Augustine Washington.

The will continues: " And whereas it has always been my intention, since my expectation of having issue has ceased, to consider the grand-children of my wife in the same light as I do my own relation, and to act a friendly part by them; more especially by the two whom we have raised from their earliest infancy, namely, *Eleanor Parke Custis* and *George Washington Parke Custis*; and whereas the former of these hath lately inter-married with *Lawrence Lewis*, a son of my deceased sister, *Betty Lewis*, by which union the inducement to provide for them both has been increased; wherefore I give and bequeath to the said *Lawrence Lewis* and *Eleanor Parke Lewis*, his wife, and their heirs, the residue of my Mount Vernon estate not already devised to my nephew, Bushrod Washington." This portion consisted of about two thousand acres, and embraced his flour-mill, distillery, and other buildings.

The will continues: " Actuated by the principle already mentioned, I give and bequeath to *George Washington Parke Custis*, the grandson of my wife, and my ward, and to his heirs, the tract I hold on Four Mile Run, in the vicinity of Alexandria, containing one thousand two hundred acres, more or less, and my entire square, No. 21, in the city of Washington "

WASHINGTON NAVY YARD.

The remainder of his estate, real and personal, was to be divided into twenty-three equal parts, and disposed of to his nephews and nieces according to a division he describes in detail,—that is, so many parts to each.

The will concludes as follows: " The family vault at Mount Vernon requiring repairs, and being improperly situated besides, I desire that a new one of brick, and upon a larger scale, may be built at the foot of what is commonly called the Vineyard Enclosure, on the ground which is marked out; in which my remains, with those of my deceased relations (now in the old vault), and such others of my family as may choose to be entombed there, may be deposited. And it is my express desire that my corpse may be interred in a private manner, without parade or funeral oration.

"Lastly, I constitute and appoint my dearly-beloved wife, *Martha Washington*, my nephews, *William Augustine Washington, Bushrod Washington, George Steptoe Washington, Samuel Washington,* and *Lawrence Lewis*, and my ward, *George Washington Parke Custis* (when he shall have arrived at the age of twenty-one years), executrix and executors of this my will and testament, in the construction of which it will be readily perceived that no professional character has been consulted or has had any agency in the draft; and that although it has occupied many of my leisure hours to digest and to throw into its present form, it may, notwithstanding, appear crude and incorrect; but having endeavored to be plain and explicit in all the devises, even at the expense of prolixity, perhaps of tautology, I hope and trust that no disputes will arise concerning them. But if, contrary to expectation, the case should be otherwise from the want of

legal expressions or the usual technical terms, or because too much or
too little has been said on any of the devises to be consonant with law,
my will and direction expressly is that all disputes (if, unhappily, any
should arise) shall be decided by three impartial and intelligent men,
known for their probity and good understanding ; two to be chosen by
the disputants, each having the choice of one, and the third by those two ;
which three men, thus chosen, shall, unfettered by law or legal construc-
tions, declare their sense of the testator's intention ; and such decision is,
to all intents and purposes, to be as binding on the parties as if it had
been given in the Supreme Court of the United States."

The will is dated July 9, 1799, and is signed in a bold, clear hand,
every page having Washington's name. The original manuscript is preserved in the record office of the Fairfax county court-house, in Virginia.

After Mrs. Washington's death, Bushrod Washington resided for some
years at Mount Vernon. He was a member of the Supreme Court of
the United States, and a jurist of profound learning and inflexible hon-
esty. He died in 1826, and the Mount Vernon estate became the property
of his nephew, John Augustine Washington. At his death, in 1832, his
son, John Augustine Washington, was the heir. He held the estate until
1860, when he disposed of it to the Mount Vernon Association.

A RECEPTION AT THE WHITE HOUSE

CHAPTER XXI.

THE INAUGURATION CEREMONIES OF PRESIDENTS OF THE UNITED STATES—THE
FIRST INAUGURATION IN WASHINGTON—ANCIENT AND MODERN CUSTOMS—THE
INAUGURATION OF PRESIDENT CLEVELAND—CEREMONY AT THE CAPITOL—TAKING
THE OATH OF OFFICE—THE GRAND PROCESSION—THE INAUGURATION BALL IN
THE NEW PENSION BUILDING.

HE first President of the United States inaugurated in the city
of Washington was Thomas Jefferson, who took the oath of
office on the 4th of March, 1801. He was the third President,
the others having been George Washington, who served two
terms, and John Adams, who served one term. Washington was inaugurated for his first term in the city of New York on April 30, 1789. The
First Congress of the United States met in New York on March 4, 1789,
but had no quorum until April 6. On that day the electoral votes for
President were counted by the Senate and House in joint session, and
immediately afterwards a messenger was despatched to Mount Vernon to
notify Washington of his election. Washington left home on April 16
for New York, and during his journey thither was the recipient of grand
popular demonstrations in the cities and towns along the route. Shortly
after twelve o'clock on April 30 a troop of light dragoons and a legion
of infantry, together with the inauguration committees of Congress and
various officials, escorted Washington from his residence in New York
to the Federal Hall, on Wall street, where Congress was sitting. On the
site of this building the sub-treasury of the United States now stands.
When Washington entered the Senate chamber, where both houses of
Congress were in joint session, all present rose and remained standing
until he had taken the seat assigned to him. In a few minutes he proceeded to the balcony of the building, to take the oath of office within
sight of the multitude assembled, who could not gain admission to the
Senate chamber. The oath was administered by Robert R. Livingston,
Chancellor of the State of New York. After the reading of the oath,
Washington inclined his head and reverently kissed the Bible, which was
held by the secretary of the Senate. Chancellor Livingston then waved

his hand to the throng in front of the balcony and shouted in a clear, ringing voice, " Long live George Washington, President of the United States!" Tumultuous cheers were given, cannon were fired, and the church bells were rung. Washington returned to the Senate chamber and delivered his inaugural address, after which he attended a special service at St. Paul's church. He wore a suit of dark brown cloth which had been woven at Mount Vernon. His lower limbs were clad in small clothes and white silk stockings, and on his feet were large, square shoes with silver buckles set with diamonds. His hair was powdered, brushed back, and tied in a queue. At his side hung a long sword with an ornamented hilt.

At the time of Washington's second inauguration, March 4, 1793, Congress was sitting in Philadelphia, which was then the national capital. The " Congress-Hall" was at the corner of Chestnut and Fifth streets, and here the inaugural ceremony was performed. Washington rode to the building in a magnificent white coach drawn by six white horses, and was escorted by a large military force. The oath of office was administered by Justice William Cushing, of the Supreme Court of the United States. Washington, who was then in mourning for his mother, was attired in a black velvet suit, with knee breeches and black silk stockings. After taking the oath he read his inaugural address, and then withdrew to his residence.

John Adams was also inaugurated in Philadelphia, on March 4, 1797. The ceremony took place in the hall of the House of Representatives, and the oath was administered by Chief Justice Oliver Ellsworth. Many distinguished persons were present.

When Thomas Jefferson was inaugurated the precise etiquette observed at the previous inaugurations was somewhat dispensed with. No military or other escort was tendered to him, as he had intimated that he did not wish one. President Adams left the city of Washington early on the morning of inauguration day, not caring to remain to see his successor inducted into office. Just before noon on March 4, 1801, Jefferson slowly rode down the muddy, unpaved Pennsylvania avenue,—a very slough of despond at that time,—courteously responding to the salutations of those who recognized him. He was unattended and rode his favorite blooded horse, " Wildair." When he arrived at the Capitol he dismounted and hitched his horse to the fence which enclosed a part of the western grounds, and then unceremoniously walked up the bank into the building. . Upon entering the crowded Senate chamber he was escorted to the chair of the Vice-President, and immediately proceeded to deliver his inaugural address, or " annual speech," as the President's remarks were then called.

When he had finished, Chief Justice John Marshall administered the oath to him. He then returned without ceremony to the White House on " Wildair," and during the afternoon and evening held a public reception. He wore a plain blue cloth suit, remarkable only for its extreme simplicity.

At Jefferson's second inauguration, March 4, 1805, about the same ceremony was observed. Chief Justice Marshall again administered the oath, and Justices William Cushing, William Patterson, and Bushrod Washington were present. On this occasion Jefferson was attired in a blue coat with brass buttons, a scarlet waistcoat, blue knee breeches, and white silk stockings.

Since Jefferson's time there have been many inaugurations at the national capital. James Madison was inaugurated in 1809 and 1813, James Monroe in 1817 and 1821, John Quincy Adams in 1825, Andrew Jackson in 1829 and 1833, Martin Van Buren in 1837, William Henry Harrison in 1841, John Tyler (after the death of Harrison) in 1841, James K. Polk in 1845, Zachary Taylor in 1849, Millard Fillmore (after the death of Taylor) in 1850, Franklin Pierce in 1853, James Buchanan in 1857, Abraham Lincoln in 1861 and 1865, Andrew Johnson (after the death of Lincoln) in 1865, Ulysses S. Grant in 1869 and 1873, Rutherford B. Hayes in 1877, James A. Garfield in 1881, Chester A. Arthur (after the death of Garfield) in 1881, and Grover Cleveland in 1885. These inaugurations were marked by special demonstrations varying in their degree of enthusiasm and interest according to the state of popular feeling at the time.

The first inauguration of Madison was, it is stated, " notable for demonstrations of joy." The ceremony took place in the hall of the House of Representatives, and it was not until the first inauguration of Monroe that the custom of delivering the inaugural address and taking the oath on the eastern portico of the Capitol was begun. A writer in 1817 said, " The difference said to have existed between the two houses in respect to the appropriation of the Representative chamber was rather fortunate than otherwise, since it caused the ceremony of the President swearing fealty to the Constitution to take place in the view, if not in the hearing, of all the people of the United States who chose to witness it. This, it appears to us, is a mode far preferable to that of being cramped up in a hall, into which, however extensive, not more than four or five hundred people can possibly have admittance." At Monroe's second inauguration the weather was too cold for the open-air exercises, and they were consequently held in the hall of the House. And when John Quincy Adams was inaugurated he preferred to have the ceremony in-doors. But from the inauguration of Jackson to the present time the Presidents have all sworn fealty to the Constitution on the Capitol portico.

PRESIDENT CLEVELAND AT HIS DESK IN THE WHITE HOUSE.

Jackson declined an escort to the Capitol on his inauguration day, and, unattended, rode his spirited war horse down Pennsylvania avenue. At every step of the way he was lustily cheered by the great throng of people who had gathered from different sections of the country to see the gallant soldier inaugurated. Daniel Webster afterwards wrote, "I never saw such a crowd here before. Persons have come five hundred miles to, see General Jackson, and they really seem to think that the country is rescued from some dreadful danger." After Jackson had delivered his inaugural address, and taken the oath administered by Chief Justice Marshall, salutes were fired, and a procession was formed to escort him to the White House.

Van Buren's inauguration was also the occasion of enthusiastic demonstrations. He had a fine military escort, and rode to the Capitol and back to the White House in a handsome phaeton constructed of wood taken from the old frigate Constitution. Chief Justice Roger B. Taney administered the oath. Harrison's inauguration called out a great crowd of spectators. The "hero of Tippecanoe" rode down Pennsylvania avenue on a white horse, accompanied by various military organizations, including a battalion of soldiers who had served under him. He read his address nearly through, then stopped, and was sworn into office by Chief Justice Taney, and then finished his address. In the evening he attended several balls given in his honor. At the inauguration of Polk and of Taylor there were about the usual exercises. Pierce and Buchanan were inaugurated with great pomp and ceremony. The attendance of strangers on both occasions was large, and the military parades were exceedingly imposing. Chief Justice Taney administered the oath to both these Presidents. Grand inauguration balls were given.

At the first inauguration of Lincoln there were apprehensions that an attempt would be made to prevent the ceremony, and the greatest precautions were taken. Lincoln was closely guarded by trusty men during the entire ceremony. There was a long procession of military and civic organizations. After the inauguration Lincoln held a reception at the White House, which was attended by several thousand people. His second inauguration was marked by a great concourse of spectators and an extensive military parade. The city was handsomely decorated for the occasion. The inaugurations of Grant and Garfield were splendid demonstrations in every particular. On these occasions the city had thousands of visitors, the inaugural processions were long and imposing, and there were magnificent fireworks and grand balls. Vice-Presidents Tyler, Fillmore, Johnson, and Arthur, who assumed the office of President, simply took the constitutional oath without public formality.

With the inauguration of Grover Cleveland as President of the United States, on the 4th of March, 1885, the Democratic party once more acquired the control of the government, after a period of twenty-four years. In magnitude and grandeur, in the diversity of its features of interest, this inauguration far exceeded all that had preceded it since the capital city was established. The day was well nigh perfect,—a clear, sunny day, with the fragrant, delightful air of spring. There was the largest outpouring of people ever known in Washington. The lowest estimate gives the number of visitors from all sections of the country at one hundred and fifty thousand, and there is good reason for the belief that there were as many as two hundred thousand. For the first time the broad, spacious city seemed crowded, but the immense multitude was accommodated with a great deal less trouble and discomfort than might have been expected. The military parade was the grandest and most extensive since the review of the army in 1865, and the civic parade was never equalled in extent and variety. About thirty thousand men were in the march with bright and handsome uniforms, glistening arms, and magnificent banners, and the long line as it stretched up Pennsylvania avenue as far as could be seen was a superb and remarkable sight. The city was decorated as it never had been before, and along the principal thoroughfares the buildings were nearly hidden by rich and brilliant decorations. Pennsylvania avenue for more than a mile was one unbroken mass of flags and bunting and decorative embellishments. All the government buildings were adorned in a beautiful manner, and some of them were notable for the extent and artistic arrangement of their decorations. Nothing occurred to mar the festivities, and the inauguration, all in all, was an event long to be remembered.

Cleveland's journey from the White House to the Capitol to be inaugurated was the first ceremony of the day. At an early hour a great crowd gathered around the hotel where the Presidential party had rooms, all eager to catch a glimpse of the man who was to guide the ship of state for four years. Shortly after ten o'clock a carriage drove up to the hotel with the committee appointed to escort Cleveland to the White House. Cleveland soon appeared on the hotel steps, and was greeted by enthusiastic cheers. He saluted the crowd in a cordial manner, and entering the carriage was driven to the White House, followed by hundreds of people, who cheered again and again as they hastened along the street. When the White House was reached President Arthur advanced and welcomed the President-elect. Hearty handshaking followed, and then the party entered the East Room to await the arrival of Vice-President-elect Hendricks. When he arrived a warm greeting was given him. An announcement was soon made that all was ready for the departure for the Capitol. Two elegant carriages had been provided for the party. The first was drawn by four bay horses and conveyed the President and the President-elect and two Senators; the second was drawn by four white Arabian horses and conveyed the Vice-President-elect and two Senators. The carriages were driven from the White House grounds to the place awaiting them in the procession which had been formed to escort the party to the Capitol. There was tumultuous cheering as the multitude recognized the occupants of the carriages. The order to march was soon given, and the procession moved rapidly down Pennsylvania avenue.

A body of United States troops headed the procession, their ranks extending entirely across the broad avenue. Then followed a battalion of the Marine Corps of the navy with the celebrated Marine Band. The Presidential party came next, escorted by General H. W. Slocum, the chief marshal, and his staff, and the First Troop Philadelphia City Cavalry, and followed by the National Democratic Committee and the Inauguration Committee in carriages. The militia of the District of Columbia, headed by the Washington Light Infantry, came next, and the escorting division was closed by various posts of the Grand Army of the Republic. The avenue was filled with a solid mass of humanity, and the Presidential party received an ovation all along the line of march. Men shouted themselves hoarse, women frantically waved handkerchiefs, and all sorts of demonstrations were made. Words would fail to give an idea of the enthusiasm and popular feeling. Cleveland kept his hat in his hand and bowed to the right and left almost constantly as his carriage rolled along. The same hearty reception was given to Hendricks, whose carriage followed. When the Presidential party reached the eastern grounds of the Capitol it was received by another demonstration of enthusiasm from a vast multitude filling every part of the extensive area. The shouts which arose were loud and prolonged, and only ceased when Cleveland and Hendricks had disappeared within the building.

Inside the Capitol a distinguished audience had gathered to witness the inaugural ceremony. The Senate chamber was crowded. All the high officials of the government were present, together with the leading officers of the army and navy, the diplomatic corps, and the justices of the Supreme Court of the United States. The Senate galleries were filled with ladies and gentlemen who had been honored with special invitations. The Senate was engaged in the closing business of the Forty-eighth Congress, but the Senators had plenty of leisure to receive their visitors. Shortly after twelve o'clock President Arthur entered the chamber, and was escorted to a seat immediately in front of the desk of the President

of the Senate. Then the announcement was made, " The President-elect of the United States," and Cleveland, attended by two Senators, appeared at the main door of the Senate. At his appearance the entire assemblage rose and applauded heartily. He advanced down the aisle, bowing first to the right and then to the left, bearing his honors with dignity and perfect self-possession, and took a seat by the side of President Arthur. Vice-President-elect Hendricks was then announced, and was received with great applause. He advanced to the desk of Acting Vice-President Edmunds and took the oath of off   Vi   P sident of the United
red a brief valedictory
day.
eat of the presiding
session. Prayer was
h the Vice-President
n in, and, after some
vas formed to escort
1 front of the central
/ was to take place.

The procession was made up as follows: Marshal of the District of Columbia and Marshal of the Supreme Court, the Justices of the Supreme Court, the Sergeant-at-Arms of the Senate, the Committee of Arrangements, the President and the President-elect, the Vice-President and the Secretary of the Senate, Members of the Senate, the Diplomatic Corps, Heads of the Departments, the Lieutenant-General of the Army, the Admiral of the Navy, and the Officers of the Army and Navy who, by name, have received the thanks of Congress, Members of the House of Representatives and members-elect, Governors and ex-Governors of States, Officers of the Senate, and Officers of the House of Representatives.   .

The procession moved through the rotunda of the Capitol, and at precisely half-past twelve o'clock emerged from the main door on to the portico. The platform erected for the inaugural ceremony was nearly one hundred feet square, and was the largest ever used for such an occasion. It was covered with two thousand chairs, for the accommodation of those who had been present in the Senate chamber, and was profusely draped with American flags. The multitude in front of the platform extended in a compact mass clear back to the edge of the eastern park, and its flanks spread out over a thousand feet to the right and left, while many thousands more were gathered on the grounds farther back. It is believed there were two hundred thousand people in this assemblage, which was the greatest ever seen at an inauguration. On the streets and avenues east of the Capitol the military and civic organizations which were to participate in the grand parade were massed in columns, and as far as could be seen were flashing bayonets, waving banners, gay uniforms, and richly-caparisoned horses, making a pageant of rare magnificence.

The seats on the platform were quickly filled by those who had formed the Presidential escort and others who had been admitted to the Capitol. In a few minutes President Arthur and President-elect Cleveland appeared on the portico, accompanied by the Chief Justice and Associate Justices of the Supreme Court of the United States and the Congressional committee, and advanced down the platform to the seats in front reserved for them. There was an outburst of applause from those on the platform, which was followed by cheer upon cheer from the vast multitude on the Capitol grounds.

After a short pause, Cleveland rose and began his inaugural address. He was dressed in a plain black suit, and appeared perfectly at ease. His voice was clear and resonant, and his words could be heard at a great distance. His address was delivered from memory, and only occasional reference was made to the notes he held in his hand. At every pause

PRESIDENT CLEVELAND TAKING THE OATH OF OFFICE.

cheers were given, and the forcible and manly style of the speaker im-
pressed all who listened to him. The address was brief, and at a few
minutes past one o'clock he had finished. Turning to Chief Justice
Morrison R. Waite, he bowed and said, " I am now prepared to take the
oath prescribed by law."

The Chief Justice rose to administer the oath, which he recited in a
distinct tone. The oath is as follows: " I do solemnly swear that I will
faithfully execute the office of President of the United States, and will, to
the best of my ability, preserve, protect, and defend the Constitution of
the United States." Cleveland said, " I swear," and reverently kissed the
open Bible, which he took in his hands. Then laying it down he shook
hands with the Chief Justice, who warmly congratulated him as the
twenty-second President of the United States. The other persons on the
platform then pressed forward and congratulated him, and the multitude
on the Capitol grounds shouted with great enthusiasm. In a few minutes

President Cleveland left the platform, walked to the basement entrance of the Capitol, and entered his carriage, to be driven in the grand procession up Pennsylvania avenue to the White House.

The Bible used in administering the oath of office was a small, well-worn volume bound in leather, which had been given to President Cleveland by his mother when he left home in his youth to seek his fortune in the world, and always had been cherished by him. On its front cover was the name, "S. G. Cleveland." By the President's special request it was used for the ceremony. It was opened by the Chief Justice without any intention of selecting a particular place, and the place that was kissed by the President was, therefore, the result purely of chance. As the type used in the Bible is small, the lips of the President touched six verses of the 112th Psalm, from verse 5 to verse 10 inclusive. They are as follows:

"A good man showeth favor, and lendeth: he will guide his affairs with discretion.

"Surely he shall not be moved forever; the righteous shall be in everlasting remembrance.

"He shall not be afraid of evil tidings; his heart is fixed, trusting in the Lord.

"His heart is established; he shall not be afraid, until he see his desire upon his enemies.

"He hath dispersed, he hath given to the poor; his righteousness endureth forever; his horn shall be exalted with honor.

"The wicked shall see it, and be grieved; he shall gnash with his teeth, and melt away; the desire of the wicked shall perish."

During the inaugural ceremony the procession had been well organized by the marshals, and when the Presidential party arrived to take its place in line the order to march was given promptly, and the column moved down Capitol Hill. General H. W. Slocum, chief marshal, rode at the head of the column, followed by his staff and members of the inauguration committee, all mounted. Then came the Presidential party in two carriages. The first carriage contained President Cleveland, ex-President Arthur, and two Senators; the second carriage contained Vice-President Hendricks and two Senators.

Then followed the first, or escort division, commanded by Brevet Major-General R. B. Ayres, United States Army. The division was headed by two battalions of United States artillery from Fort McHenry and Fortress Monroe, Light Battery A, and a battalion of the United States Marine Corps. Then came the militia organizations of the District of Columbia, as follows: Washington Light Infantry, Union Veteran Corps, National Rifles, Washington Continentals, Emmet Guard, Wash-

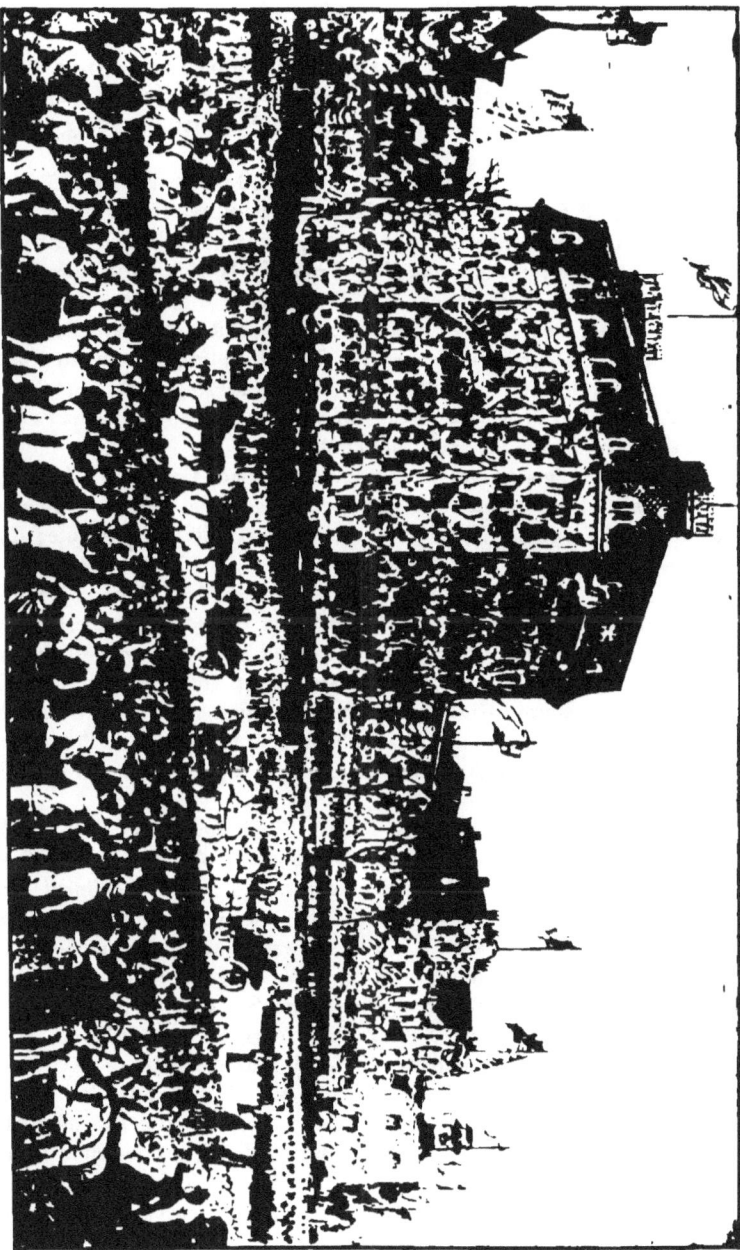

THE INAUGURAL PROCESSION ON PENNSYLVANIA AVENUE.

Pension Office   President Cleveland's Carriage.   Vice-President Hendricks' Carriage

ington Rifle Corps, Butler Zouaves, Washington Cadet Corps, Capitol
City Guards, and Webster Rifles. The division was closed by the Grand
Army of the Republic, Department of the Potomac, parading with ten
posts.

The second division was entirely composed of the National Guard of
the State of Pennsylvania, Major-General John F. Hartranft, commanding.
The first brigade consisted of the First, Second, Third, and Sixth Regi-
ments, the State Fencibles, the First Troop Philadelphia City Cavalry, the
Gray Invincibles, and Battery A. The second brigade consisted of the
Fifth, Tenth, Fourteenth, Fifteenth, Sixteenth, and Eighteenth Regiments,
the Sheridan Troop, and Battery B. The third brigade consisted of the
Fourth, Eighth, Ninth, Twelfth, and Thirteenth Regiments, and Battery
C. About 7500 men were in this division, and each brigade had a band,
and each regiment a fife and drum corps.

The third division was in command of Major-General Fitzhugh Lee,
of Virginia. First in line were troops composing the Virginia Volunteers,
as follows: Corps of Cadets from the Virginia Military Institute; Companies A, B, and D, First Regiment of Virginia; Richmond Light Infantry Blues; St. John's Academy Cadets, Alexandria; Second Regiment
of Virginia; Harrisburg Guards; Anderson Guards; Winchester Light
Infantry; Berneville Company; Warren Light Infantry; Third and
Fourth Regiments of Virginia; Wise Light Infantry; Norfolk City
Guard; Petersburg Grays; Second Battalion Virginia Volunteers;
Langston Guard; Virginia Guard; Seaboard Elliot Grays, Portsmouth;
National Guard; Hannibal Guard; Garfield Light Infantry, Fredericks-
burg; State Guard, Richmond.

Then followed the American Rifles, Wilmington, Del.; Phil Kearney
Guard, Elizabeth, N. J.; Governor's Guards, Columbia, S. C.; Clarke
Light Infantry, and Clinch Rifles, Augusta, Ga.; Fifth Regiment Mary-
land National Guard; Governor's Guards, Annapolis, Md.; Bond Guard,
Catonsville, Md.; Towson Guards, Towson, Md.; Monumental City
Guards, Baltimore; Baltimore Rifles; Washington Infantry, Pittsburg,
Pa.; South Carolina Volunteers, Charleston, S. C.; Sixty-ninth Regiment
National Guard, State of New York; Jackson Corps, Albany, N. Y.;
Thirty-first Separate Company National Guard, State of New York,
Mohawk, N. Y.; Washington Continentals, Schenectady, N. Y.; Des
Grenadiers Rochambeau, New York City; Hornet's Nest Riflemen, Char-
lotte, N. C.; Forsythe Riflemen, Winston, N. C.; Edgecombe Guards,
Tarborough, N. C.; Meagher Guards, Providence, R. I.; Busch Zouaves,
St. Louis, Mo.; High School Cadets, Corcoran Cadets, National Rifles'
Cadets, Gonzaga Cadets, Washington, D. C.; Light Guards, Sandusky, O.

All the military organizations had bands of music or fife and drum corps.

The fourth division was in command of Major Thomas J. Luttrell, and was composed of civic organizations, as follows: Jackson Democratic Association, Washington, D. C.; Society of Tammany, Irving Hall Democratic Club, and the County Democracy, New York City; Democratic Phalanx, Albany, N. Y.; Kings County Democracy, and the Cleveland and Hendricks War Veterans, Brooklyn, N. Y.; Democratic Club, Harlem, N. Y.; Thomas Jefferson Club, New York City; Young Men's Democratic Club, Washington, D. C.; Bayard Legion, Wilmington, Del.; Joel Parker Association, and the Kruger Engineers, Newark, N. J.; New Jersey Democratic Battalion, Camden, N. J.; Iroquois Club, and the Cook County Democracy, Chicago, Ill.; Duckworth Club, Cincinnati, O.; Democratic Legion, Buffalo, N. Y.; Jefferson Club, Cincinnati, O.; Jackson Club, and the Democratic Glee Club, Columbus, O.; Americus Club, Samuel J. Randall Association, R. S. Patterson Association, Moyamensing Legion, Hancock Veteran Association, Sensenderfer Young Men's Democratic Association, Eleventh Ward Randall Club, Samuel J. Randall Association of First Congressional District, Continental Club, Monroe Club, Andrew Jackson Club, and First Ward Democratic Association, Philadelphia, Pa.; Americus Club, Reading, Pa.; Central Democratic Club, Harrisburg, Pa.; Calumet Club, Crescent Club, Taney Club, German American Democratic Association, Stonewall Club, and Bohemian Club, Baltimore, Md.; Monumental Club, and the Madison Club, Washington, D. C.; Democratic Inauguration Club, Portland, Me.; First Cleveland Flag Escort, Moberly, Mo.; Davis Democratic Club, Piedmont, W. Va.; Young Men's Democratic Club, Wheeling, W. Va.; Democratic Flambeau Club, Topeka, Kan.; Democratic Club, Kansas City, Mo.; Flag Cavalry of the Two Hundred and Nineteen Electoral Votes, Washington, D. C.; Lewinsville Cleveland and Hendricks Club, Fairfax County, Va.; Veteran Firemen's Association, New York City; Fire Department of the District of Columbia. The clubs and associations were accompanied by bands of music, and carried elegant banners.

As the procession moved up Pennsylvania avenue it presented a most magnificent spectacle. Constant applause and cheers were given the Presidential party, and the various military and civic organizations were received with enthusiastic demonstrations. The avenue, the broadest in the world, was densely packed with spectators. All the public reservations had stands extending their entire length, and these were filled to overflowing. Upon the front of nearly every building a stand was erected from one to three stories in height, and all these stands were crowded.

The military marched in company front, and the clubs and associations marched as compactly as possible, yet the procession, moving rapidly, was three hours passing a given point. The route of march was four miles long.

When the head of the procession reached the Treasury building a halt was made for a few minutes to allow President Cleveland to leave the line for the reviewing stand on Pennsylvania avenue, directly in front of the White House. The stand was profusely decorated with flags and bunting, and contained many prominent people. The President stood on a projecting platform covered with flags, and remained standing during the entire review, cordially responding to the salutes of the various organizations as they passed. It was past five o'clock when he retired to the White House.

The festivities of the evening included a magnificent display of fireworks on the White House grounds, and the grand inauguration ball in the new Pension building. A vast assemblage witnessed the fireworks, which were the finest ever seen in Washington. The display embraced flights of hundreds of rockets at a time, producing a mass of gold, silver, and variegated lights, which had a superb effect. Japanese shells and great bombs were exploded in immense numbers, and there were many varieties of mines of stars and serpents, floral fountains, batteries with signal rockets, etc., making mammoth sprays of colored fire. There were three prominent set pieces. The first consisted of a portrait of Thomas Jefferson, sixty feet high, which was festooned with banners in national colors, and presented a beautiful appearance. The second represented the eastern front of the Capitol, with portraits of Cleveland and Hendricks on the sides, while on one corner appeared the figure of a sailor, and on the other that of a mechanic, and the motto " Peace and Prosperity" was displayed above the dome. This piece was one hundred and sixty feet long and seventy-five feet high, and was the most elaborate one ever fired in the United States. The third set piece was a representation in vivid golden fire of Niagara Falls. It was nearly three hundred feet long, and was a faithful presentation of that great natural wonder. The display concluded with the flight of five thousand rockets, forming a gigantic outburst of colored fire in mid-air.

The inauguration ball was a brilliant finale to the ceremonies of the day. It was held in the unfinished Pension building on Judiciary Square. The building has an interior court-yard more than three hundred feet long and more than one hundred feet wide, and this was roofed over, a smooth floor laid, and the whole interior transformed by skilful hands into a veritable palace of beauty.

THE CLEVELAND INAUGURATION BALL IN THE NEW PENSION BUILDING.

The custom of having inauguration balls dates back to the second inauguration of President Washington, in Philadelphia, 1793. At that time
the following invitation was published: "The members of the Senate and
the House of Representatives of the United States are respectfully invited
to a ball on the 4th of March, 1793, to be given by the Dancing Assembly,
in honor of the unanimous re-election of George Washington, the President of the United States, the anniversary of the present form of government of the United States, and a parting leave with the members of the
present Congress."

The first inauguration ball given at the national capital was when
James Madison was inaugurated, in 1809. It took place at Long's
Hotel, and was attended by about four hundred persons, including ex-
President Jefferson, the high officials of the government, members of
Congress, and the foreign ministers, and was declared "a most brilliant
affair." Carusi's Saloon, on Eleventh street, now used as a variety
theatre, was for years the fashionable ball-room of the city, and here the
inauguration balls were usually held until the incoming of President
Taylor. The ball in his honor was given in a structure erected for the
occasion, as were the balls given for Presidents Pierce and Buchanan.
At the first inauguration of President Lincoln a temporary structure was
used for the ball, but at his second inauguration the ball was held in the
Patent Office building. The first Grant inaugural ball was held in the
north wing of the Treasury building, and the second in a building
erected on Judiciary Square. The National Museum was used for the
Garfield ball.

The ball-room in which the Cleveland inauguration ball was held was
remarkable for its size and elaborate decorations. It was the largest ever
used for a Presidential fete. The floor had a waxed surface three hundred and sixteen feet long and one hundred and sixteen feet wide. Eight
ponderous columns in the centre divided the huge quadrangle into what
might be called three separate rooms, but did not interfere with the dancing
or promenading from end to end of the long court. The floor was surrounded by capacious galleries, and there were reception-rooms, supper-
rooms, etc., at the ends and sides of the building. The arrangement of
columns and galleries gave ample opportunity for decoration, and flags,
banners, and bunting of every description were used in a lavish manner
to make the great room a scene of rare beauty. The central columns
supporting the roof were covered with white muslin, and had entwined
around them broad bands of evergreens. Between the evergreens were
leaves of the palmetto plant, placed in irregular Japanese designs half-way
up the columns. The smaller columns supporting the galleries were

INAUGURATION BALL

MARCH 4TH 1885.

COMMEMORATIVE OF THE INAUGURATION OF

OF THE UNITED STATES.

J. A. Hendricks

SOUVENIR TICKET OF THE INAUGURATION BALL

decorated with palmetto leaves at their base, and at their top silken banners
with stars of gold were suspended. The front of the galleries was covered
with drapery of maroon velvet, in which handsome designs in golden
thread were woven. Trophy pieces, consisting of small silk flags mounted
on silver-tipped spears and upholding a national shield, were placed along
the front of the galleries. The ceiling, which was at a height of seventy-
five feet, was entirely hidden by masses of gayly-colored bunting, and
from a central point in each of the divisions hung hundreds of broad
pennants, interspersed with ropes of evergreens, which were brought down
and looped against the wall. The bannered ceiling was very beautiful,
and the innumerable flags, festoons, and streamers composing it had a very
pleasing effect. Great electric lamps hanging from the ceiling flooded the
vast room with a soft, clear light, and all the details of form and decoration were distinctly brought out.

At the east end of the room there was a large, brilliant star of colored
lights, and just below this was a magnificent Venetian mirror, with a
frame composed of hundreds of pieces of cut glass, which reflected the
colors of the rainbow. Plants and flowers were grouped here and there,
adding color and fragrance. The walls of the building were concealed
by flags of varied nationalities, and at short intervals were silken banners
bearing the arms of all nations finely embroidered in glowing tints. The
entrances to all the rooms leading from the ball-room were draped with
damask silk curtains of blue, red, and old gold. Between the rows of
columns in the centre of the room were two music stands, one for the
dance music and the other for the concert music. Each was decorated
with damask silk and maroon velvet. The stairways leading to the galleries were draped with the flags of all nations.

The room set apart for the use of President Cleveland and the
members of his party was artistically decorated and elegantly furnished.
A Wilton carpet covered the floor, and the furniture was of mahogany
upholstered in maroon and blue velvet. The walls were lined with satin
banners, and the windows were draped with rich ecru and garnet tapestry
curtains. Vines of smilax festooned the ceiling, making a beautiful green
bower, and roses and exotics were profusely displayed. Life-size paintings
of Jefferson and Cleveland hung on the west wall, and on the east wall
were landscape paintings.

The parlor used by the reception committee was handsomely decorated. In addition to the flowers and tropical plants there were eight
large floral designs specially arranged to represent the White House and
the executive departments of the government. The White House was
represented by a design of the President's chair made of red and white

roses, under a canopy of smilax and flowers. For the Department of State there was a floral device of the coat of arms of the United States surmounted by an eagle; for the Treasury Department, a large combination safe; for the War Department, two cannons crossed; for the Navy Department, a full-rigged war ship; for the Post-Office Department, a mail-bag marked U. S. M., and a letter addressed to President Grover Cleveland, and postmarked Washington, D. C., March 4th, 9 P.M.; for the Department of the Interior, a stump of a tree with an axe imbedded in it, and a plough, a scythe, and a sheaf of wheat at its base; for the Department of Justice, a desk and an open book, and the scales of justice, with the motto, " Fiat Justitia." All these designs were artistically executed in immortelles, roses of various kinds, and lilies of the valley.

It was not until ten o'clock that the ball-room began to be crowded, but from this time until far into the morning the huge floor was filled with a gay company, and the galleries contained a great throng of spectators. Nearly ten thousand people were present, and the receipts from the sale of tickets amounted to about $40,000. The scene presented was, doubtless, the most magnificent ever witnessed in a ball-room in America, and surpassed the most sanguine expectations. The rich and handsome toilets of the ladies, the varied uniforms of the military and naval officers, the splendid decorations, the great masses of flowers, the high, long room with its bannered ceiling, all combined to form a spectacle of entrancing effect. Music for promenading was furnished by the United States Marine Band, and music for dancing by the Germania Orchestra of Philadelphia.

President Cleveland and Vice-President Hendricks. accompanied by a distinguished party, arrived at the ball about eleven o'clock. After holding a reception. the Presidential party made the tour of the ball-room, and departed soon after midnight. The ball was the greatest social success ever known in Washington, and fitly closed the memorable inauguration.

CHAPTER XXII.

THE CHURCHES OF WASHINGTON—SKETCHES OF THE ANCIENT RELIGIOUS ORGANIZA-
TIONS—CHURCHES THAT WERE ATTENDED BY THE PRESIDENTS—THE PROMINENT
CHURCHES—THE COLORED POPULATION—HOW EMANCIPATION WAS ACCOMPLISHED
IN THE DISTRICT OF COLUMBIA.

HERE are many fine church edifices in Washington, and the number is rapidly increasing from year to year. During the past decade there has been a marked improvement in church architecture, and a strong desire has been manifested by all the denominations erecting new churches to have them conform, in some degree at least, with the ornate architectural forms employed throughout the city for other buildings. Washington is a city of churches, and even Brooklyn, which has for a long time assumed this title, does not now number as many churches in proportion to the population. The church organizations with but few exceptions are in a prosperous condition, and are constantly extending their fields of labor and increasing their influence and means. Many years before the District of Columbia was set apart for the use of the government a church was erected on Rock creek, a short distance above the present limits of Washington. Its erection was largely owing to the efforts of John Bradford, one of the early settlers of the district. He gave a large tract of land for the church, and imported bricks from England to build it. In 1719 it was dedicated, and it is, therefore, one of the oldest in the country, antedating the old Christ Church in Alexandria by forty-six years. It is known as St. Paul's Church, of Rock Creek Parish, and is of the Episcopal denomination. The edifice has been remodelled within a few years, but the original walls remain in a good state of preservation. In the cemetery attached to the church a large number of the early residents of the District of Columbia are buried.

Another ancient church is the Christ Episcopal Church, situated in the southeast quarter of Washington, near the navy-yard. This is the oldest church in the city, it having been erected in 1795, five years before the government took possession of the national capital. At that

ASCENSION EPISCOPAL CHURCH.

time the city was little more than a " howling wilderness," and the founders
of the little church had a hard struggle for some years to maintain it.
But they were hopeful, patient, and courageous, and year by year made
progress towards a permanent establishment. In 1807 the society of
Christ Church, with the help of citizens of the eastern part of Washington, laid out the " Washington Parish Burial-Ground," on the banks of the
Anacostia river. Afterwards Congress appropriated money for the burial-
ground, and its name was changed to " Congressional Cemetery." Some
of the early Presidents attended divine service in Christ Church, and it is
noted in the church records that a committee waited on President Monroe
soon after his inauguration in 1817, and informed him that the vestry of
the church had passed a resolution assigning " pew number one" for his
use during his term of office. Monroe accepted the pew, and became a
warm friend and liberal supporter of the church. He attended service
every Sunday morning with his family, and was also frequently present at
other services.

In 1816 another Episcopal church was erected in the northwest quarter of the city. This was St. John's Church, on the corner of H and 16th streets. The services of Benjamin Henry Latrobe, the architect of the central part of the Capitol, were secured to design and construct the church, and he produced a work which was greatly admired in those days. President Madison worshipped in this venerable church, and other Presidents have been regular worshippers. All through his official term President Arthur regularly attended the morning service here.

The Trinity Episcopal Church, corner of Third and C streets northwest, was erected soon after St. John's. Among the other leading churches of this denomination are the Church of the Ascension, corner of Massachusetts avenue and Twelfth street, and the Church of the Epiphany, on G street northwest. There are twenty-six Episcopal churches in the city.

The First Presbyterian Church, on Four and one-half street, near Judiciary Square, which is attended by President Cleveland, has numbered several Presidents among its attendants. President Jackson worshipped in it during his second term, but during most of his first term he worshipped in the Second Presbyterian, now known as the New York Avenue Church. It is stated that in President Jackson's first term "occurred that famous quarrel among the members of his Cabinet in regard to the social recognition of Mrs. General Eaton, the wife of the Secretary of War. Before her marriage with General Eaton she was known as Peggy O'Neil, the daughter of the proprietor of the leading hotel in Washington, and she was a famous beauty. President Jackson warmly espoused the cause of Mrs. Eaton, and in his characteristic style determined that every one else should do the same. This episode was taken advantage of by the factions then existing in the Democratic party, led respectively by Martin Van Buren and John C. Calhoun, and, as the result, the entire Cabinet was reorganized, and the political effects of what was alleged to be jealousy on the part of the ladies toward beautiful Peggy O'Neil went far beyond what such an apparently slight cause would seem to justify in the calm light of history. At any rate, the Mrs. Eaton quarrel extended to the church, and the pastor of the Second Presbyterian refused to recognize Mrs. Eaton, and so Old Hickory, in high dudgeon, left the church and went to the First Presbyterian, where he remained until his second term as President expired, in 1837, and he retired to his home in Tennessee."

The First Presbyterian Church was also attended by Presidents Polk, Pierce, and Buchanan. The church society was organized in 1795, and at first held its meetings on the Sabbath, in a small building on the White

House grounds used by the carpenters employed in constructing the Presidential mansion. When the Capitol was erected the society obtained permission to hold meetings in the chamber occupied by the Supreme Court, and, until the Capitol was burned by the British invaders, services were held every Sunday in the court chamber. Afterwards, for nearly two years, the society was compelled to suspend its services, as no place of meeting could be obtained, but finally a small church was erected south of the Capitol. This church was used until 1828, when it was sold, the location on Four and one-half street secured, and a new church erected. In 1859 the present church was constructed. The pastor of the First Presbyterian, Rev. Dr. Byron Sunderland, has occupied the pulpit for thirty-two years, and during his long pastorate has witnessed many changes. There are twenty-one Presbyterian churches in the city, the

FIRST PRESBYTERIAN CHURCH.

19

NEW YORK AVENUE PRESBYTERIAN CHURCH.

New York Avenue Church being the leading one. President Lincoln attended this church.

The All Souls' Church, on Fourteenth street northwest, is the only Unitarian church in the city. It was dedicated in 1878. The first church of this denomination was erected in 1822, and was attended by John Quincy Adams before and after he became President. During the Civil War the church was used by the government as a hospital, and the society was granted the privilege of holding its Sunday services in the hall of the House of Representatives.

The Church of Our Father, on Thirteenth street northwest, is the only Universalist church in Washington. It was occupied by the Universalist society in 1883. Previous to that time the society held its meetings in the Masonic Temple and other halls for a number of years.

There are fifty-two Methodist churches in the city. The principal ones are the Metropolitan Church, on Four and one-half street, which

was attended by President Grant, and the Foundry Church, on G street northwest, which was established in 1815. The Baptists have forty-five churches. The First Baptist Church was established in 1803. There are four Congregational and ten Lutheran churches.

The Garfield Memorial Church, named in honor of President Garfield, is situated on Vermont avenue, and is of the Christian or Campbellite faith. During the many years that Garfield served in Congress he was a regular attendant at the little chapel which formerly stood on the site of this church, and was deeply interested in the Campbellite society. When he was elected President the society determined to erect a new church, which should be the leading one of the faith in the country. The church was not finished at the time of the President's death. In the church is the pew formerly used by him and his family in the old chapel. It is draped in black, and is preserved by the society as a sacred relic.

The principal Catholic church is St. Patrick's, on G street northwest, which was dedicated in 1884. The original church, which stood on the

ALL SOULS' UNITARIAN CHURCH.

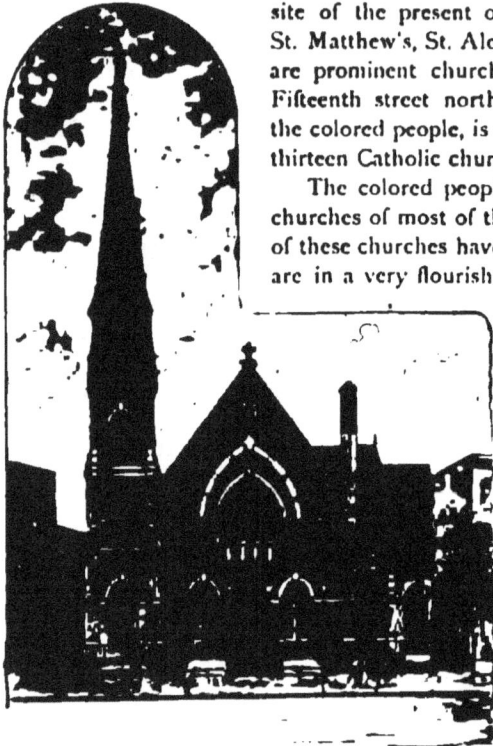

GARFIELD MEMORIAL CHURCH.

site of the present one, was erected in 1804. St. Matthew's, St. Aloysius', and St. Dominic's are prominent churches. St. Augustine's, on Fifteenth street northwest, which is used by the colored people, is one of the largest of the thirteen Catholic churches of the city.

The colored people are well supplied with churches of most of the denominations. Many of these churches have a large membership and are in a very flourishing condition. Some of the Baptist and Methodist church organizations are very liberally sustained, and have large and handsome edifices.

At the present time there is a colored population in Washington of nearly 50,000. When the city was first taken possession of by the government the colored people numbered about two thousand. They were mostly the slaves of the planters who owned the land on which the "Federal city" was located. For some years after this part of Maryland was designated as the District of Columbia the slaves were employed in agricultural labor, as a large number of the plantations remained as they were before the government occupied the district, and were cultivated with great care. In 1860 the colored population had increased to 14,316, but the greater number were freed people. As soon as the Civil War began hundreds of slaves from all the adjacent country came to Washington, and in a short time the colored population was very large. The government employed many of the colored people in various kinds of work pertaining to the organization and equipment of the army, and they were found to be very useful as laborers.

In 1861 the question of the emancipation of the slaves within the District of Columbia was agitated, and on the 16th of December of that

ST. PATRICK'S CATHOLIC CHURCH.

year a bill for that purpose was introduced in the Senate by Henry Wilson. The bill provided that all persons of African descent held to service in the District of Columbia should be liberated, and that slavery or involun tary servitude in the district should forever cease, except as a punishment for crime. The bill also provided that compensation should be given to the owners of the slaves, and the President was authorized to appoint, three commissioners to make an appraisement of the value of all the slaves liberated. One million dollars were appropriated by the bill to pay for the slaves. When the bill was called up for action in the Senate it was debated for some time with a good deal of earnestness and met with considerable opposition, but finally the Senate passed it on April 3, 1862. A week later it was debated by the House of Representatives. The House passed it without much difficulty, and on April 16 it was signed by President Lincoln and became a law. The President, in announcing to Congress his signature to the bill, took occasion to say that he had "never doubted the constitutional power of Congress to abolish slavery in the District of Columbia."

Commissioners were at once appointed to make the appraisement of the value of the slaves, and they engaged as an expert a well-known dealer in slaves from Baltimore, who was to fix the value of each slave liberated under the law. It is stated that "the slaveholders were required to pre- sent their petitions setting forth the names, ages, and estimated value of the slaves, with the nature of the title by which they were held. They were required to swear to the petitions, and to take and subscribe to what is known as the 'iron-clad oath' of allegiance and non-participation in the rebellion; but these oaths were not to be received by the commis- sioners as conclusive proof of the facts sworn to. The commissioners were required to invite and receive testimony in regard to the loyalty of the claimants, the validity of their titles, and to the value of the slaves."

The commissioners held their sessions in the old City Hall, now the District Court-House, and to this building "the claimants came with their troops of slaves" to be examined. Every day a large number of slaves were examined by the expert, under the supervision of the commissioners. The slaves were examined very carefully, and the expert even had most of them "open their mouths, in order that he might see their teeth. He considered sound teeth as an indication of sound health." Crowds of citizens were in attendance, and there was a good deal of merriment over the examinations. The liberated slaves were jubilant, and freely dis- played their characteristics, laughing and singing and making many funny speeches. The commissioners were in session about nine months, and

ST. AUGUSTINE'S CATHOLIC CHURCH.

disbursed during that time $914,942 as compensation to the slaveholders and for expenses. Compensation was allowed for 2989 slaves. There were one hundred and one slaves who were too old or too feeble to be worth anything, and compensation for them was refused. The highest sum allowed for a slave was $788, and the lowest $10.95. In the latter case the slave was an infant. The largest slaveholder in the district had sixty-nine slaves, and he received $17,771 for them.

In the act of emancipation there was a provision for the colonization in Hayti or Liberia of such of the liberated slaves as desired to emigrate to either of those countries, and the sum of $100,000 was appropriated to carry out the provision. Some effort was made towards colonization, but it was found that few of the freed people cared to leave the United States, and, therefore, this part of the act was of very little effect.

Since 1862 the colored people of the District of Columbia have annually celebrated "emancipation day," and the 16th of April is always made the occasion of great rejoicing.

CHAPTER XXIII.

HE city of Washington, unlike many other cities of the country, continually grows in beauty as it grows in greatness. With the increase in population and wealth, and the advancement of all its material interests, the city is steadily assuming grace and attractiveness. The great change that has taken place everywhere within its borders during the past ten years astonishes those who recollect it in the war period, and even for some time after the war, and who contrast it as it was then with the city of to-day,—the new and magnificent Washington, with its miles of smooth pavements on which carriage riding is delightful, its lovely small parks in every quarter filled in the spring and summer with rare plants and flowers, its elegant homes and business structures, and its appearance of thrift and enterprise. Thousands of people in different parts of the country who have not visited the city for a long time, and who remember with a feeling of repugnance its muddy, unpaved streets and generally dilapidated condition in years past, can hardly credit the current stories of the vast improvements that have been made. The improvements extended to all parts of Washington, and were so comprehensive and thorough that the transformation was complete. The national capital emerged from its stagnant, morbid condition, and became vigorous, progressive, and alert. Old forms and ideas were discarded, and there was developed a strong desire for all those things which make an admirable city, alike agreeable to its people and to strangers. Year by year much has been done in the line of progression, and those who now look on the city for the first time find it hard to believe that it ever was commonplace and unpleasant. In the days when it was struggling for an existence, and for a long while afterwards, the city had to meet the contempt and indifference of the people of the country, who seemed to have no feeling of pride in the progress and

296

THE ANCIENT SEWARD MANSION.

development of their seat of government, but, instead, had a feeling of jealousy, of anger and resentment, because it was located on the banks of the Potomac. Congress was always indifferent, and to this day has to be spurred by public opinion to give to the city the things it needs, and which should be given to it. But, in spite of all its drawbacks, the city has grown to be a capital of great beauty, and is constantly adding attractive features and acquiring fame throughout the land. It is the fashion now to admire Washington, and to talk and write of it in glowing terms. The tide of popular favor flows hitherward, and is likely so to flow for many a year.

It is believed that within a very short time Washington will become the social and intellectual, as well as the political, centre of the United

RESIDENCE OF JAMES A. GARFIELD WHILE A
MEMBER OF CONGRESS.

States. It possesses many advantages for persons of wealth and leisure, for those engaged in literary occupations, in art and in the professions, and every year these advantages are better appreciated and sought after. A social life not to be found elsewhere in America can be enjoyed even by men and women of moderate means. Interesting people from all parts of the country,—people of refinement, wide experience, and great ability,—who talk well, who have bright ideas, who are not fettered by local prejudice or illiberality, are constantly met with. The city is always full of people of national fame,—statesmen, jurists, authors, artists, scientists, great soldiers and sailors, explorers, inventors,—and in all the social gatherings they are to be seen and their society can be enjoyed. In this respect alone Washington is far in advance of all other cities of the country. A well-informed writer says: "Of course no one will be rash enough to assert that Washington must ever remain the national capital, but after the millions spent upon public buildings and improvements, and since annihilation of space by modern invention and discovery makes neighbors of all parts of the country, a change is not probable. Therefore, as years go by, Americans will look to Washington as the Mecca of thought in all phases. The bigger the republic grows the more necessary will a rallying point become. The North, South, East, and West will meet in Washington on common ground. Sectional egotism will disappear in the full light of national glory, and as to-day a trip to Europe is considered necessary to a liberal education, so, in a not distant to-morrow, a sojourn in Washington will be regarded as necessary to all who would have a thorough knowledge of this republic."

Washington is a favorite winter resort, and even in summer it is preferable to many cities of the North, as of late years it has been found that the heat was not near as great as in New York, Philadelphia, and even Boston. The records of the Weather Bureau show this conclusively. The city in summer is a mass of foliage, every street having rows of trees

RESIDENCE OF WILLIAM W. CORCORAN.

RESIDENCE OF JEROME NAPOLEON BONAPARTE.

which afford grateful shade, and at all times there are cooling breezes from the wooded hills which encircle the city. Newport and Saratoga in July and August are hotter and more uncomfortable than Washington, and this has been so thoroughly demonstrated that it is now quite the custom for many families who formerly visited those resorts to remain at home during the heated term, and make their vacation trips in the spring and fall. Washington is the only thoroughly sylvan city in the United States. Tree-planting is done by a regular, competent system, and no part of the city, not even the poorest quarter, is devoid of fine shade trees, which on many streets completely cover the walks. Rows of trees are planted on all new streets as soon as they are graded and open to travel, and the parking commission carefully watches the growth of the trees from month to month. In the parks, squares, and circles thousands of beautiful, aromatic plants and flowering shrubs are set out every spring by the government, and roses and all the favorite flowers are to be seen in great profusion in the public and private gardens. In the Capitol park and in the splendid gardens of the Department of Agriculture, from May to November, are to be found the choicest floral productions, embracing many varieties of foreign origin seldom, if ever, seen elsewhere in the country. All the parks and gardens are open to the public every day, comfortable seats are provided, and plenty of fountains supply pure drinking water.

At an early day a great park with nearly three thousand acres of land is to be laid out along the banks of the picturesque Rock creek, which flows north of the city. Massachusetts avenue will be extended across the creek, and will, doubtless, be lined with fine houses, and, beginning north of the extension, the park will be laid out for three miles. Rock creek is a beautiful stream. It winds among the wooded hills of the northern part of the District of Columbia, and has a great deal of romantic scenery. In the course of a few years the Rock creek park will be one of the loveliest and most attractive pleasure places to be found in the world.

There will also be another park of extensive area situated partly along the Potomac. The Potomac flats or marshes, which have been exceedingly unpleasant to look at and a great breeding-place for malaria, are being rapidly improved by the government, and ere long will be transformed into a beautiful park, with drives along the river bank for two miles. It is likely that when the improvement of the flats is completed the extensive grounds of the arsenal at Greenleaf's Point, where the waters of the Anacostia and Potomac mingle, will be given up for park purposes, and the quarters of the army removed to another location. If this is done, no city in the world will have such a public resort as this park along the Potomac. .From Greenleaf's Point there is a charming,

RESIDENCE OF ALEXANDER GRAHAM BELL.

RESIDENCE OF STILSON HUTCHINS.

far-reaching view. The course of the river can be traced for miles and miles, and on the sides come plainly in the range of vision the luxuriant lands of Maryland and Virginia, dotted here and there with farm-houses and villas. The park will include the grounds of the Washington Monument and the grounds of the mall, and, taken together, will enable one to drive or walk for hours on shaded roads, past lawns and gardens, with a background of river and wooded hills, and all without leaving the central part of the city very far behind. The outlook then from the south windows of the White House will be even more pleasing than it is at present, as it will embrace that portion of the park laid out on the river bank.

It has been very cleverly said, " Think of the transformation that

Washington has undergone since the war! To-day it is the only well-paved city in this country. So clean and smooth are its streets that pedestrians walk on their asphalt in preference to the brick or stone sidewalks. Bicycles abound in consequence, and the lovers of driving and riding heave a sigh of relief at the absence of the noise, holes, and cobblestones peculiar to our great towns, hideous facts that make exercise on wheels or in the saddle an agony instead of a pleasure. Magnificent private dwellings line the West End of the capital; still better houses are about to be built. At last it begins to look as though the student, the artist, the statesman, the retired trader, the man and woman of the world may find a place on this continent where escape from the din of money-grabbing is possible, where culture can shake hands with genius in all forms, where merit, not money or grandfathers, is the entrée to society, where persons of leisure may hobnob with other persons of leisure and not be regarded as public nuisances, and where the stock market is not the chief end of man. If ever a people needed to escape from themselves and cultivate repose it is ourselves. If ever this repose is acquired it will be in Washington. So convinced have some Americans become of these probabilities as to have metamorphosed the national capital. People of

RESIDENCE OF MRS. M. T. DAHLGREN.

RESIDENCE OF GENERAL ANDERSON.

fortune are making it their home, in order to
enjoy life under the most favorable circumstances. For similar reasons people of mod-
erate and settled incomes are lured there also. Comparative poverty is
no badge of disgrace where ladies and gentlemen serve the government
for moderate salaries, where retired army and navy officers rank above
the wealthiest of nouveaux riches while living modestly on half pay."

Taxation is light in Washington as compared with most cities of its
size, particularly those of the West. Real estate is taxed $1.50 per $100.
House rents are much lower than in New York and other large cities.
Though the climate is by no means perfect, the winter is a great deal
milder than in the Northern cities, and the spring is a month earlier.
The splendid public markets, five in number, all occupying capacious
brick buildings constructed with every convenience, are without a rival in
the country. They are filled to overflowing with good marketing. The
meats are the very best, and they are cheaper than in New York, and fish,
game, vegetables, and fruits are to be had in profusion at reasonable
prices. Washington is situated in the centre of one of the finest agricultural districts in the United States. More wheat to the acre can be raised
in this vicinity than in any Western state, and all kinds of vegetables
grow in these fertile lands with remarkable exuberance. The shad and

RESIDENCE OF LIEUT. W. H. EMORY.

herring caught in the Potomac within sight of the city are noted for their lusciousness. Forty miles down the river are the famous ducking shores, where from November to April vast numbers of canvas-backs, black- and red-heads, and whistle-wings feed on the great beds of wild celery which there abound. The forests of Virginia, within a few miles of Washington, across the Potomac, are filled in the autumn with wild turkeys, which are shot by thousands for the city markets, and the bottom-lands along the river supply great quantities of quail and other game birds. On the upper Potomac the fishing cannot be excelled. No large city is so favored in this respect, and, in consequence, the food supplies are plentiful and cheap.

THE BLAINE MANSION.

The libraries and museums of the city afford advantages to students and professional men and women which few cities can present. The wonderfully comprehensive National Library, with its half million of books upon all subjects, is open to the public daily, and every facility is given to those who desire to use the valuable literary and historical collections. Besides this library there are great collections of books on special subjects in all the government departments, and most of these can be freely used by the public. The National Museum opens its doors to every one, and students of natural history have the privilege of inspecting one of the finest and largest collections of natural and industrial products to be found in the world. The museum of agriculture and of medical objects, the museums of war and naval implements, the museum of the signal office, are all admirably arranged and very complete for purposes of study and research. The Corcoran Gallery of Art has the only complete set of casts of antique statuary in the United States, and has also many famous original statues and paintings. The schools and colleges of the city are equal to any. A writer says, " Comparatively low rents, good climate,—as climates go, —good markets, good roads, good libraries, good company. What other American city can show as good a record ?"

The improvement of what is known as the West End is one of the astonishing features of the sudden and grand development of Washington. This extensive region, comprising an area of about five miles, now covered with costly and beautiful residences, was but a few years ago only hillocks and swamps, which could be had almost for the asking. Acres and acres of it were held by people who despaired of ever disposing of their lands. No one dreamed that it would eventually contain the finest mansions in the city, and be held at a large sum per foot. Rude cabins, inhabited by colored people, dotted the region here and there, but there were no graded streets or marks of improvement. In the spring of 1872 there was a "boom" in real estate, caused by the beginning of the vast improvements under the direction of the Board of Public Works, at the head of which was Governor Shepherd. Syndicates were organized by speculators

RESIDENCE OF JUSTICE CHARLES P. JAMES.

to obtain control of all the desirable properties in the city. One known as the "California Syndicate" purchased for a small sum squares and large blocks of land in the neighborhood of what is now Dupont Circle ; another purchased land around Iowa Circle ; and others acquired tracts in other sections of the West End. Much of the land was obtained for ten, twenty, and twenty-five cents per foot, and in no case was more than seventy-five cents per foot paid, and this was for land that had been somewhat improved. The square on which the residence of the English legation is now located was purchased by the speculators for thirty-five cents per foot, and shortly afterwards sold to the English government for fifty cents.

Shepherd began at once to improve the West End. The hills were cut down, and the earth used to fill in the swamps. Streets and avenues were laid out, and everything necessary was done to make the region a desirable part of the city for the residences of wealthy people. When

RESIDENCE OF BELDEN NOBLE.

the English government, in 1875, erected its splendid legation residence a great impetus was given to building in the West End, and, in rapid succession, fine mansions were erected over its territory. The price of land advanced constantly. One dollar per foot was demanded, then two dollars, then three, and at present very little of this section can be bought for less than five dollars, and some of it is held at a much higher price. The speculators who first invested in these waste lands realized great profits, and others who afterwards

RESIDENCE OF MRS. F. H. PLUMMER.

took advantage of the "boom" made fortunes by shrewd purchases.

During the past five years large sums have been invested by Northern capitalists in the West End, and also in other quarters of the city, as it is believed that the future of the national capital is assured, and that it

RESIDENCE OF SAMUEL SHELLABARGER.

will within a short period become a very large and flourishing city. The population increases rapidly, because the attractions of the city appeal not only to politicians and those connected with the government, but to people of culture and refinement who find in it congenial surroundings and associations. The improvement of the city by the erection of beautiful houses and business edifices goes on steadily, and every year there are many additions to the number. It is a well-known fact that in no other city of the United States can there be seen such a great variety of elegant, unique residences and so little sameness and monotony in architecture as Washington displays on every prominent street and avenue. If the desire for diversity and novelty prevailing at present is maintained with the city's growth and expansion, it will eventually have an extensive fame as a capital of singularly pleasing and attractive architecture.

Before the era of improvement Washington had a number of stately mansions, mostly constructed after the Southern style, but in general its architecture, both in the resident and business sections, was commonplace and quite often very mean. It is related of the first "Queen Anne" house erected in the city that " it was for a commodore who knew more of ships and guns than of houses, and so the architects were told to give their fancy rein, and work out some new and pleasing structure without bothering the future occupant with details. The house was built, and did not please the conservative Washington of that day. The owner was influenced by the criticisms of his neighbors, and was much troubled and dispirited. He had been imposed upon by some new-fangled thing which was laughed at, and he knew not whether to live in it or abandon it. The momentous question was settled by visiting Boston friends who pronounced the house 'quite too lovely for anything.' That was sufficient. If Boston approved, who dare dispute? The stern face of the commodore relaxed, and the architects were congratulated. What might have been the character of new Washington if that first ' Queen Anne' had remained under the seal of condemnation, it is distressing to contemplate."

RESIDENCE OF GARDNER G. HUBBARD.

RESIDENCES OF GENERAL DRUM AND COMMODORE ENGLISH.

While the " Queen Anne" style is seen to a considerable extent in the fashionable quarter and elsewhere, there are also many other styles, or artistic combinations, embracing numerous forms of the antique and mediæval, most of which make very attractive houses. Some of the latest houses erected have a good deal of ornamentation produced by means of brick-work. Bricks are constructed for the purpose after special designs. Large bricks, fan-shaped, octagonal, and in other forms, are set in the walls and in the arches over the windows and doors, giving variety and richness, and some very fine effects are produced in this way. Most of the houses, large or small, in the city are constructed of brick. There are many brickyards in this vicinity, and a superior sort of brick is made in them, the clay of the region being particularly adapted to brickmaking. The brick has a bright red color, very pleasing to the eye. There is some use of brownstone, sandstone, and the peculiar mottled greenstone found

in Pennsylva-
nia, but the ma-
jority of the
new houses are
of brick. Mar-
ble is seldom
used.

Several ele-
gant houses
have lately been
constructed
after the Mexi-
can style. These
are two stories
in height, and
have a large
interior court,
with balconies
around the

RESIDENCE OF EX-SENATOR STEWART,
KNOWN AS "STEWART CASTLE."

court, into which the rooms in the second story
open. It is a rather unique style of architecture
for this latitude, but seems to be growing in
favor. A few years ago there was a decided tendency to build large,
massive houses, but of late smaller houses are built even by the wealthiest
people. These small houses are given every form of ornament considered
to be proper and tasteful, and many of them are notable for exquisite
beauty.

• There is very little doubt that the West End and all the contiguous
territory, which has been selected by common consent for the residences
of wealthy and fashionable people, will eventually become a very magnificent section. A vast sum has already been expended upon it, and on
all its streets and avenues there are scores of artistic and costly houses,
and new ones are being erected every season. It has a good deal of land
yet to be improved, and can accommodate many more houses of the
better sort, and these houses, there is every reason to believe, will, before
ten years have rolled away, cover every available space of the extensive
region. In that case, Washington can claim one of the grandest resident
sections in the world, and one that will have a distinctive grandeur. The
seal of fashion has been deeply set on this section, and there is no possi-
bility that it will ever be less fashionable than it is at present. Other
parts of the city may become in time noted for elegant residences, as, for

instance, a certain portion of Capitol Hill, which has already begun to have numerous beautiful homes, and which is preferred by some for various reasons; but, however large may be the growth and development elsewhere in this way, the West End is likely to retain its pre-eminence as the quarter for the world of wealth and fashion, whose votaries now so numerously inhabit its hundreds of splendid mansions.

RESIDENCE OF GEORGE BANCROFT

The West End has many broad streets and avenues all paved with concrete, and within the section are the most prominent public squares and circles adorned with statues of America's distinguished soldiers. Connecticut avenue, which extends from Lafayette Park to the northern limits of the city, is the main thoroughfare, and has a roadway one hundred and thirty feet wide.

RESIDENCE OF EX-SENATOR GEORGE H. PENDLETON.

RESIDENCE OF SENATOR J. DONALD CAMERON.

Massachusetts, Rhode Island, New Hampshire, and Vermont avenues also traverse the section. From Dupont Circle, which may be said to bound the extreme western part of the West End, ten streets and avenues diverge, and from the other circles and squares there are numerous diverging thoroughfares. The streets are laid out at right angles, as they are in all the other parts of the city, and the avenues cross them diagonally. Where the streets and avenues intersect are triangular lots, which permit of the erection of oddly-shaped houses. On many of these triangles one will see some of the most beautiful forms of all the West End architecture—quaint, even fantastic structures, which give a measureless amount of picturesqueness to the section.

The illustrations presented in this chapter include many of the notable residences of the West End and of other localities. The leading styles of architecture are given. It is not proposed to describe the residences, as the illustrations clearly show the architectural designs, and descriptions seem unnecessary.

There are numerous houses in Washington of historical interest. On Fifteenth and one-half street (Lafayette Square) is the ancient house occupied by Secretary of State William H. Seward at the time the attempt on his life was made by Payne, one of the conspirators in the Lincoln assassination. Previous to its occupancy by Secretary Seward it had been used as a club-house for some time, and in front of it General Daniel E. Sickles shot and killed Philip Barton Key as he stepped from its door one evening in 1859. Sickles was tried for murder in the District Court-House and acquitted.

The residence now owned and occupied by William W. Corcoran, at the corner of H and Seventeenth streets, fronting Lafayette Park, was occupied by Daniel Webster for a number of years. At the rear of the house is a large garden containing a fine collection of plants and fruit-trees.

During most of the time that the lamented President Garfield was a member of Congress he resided in the house at the corner of I and Thirteenth streets, near Franklin Park. It is a plain brick structure.

The Van Ness mansion, at the foot of Seventeenth street, near the Potomac river, is now fast going to ruin. It was designed and con-structed by Latrobe three-quarters of a century ago, and was a famous house in the early years of the city. Within its walls there have been many brilliant assemblages. General John P. Van Ness was one of the notable men of Washington, and his wife, Marcia Burns Van Ness, was a leader in society for many years. The cabin of David Burns, the father of Mrs. Van Ness, is also standing near the Van Ness mansion, but is in the last stages of decay.

RESIDENCE OF GENERAL M. C. MEIGS.

RESIDENCE OF CHARLES T. MURRAY.

On New York avenue, at the corner of Eighteenth street, is the ancient Octagon House, erected in 1798 by Colonel John Tayloe, a wealthy Virginia planter who acquired a large amount of property in Washington, and resided in the city for a number of years. His wife was the daughter of Governor Ogle, of Maryland. Tayloe had an income of about $80,000 a year, one-half of which he expended in the purchase of land in the District of Columbia. He was considered the wealthiest man in the district. He died in the Octagon House in 1828, and his widow died in 1855.

The Duddington Manor-House, on North Carolina avenue (Capitol Hill), once the residence of Daniel Carroll, still remains as a memento of the past age. The descendants of Carroll have occupied the house many years. It is a stately building, arranged somewhat like the old mansions of England. Extensive grounds covered with noble trees surround the house.

The fine, spacious mansion erected in 1805 by Joel Barlow, the poet, politician, and wealthy merchant, is standing on Kalorama Hill, just beyond the northern boundary of Washington. Barlow lived here until he went abroad as Minister to France. He never returned to America, and his mansion for a time was occupied by the family of Commodore Decatur. On the grounds is a tomb in which reposed the remains of Decatur until they were removed to Philadelphia in 1846. An illustration of the mansion is given on page 45.

On Meridian Hill, Joaquin Miller has erected a log cabin for his residence. Here the poet of the Sierras performs his literary work and enjoys life after his own fashion. From Meridian Hill a charming view of the city of Washington can be obtained.

Georgetown has a number of old mansions once occupied by families prominent in the early years of the district. Most of these mansions have spacious grounds filled with majestic trees and flowering plants. The town in the first part of the century was noted for its wealthy, aristocratic families, who lived gayly and luxuriously " in fine old English style." The opulent planters of the adjacent region usually spent the winter in the town, and balls, parties, and dinners were given frequently

RESIDENCE OF D. R. MCKEE.

through the season. The annual races in the vicinity of Georgetown were always attended by the prominent people. An English traveller wrote, in 1803, as follows: "In November in each year there are horse-races at the capital of America. I happened to arrive just at this time, on horseback, at Georgetown, which is about two miles from the race-ground, and at an early hour proceeded to the turf. Though the day was raw, cold, and threatening to rain or snow, there were abundance of ladies decorated as if for a ball. In this year Congress was summoned early by President Jefferson upon the contemplated purchase of Louisiana. Many scores of American legislators, who are allowed six dollars a day besides their travelling expenses, went on foot from the Capitol, above four English miles, to attend the sport; nay, it is an indisputable fact that the houses of Congress adjourned at an early hour to indulge the members for this purpose. It rained during the races, and thus the law-makers of the country were driven into the booths, and thereby compelled to eat and pay for what was there called a dinner, while their contem-plated meal remained untouched at their respective boarding-houses."

Opposite Georgetown, in the Potomac river, is Analostan Island, where General John Mason and his descendants resided for more than half a century. The island is about seventy acres in extent, and for some years

RESIDENCES OF MRS. B. B. FRENCH AND W. S. LINCOLN.

RESIDENCE OF NATHANIEL WILSON.

has been used as a pleasure resort. General Mason's house, which was erected in the latter part of the eighteenth century, was destroyed during the Civil War. It was situated on an eminence fifty feet above the river, and commanded a charming view of Washington and all the surrounding country. In his " Historical Sketches," published in 1830, Jonathan Elliot says that "the house, which you approach through a fine avenue of trees, is extensive, with a number of convenient buildings attached. Its interior is finished with taste and in a costly style. The garden is kept in fine order; ornamental trees, shrubs, and rare plants are a source of attraction to the botanist, whilst the kitchen garden affords excellent roots of the choicest varieties. The south side of the island is substantially walled and dotted with neat white cottages for servants."

General Mason was famed for his profuse hospitality, and his picturesque island was constantly visited by the select society of Washington and Georgetown. He entertained many distinguished Europeans. He was an ardent agriculturalist, and always kept the island in a high state of cultivation. Some cotton was raised, and, among other things, a species of maize was cultivated, the deep purple leaves of which were

RESIDENCE OF DAVID FERGUSON.

used as a dye. Some of the seeds of this maize were carried from the island to France and presented to the Empress Josephine, "who sowed them with her own hand in the garden of Malmaison, where they gave a luxuriant produce."

In 1816 a little book was published in Paris with this title : "A Chorographical and Statistical description of the District of Columbia, the Seat of the General Government of the United States." The book was written by D. B. Warden, and dedicated to Mrs. George Washington Parke Custis. The author says in the preface that he had occupied his leisure hours at Washington "in examining the interesting objects of that magnificent situation," and that he thought "a publication of this kind is now called for not only by citizens of the United States, but also by foreigners, who, from motives of curiosity or interest, seek minute information concerning the present state of the American metropolis." Warden's book was the first ever written about the District of Columbia, and, although it does not give much "minute information" of value at this time, it has some interesting statements.

Warden says : "About a mile beyond Georgetown, on the Potomac river, there is a cannon foundry belonging to Mr. Foxhall, a native of England, the machinery of which was erected by a Scotsman of the name of Glasgow. There are two boring-mills situated near each other. In one, five cannons are bored at the same time ; in the other, three. The streams which move the machinery are small, but the water falls to great advantage over an overshot wheel of twenty-nine feet in diameter. By the aid of dams, which receive rain water, there is a constant supply during the summer. About thirty workmen are employed, chiefly emigrants from Europe. Foremen have two dollars; moulders, one dollar and a half; and common workmen, two-thirds of a dollar per day. The iron ore, of an excellent quality, is brought from the banks of the Potomac, near Harper's Ferry. It is rare that a gun bursts in firing it with a double charge. A cannon was lately cast at this foundry, of a hundred pound ball, to which was given the name of Columbiad. It requires two days to make a cannon, and two to bore it. The price is fifty pounds currency per ton. The profits of this establishment are very considerable."

In describing Georgetown, Warden states that "the houses, chiefly of brick, have a neat appearance. Several were built before the streets were

JOAQUIN MILLER'S LOG CABIN ON MERIDIAN HILL.

21

formed, which gave rise to an observation from a French lady, that Georgetown had houses without streets, and Washington streets without houses." It is stated that there were two bridges over Rock creek, which divides Georgetown from Washington, and that the one nearest to its mouth had three arches, and was a hundred and thirty-five feet in length and thirty-six feet in breadth. The other, at a distance of six hundred and fifty yards, was supported by piles two hundred and eighty feet long and eighteen feet wide. There was a daily communication between Georgetown and Alexandria by means of a packet-boat.

About five miles from Washington is the quaint, old-fashioned town of Bladensburg, Maryland, which was founded in 1750, and named after Thomas Bladen, who was governor of Maryland in 1742. Before the Revolutionary war it had considerable commerce, and many vessels laden with tobacco sailed from its wharves down the Anacostia. For a number of years it was a fashionable summer resort, as it had a mineral spring reputed to be efficacious in the cure of numerous diseases, and throngs of people went to drink of the water. Near the town the British troops defeated the Americans, August 24, 1814, and then invaded Washington. During the first half of the century Bladensburg was noted as a duelling ground, and on its fields many prominent men have fought to satisfy their "honor." The memorable duel between Commodore Decatur and Commodore Barron took place near the ancient cemetery of the town, on March 22, 1820. Decatur was fatally wounded, and died that night at his residence in Washington. For nearly thirty years no duels have been fought in this locality. The old town long since lost its commerce, its thrift and enterprise. It has a picturesque location, and is one of the pleasant environs of Washington.

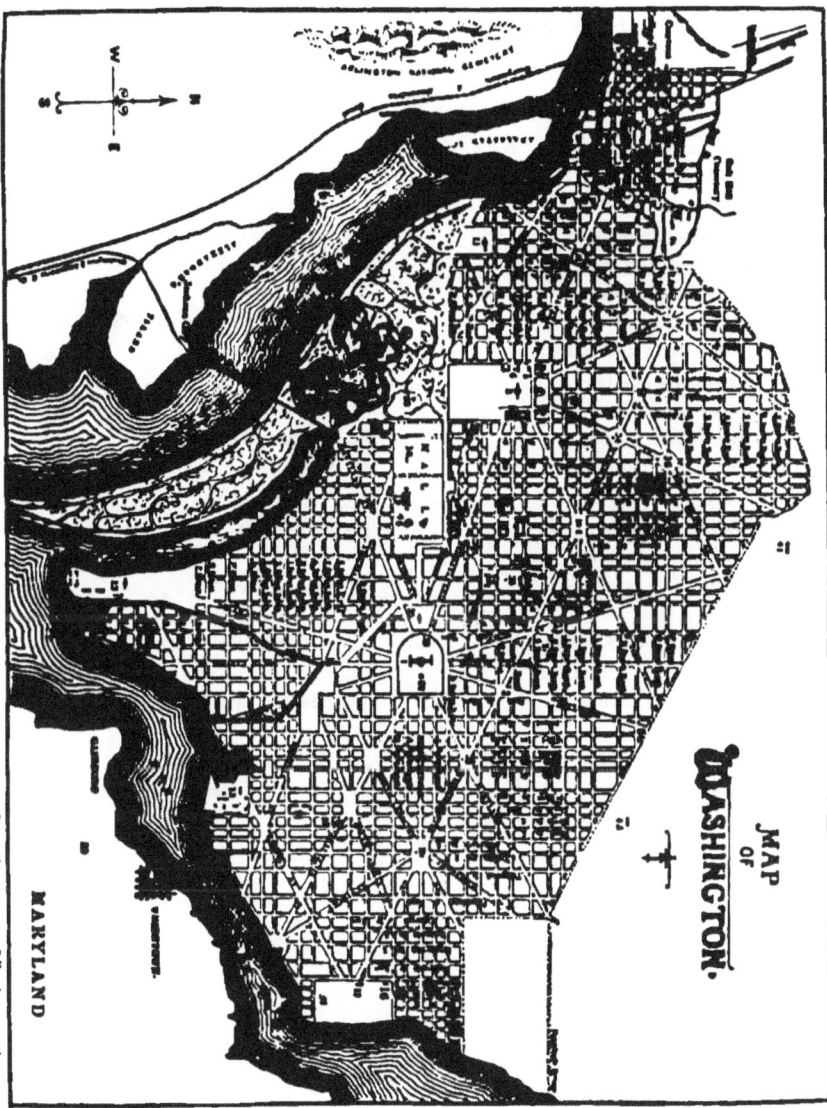

MAP
OF
Washington.

MARYLAND

(For reference, see following page.)

REFERENCES TO MAP OF WASHINGTON.

1. The Capitol.
2. White House.
3. Department of State.
4. Treasury Department.
5. War Department.
6. Navy Department.
7. Patent Office
8. Post Office Department.
9 Department of Justice.
10. Department of Agriculture.
11. Naval Observatory.
12. United States Arsenal.
13. Navy Yard.
14. Marine Corps Barracks.
15. District Court-House.
16. District Jail.
17. City Asylum.
18. Mount Vernon Square.
19. Smithsonian Institution.
20. Washington Monument.
21. Washington Circle.
22. Statue of Washington.
23. Lafayette Park.
24. Corcoran Gallery of Art.

25. National Botanical Garden.
26. Congressional Cemetery.
27. Naval Hospital.
28. Lincoln Park.
29. Rawlins Square.
30. Scott Square.
31. Government Printing-Office.
32. Greene Square.
33. Naval Monument.
34. Thomas Circle.
35. Judiciary Square.
36. McPherson Square.
37. Dupont Circle.
38. Iowa Circle.
39. Government Hospital for Insane.
40. Center Market.
41. Howard University.
42. National Deaf-Mute College.
43. Bureau of Engraving and Printing.
44. New Pension Building.
45. Army Medical Museum.
46. National Museum.
47. Potomac River Park.

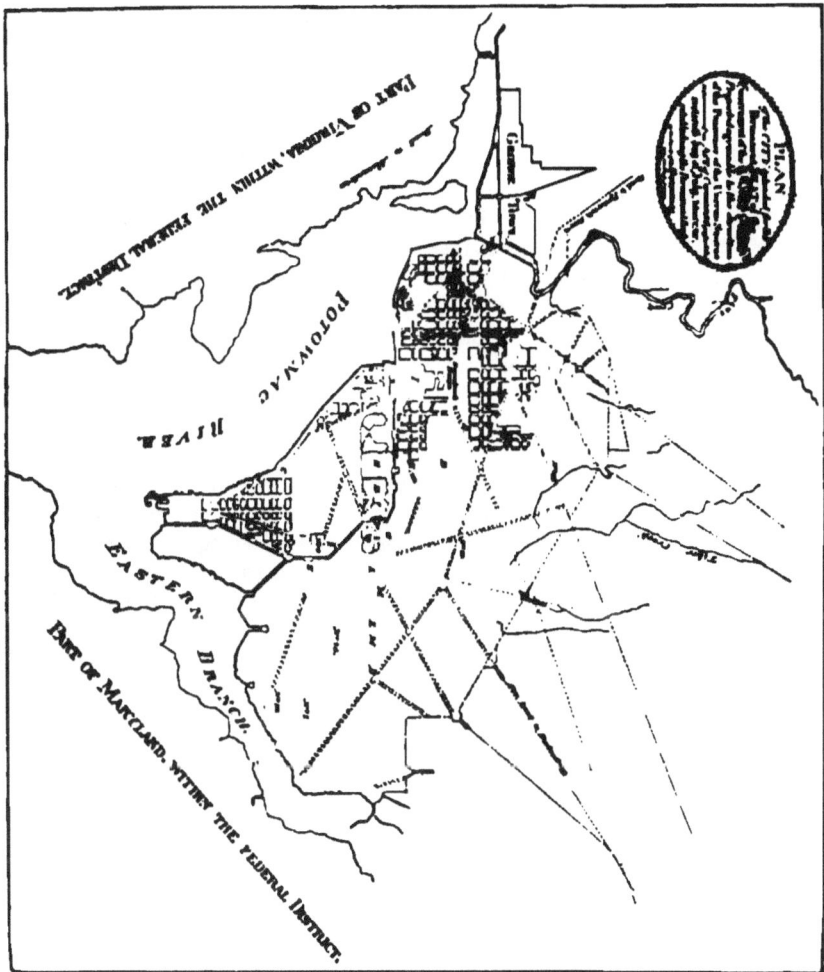

L'ENFANT'S ORIGINAL PLAN OF WASHINGTON.

(For reference and observation, see following pages.)

L'ENFANT'S PLAN OF WASHINGTON.

HE original plan of the city of Washington, as drawn by Pierre Charles L'Enfant in 1791, is presented on the preceding page. For particulars in reference to L'Enfant, see page 33.

"Observations explanatory of the plan" were made by L'Enfant, as follows:

"I. The positions for the different grand edifices and for the several grand squares or areas of different shapes, as they are laid down, were first determined on the most advantageous ground, commanding the most extensive prospects and the better susceptible of such improvements as the various intents of the several objects may require.

"II. Lines or avenues of direct communications have been devised to connect the separate and most distant objects with the principal, and to preserve through the whole a reciprocity of sight at the same time. Attention has been paid to the passing of those leading avenues over the most favorable ground for prospect and convenience.

"III. North and South lines, intersected by others running due East and West, make the distribution of the city into streets, squares, etc., and those lines have been so combined as to meet at certain given points with those divergent avenues, so as to form on the spaces first determined the different squares and areas, which are all proportional in magnitude to the number of avenues leading to them.

"Breadth of the streets. Every grand transverse avenue, and every principal divergent one, such as the communication from the President's House to the Congress House, etc., are 160 feet in breadth, and are thus divided: 10 feet of pavement on each side; 30 feet of gravel walk, planted with trees, on each side; 80 feet in the middle for carriage way. The other streets are of the following dimensions, viz.: those leading to public buildings or markets, 130 feet; others, 110 and 90 feet.

"In order to execute the above plan, Mr. Ellicott drew a true meridianal line by celestial observation, which passes through the area intended

326

for the Congress House; this line he crossed by another due East and West, which passes through the same area. These lines were accurately measured, and made the bases on which the whole plan was executed. He ran all the lines by a transit instrument, and determined the acute angles by actual measurement, and left nothing to the uncertainty of the compass."

L'Enfant noted the following references to sites, designated on the plan by letters:

" A. The equestrian figure of George Washington, a monument voted, in 1783, by the late Continental Congress.

" B. An historic column. Also intended for a mile or itinerary column, from whose station (a mile from the Federal House) all distances of places through the continent are to be calculated.

" C. A naval itinerary column, proposed to be erected to celebrate the first rise of a Navy, and to stand a ready monument to consecrate its progress and achievements.

" D. This site is for a church intended for national purposes, such as public prayer, thanksgivings, funeral orations, etc., and assigned to the special use of no particular sect or denomination, but equally open to all. It will be likewise shelter for such monuments as were voted by the late Continental Congress for those heroes who fell in the cause of liberty, and for such others as may hereafter be decreed by the voice of a grateful nation.

" E. Five grand fountains, intended with a constant spout of water. There are within the limits of the city above 25 good springs of excellent water, abundantly supplied in the dryest season of the year.

" F. Grand cascade formed of the water from the sources of the Tiber.

" G. Public walk, being a square of 1200 feet, through which carriages may ascend to the upper square of the Federal House.

" H. Grand avenue, 400 feet in width, and about one mile in length, bordered with gardens, ending in a slope from the houses on each side. This avenue leads to the monument, A, and connects with the

" I. President's Park and the

" K. Well-improved field, being a part of the walk from the President's House, of about 1800 feet in breadth and three-fourths of a mile in length.

" L. Around this square and all along the

" M. Avenue from the two bridges to the Federal House the pavement on each side will pass under an arched way, under whose cover shops will be most conveniently and agreeably situated. This street is 160 feet in breadth and a mile long."

L'Enfant says, " The squares colored yellow, being fifteen in number, are proposed to be divided among the several states in the Union, for each of them to improve or subscribe a sum additional to the value of the land for that purpose, and the improvements around the squares to be completed in a limited time.   The centre of each square will admit of statues, columns, obelisks, or any other ornaments such as the different states may choose to erect to perpetuate not only the memory of such individuals whose counsels or military achievements were conspicuous in giving liberty and independence to this country, but also those whose usefulness hath rendered them worthy of general imitation to invite the youth of succeeding generations to tread in the paths of those sages or heroes whom their country has thought proper to celebrate.   The situation of these squares is such that they are the most advantageously and reciprocally seen from each other, and as equally distributed over the whole city district, and connected by spacious avenues round the grand Federal improvements, and as contiguous to them and at the same time as equally distant from each other as circumstances would admit.   The settlements round these squares must soon become connected.   This mode of taking possession of and improving the whole district at first must leave to posterity a grand idea of the patriotic interest which promoted it.

   " The squares colored red are intended for the use of all religious denominations, on which they are to erect places of worship, and are proposed to be allotted to them in the manner as those colored yellow to the different states of the Union, but no burying-ground will be admitted within the limits of the city, an appropriation being intended for that purpose without.   There are a number of squares or areas unappropriated, and in situations proper for colleges and academies, and of which every society whose object is national may be accommodated.

   " Every lot deep-colored red, with green plots, designates some of the situations which command the most agreeable prospects, and which are the best calculated for spacious houses and gardens, such as may accommodate foreign ministers, etc.

   " Every house in the city will stand square on the streets, and every lot, even those of the divergent avenues, will run square with their fronts, which on the most acute angle will not measure less than fifty-six feet, and many will be above one hundred and forty feet."

   The figures on the plan refer to the sites for the public buildings, and to certain squares, etc., concerning which some details were given.

LADIES' RECEPTION ROOM

EASTERN LOBBY

VICE PRESIDENT'S ROOM

COAT ROOM

SOUTHERN LOBBY

THE MARBLE ROOM

SENATOR'S LOBBY

V. P.

L. C.   C. C.   N. C.

COAT ROOM

PRESIDENT'S ROOM

WESTERN LOBBY

V. P., Vice-President.   S., Secretary.   D., Doorkeeper.   L. C., Legislative Clerk.   C. C., Chief Clerk.

N. C., Minute Clerk.   S., Sergeant-at-Arms.   R., Official Reporters.

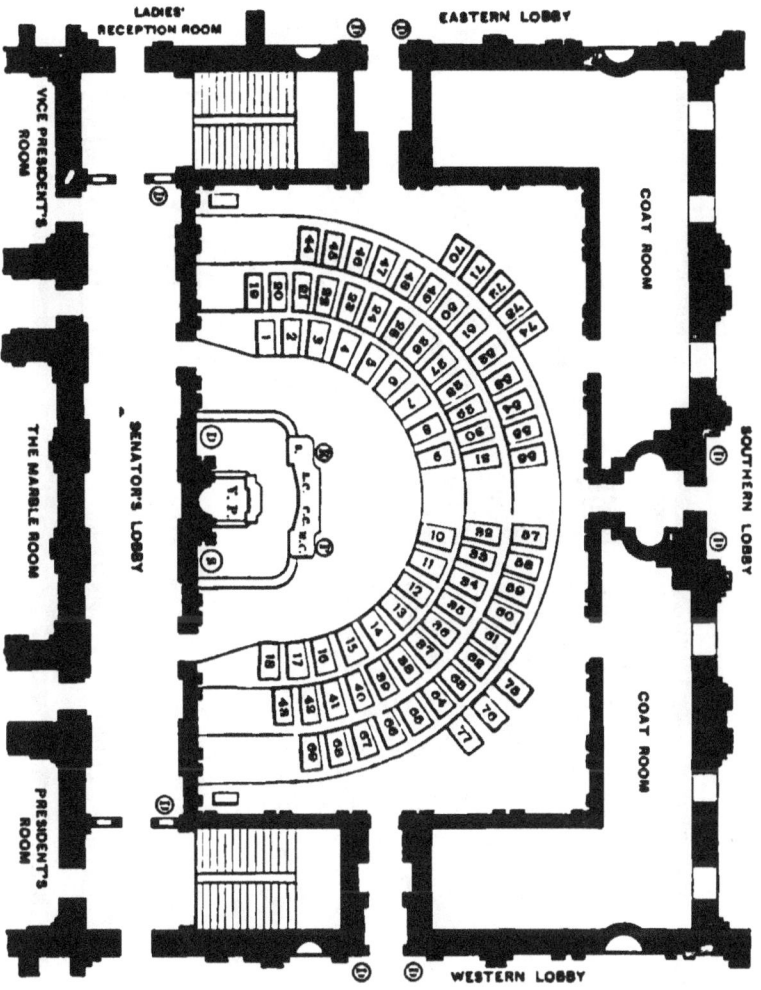

PLAN OF THE SENATE CHAMBER.

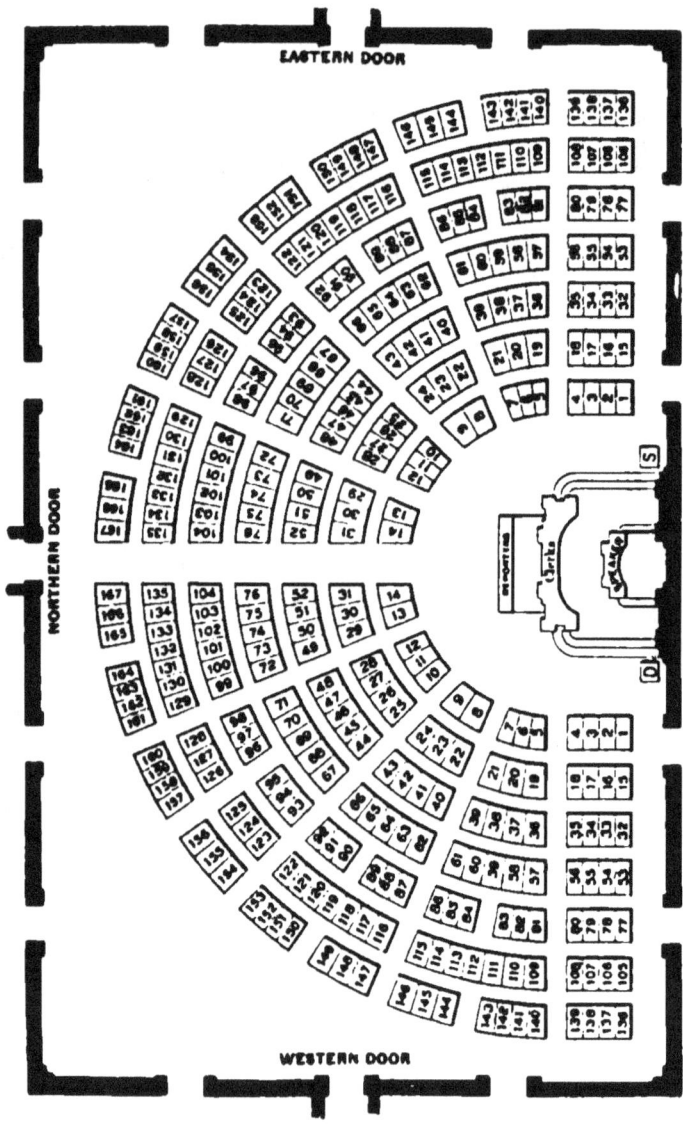

PLAN OF THE HALL OF THE HOUSE OF REPRESENTATIVES.   S., Sergeant-at-Arm.   D., Doorkeeper.

THE PUBLIC SERVICE.

THE following is a list of the officials, clerks, and employés in the various departments of the government, together with the salary attached to each office. There are four classes of graded clerks. The clerks of the first class have salaries of $1200; of the second class, $1400; of the third class, $1600; of the fourth class, $1800. Ungraded clerks have salaries from $700 to $1000. The Cabinet Ministers and the heads of the divisions of the War and Navy departments are not given in the list.

DEPARTMENT OF STATE.

First assistant secretary of state, $4500; two assistant secretaries of state, $3500 each; chief clerk, $2500; five chiefs of bureau and one translator, $2100 each; twelve clerks of class 4, four clerks of class 3, three clerks of class 2, ten clerks of class 1; four clerks, $1000 each; ten clerks, $900 each; one superintendent of the watch, $1000; one assistant, $800; chief engineer, $1200; assistant engineer, $1000.

TREASURY DEPARTMENT.

Secretary's Office.—Chief clerk and ex-officio superintendent of the Treasury building, $2700; stenographer to the secretary, $2000; one chief of division of warrants, estimates, and appropriations, and one chief of division of customs, $2750 each; one assistant chief of division of warrants, estimates, and appropriations, $2400; six chiefs of division, $2500 each; two assistant chiefs of division, $2100 each; six assistant chiefs of division, $2000 each; two disbursing clerks, $2500 each; government actuary, under control of Treasury Department, $2000; forty clerks of class 4, twenty-five clerks of class 3, twenty-one clerks of class 2, fifteen clerks of class 1; eleven clerks, $1000 each; fifty female clerks, $900 each; superintendent of the Treasury building, $300; one captain of the watch, $1400; one engineer, $1400; one assistant engineer, $1000; one machinist and gas-fitter, $1200; one storekeeper, $1200.

Supervising Architect's Office.—Supervising architect, $4500; assistant and chief clerk, $2500; photographer, $2000; one principal clerk, $2000; two clerks of class 3, three clerks of class 1 ; one clerk, $900.

First Comptroller's Office.—First comptroller of the Treasury, $5000; deputy comptroller, $2700; four chiefs of division, $2100 each; five clerks of class 4, ten clerks of class 3, ten clerks of class 2, seven clerks of class 1 ; four clerks, $1000 each ; seven clerks, $900 each.

Second Comptroller's Office.—Second comptroller of the Treasury, $5000; deputy comptroller, $2700; five chiefs of division, $2100 each ; eight clerks of class 4, twelve clerks of class 3, thirteen clerks of class 2, twelve clerks of class 1 ; three clerks, $1000 each ; nine clerks, $900 each.

Commissioner of Customs.—Commissioner of customs, $4000; deputy commissioner, $2250; two chiefs of division, $2100 each ; two clerks of class 4, four clerks of class 3, ten clerks of class 2, nine clerks of class 1 ; three clerks, $1000 each.

First Auditor's Office.—First auditor of the Treasury, $3600; deputy auditor, $2250; four chiefs of division, $2000 each ; seven clerks of class 4, nine clerks of class 3, ten clerks of class 2, sixteen clerks of class 1 ; three clerks, $1000 each ; three copyists and two counters, $900 each.

Second Auditor's Office.—Second auditor, $3600; deputy auditor, $2250; five chiefs of division, $2000 each ; nine clerks of class 4, twenty-nine clerks of class 3, additional to one clerk of class 3 as disbursing clerk, $200; sixty clerks of class 2, twenty-three clerks of class 1 ; eight clerks, $1000 each ; twelve additional clerks of class 1.

Third Auditor's Office.—Third auditor, $3600; deputy auditor, $2250; five chiefs of division, $2000 each ; six clerks of class 4, sixteen clerks of class 3, fifty-seven clerks of class 2, forty-three clerks of class 1 ; seven clerks, $1000 each ; nine clerks, $900 each.

Fourth Auditor's Office.—Fourth auditor, $3600; deputy auditor, $2250; three chiefs of division, $2000 each; two clerks of class 4, fourteen clerks of class 3, eight clerks of class 2, nine clerks of class 1 ; three clerks, $1000 each; five clerks at $900 each.

Fifth Auditor's Office.—Fifth auditor, $3600; deputy auditor, $2250; two chiefs of division, $2000 each; two clerks of class 4, five clerks of class 3, four clerks of class 2, five clerks of class 1 ; two clerks at $1000 each ; three clerks, $900 each.

Sixth Auditor's Office.—Sixth auditor, $3600; chief clerk, $2000; deputy auditor, $2250; eight chiefs of division, $2000 each; thirteen clerks of class 4, and additional to one clerk as disbursing clerk, $200; fifty-eight clerks of class 3, sixty-nine clerks of class 2, fifty clerks of class 1; thirty clerks, $1000 each; eighteen female assorters of money orders, $900 each; one skilled laborer, $1000.

Treasurer's Office.—Treasurer of the United States, $6000; assistant treasurer, $3600; cashier, $3600; assistant cashier, $3200; chief clerk, $2500; five chiefs of division, $2500 each; one principal book-keeper, $2500; one assistant book-keeper, $2400; two tellers, $2500 each; two assistant tellers, $2250 each; twenty-five clerks of class 4, seventeen clerks of class 3, fifteen clerks of class 2, twenty-three clerks of class 1; five clerks, $1000 each; eighty clerks, $900 each.

The Redemption Bureau.—Superintendent, $3500; one principal teller and one principal book-keeper, $2500; one assistant book-keeper, $2400; and one assistant teller, $2000; two clerks of class 4, three clerks of class 3, four clerks of class 2, twenty clerks of class 1; ten clerks, $1000 each; ten clerks, $900 each.

Register of the Treasury.—Register of the Treasury, $4000; assistant register, $2250; five chiefs of division, $2000 each; eighteen clerks of class 4, seventeen clerks of class 3, fifteen clerks of class 2, twenty clerks of class 1; four clerks, $1000 each; sixty copyists, $900 each.

Comptroller of the Currency.—Comptroller of the currency, $5000; deputy comptroller, $2800; four chiefs of division, $2200 each; one stenographer, $1600; eight clerks of class 4, eleven clerks of class 3, eight clerks of class 2, eight clerks of class 1; two clerks, $1000 each; twenty-five clerks, $900 each.

Superintendent of Currency.—One superintendent, $2000; one teller and one book-keeper, $2000 each; one assistant book-keeper, $2000; nine clerks, $900 each.

Lighthouse Board.—Chief clerk, $2400; two clerks of class 4, two clerks of class 3, one clerk of class 2, three clerks of class 1; one clerk, $900.

Bureau of Statistics.—Officer in charge, $3000; chief clerk, $2000; four clerks of class 4, five clerks of class 3, five clerks of class 2, six clerks of class 1; three clerks, $1000 each; five copyists, $900 each.

Bureau of Engraving and Printing.—Chief of bureau, $4500; one assistant, $2500; accountant, $2000; stenographer, $1600; one clerk of class 3, one clerk of class 2, four clerks of class 1; one clerk, $1000, three copyists, $900 each.

Office of Life-Saving Service.—General superintendent, $4000; assistant general superintendent, $2500; one principal clerk and accountant,

$1800; two clerks of class 3. one clerk of class 2, three clerks of class 1; two clerks, $1000 each; four clerks, $900 each.

Commissioner of Internal Revenue.—Commissioner of internal revenue, $6000; one deputy commissioner, $3200; two heads of division, $2500 each; five heads of division, $2250 each; one stenographer, $1800; twenty-three clerks of class 4, twenty-six clerks of class 3, thirty-six clerks of class 2; twenty-one clerks of class 1; thirteen clerks, $1000 each; fifty clerks, $900 each.

Assistant Treasurer at Baltimore.—Assistant treasurer, $4500; cashier, $2500; three clerks, $1800 each; two clerks, $1400 each; two clerks, $1200 each.

Assistant Treasurer at Boston.—Assistant treasurer, $5000; chief clerk, $2500; paying teller, $2500; assistant paying teller, $2000; chief interest clerk, $2500; receiving teller, $1800; first book-keeper, $1700; second book-keeper, depositors' accounts, $1500; specie clerk, $1500; assistant specie clerk, $1400; clerk, $1800; two coupon clerks, $1400 each; two clerks, $1200 each; assistant book-keeper, $800; two clerks, $1000 each; assistant currency redemption clerk, $1100.

Assistant Treasurer at Chicago.—Assistant treasurer, $4500; cashier, $2500; paying teller, $1800; book-keeper and receiving teller, $1500 each; two clerks, $1200 each.

Assistant Treasurer at Cincinnati.—Assistant treasurer, $4500; cashier, $2000; book-keeper, $1800; receiving teller, $1500; check clerk and interest clerk, each $1200; fractional currency and minor coin clerk, $1000.

Assistant Treasurer at New Orleans.—Assistant treasurer, $4000; cashier, $2250; receiving teller, $2000; book-keeper, $1500; one clerk, $1000; and porter, $900.

Assistant Treasurer at New York.—Assistant treasurer, $8000; cashier and chief clerk, $4000; deputy assistant treasurer, $3600; chief of coin division, $3600; chief of note paying division, $3000; chief of note receiving division, $2800; chief of check paying division, $2800; chief of registered interest division, $2600; chief of coupon interest division, $2400; chief of minor coin division, $2400; chief of bond division, $2250; chief of cancelled check and record division, $2000; two clerks, $2250 each; six clerks, $2100 each; ten clerks, $2000 each; eleven clerks, $1800 each; four clerks, $1700 each; seven clerks, $1600 each; four clerks, $1500 each; twelve clerks, $1400 each; five clerks, $1200 each; keeper of building, $1800; chief detective, $1800; two assistant detectives, $1400 each; one engineer, $1000.

Assistant Treasurer at Philadelphia.—Assistant treasurer, $4500; cashier and chief clerk, $2500; book-keeper, $2500; chief interest clerk.

$2200; chief registered interest clerk, $1900; assistant book-keeper, $1800; coin teller, $1700; redemption clerk, $1600; assistant coupon clerk, $1600; assistant registered interest clerk, $1500; assistant cashier, $1400; assistant coin teller, $1400; receiving teller, $1300; assistant receiving teller, $1200; superintendent of building, $1100; four female counters, at $900 each.

Assistant Treasurer at St. Louis.—Assistant treasurer, $4500; chief clerk and teller, $2500; assistant teller, $1800; book-keeper, $1500; assistant book-keeper, $1200.

Assistant Treasurer at San Francisco.—Assistant treasurer, $5500; cashier, $3000; book-keeper, $2500; one chief clerk, $2400; assistant cashier, $2000; assistant book-keeper, $2000; one clerk, $1800.

Depositary at Tucson.—In addition to his pay as postmaster, $1500; one watchman, $900.

Director of the mint, $4500; examiner, $2300; computer, $2200; adjuster of accounts, $2000; one clerk of class 3, one clerk of class 2, two clerks of class 1; one translator, $1200; one copyist, $900.

Superintendent of mint at Philadelphia, $4500; assayer, melter and refiner, coiner and engraver, $3000 each; assistant assayer, assistant melter and refiner, and assistant coiner, $2000 each; cashier, $2500; chief clerk, $2250; book-keeper, deposit clerk and weigh clerk, $2000 each; one clerk, $1600.

Superintendent of mint at San Francisco, $4500; assayer, melter and refiner, and coiner, $3000 each; chief clerk and cashier, $2500 each; four clerks, $1600 each.

Superintendent of mint at Carson, $3000; assayer, melter and refiner, and coiner, $2500 each; chief clerk, $2250; cashier, book-keeper, and weigh clerk, $2000 each; voucher clerk, and computing clerk, $1800 each; assayer's clerk, $1200.

Superintendent of mint at New Orleans, $3500; assayer, melter and refiner, and coiner, $2500 each; cashier and chief clerk, $2000 each; weigh clerk, deposit clerk, book-keeper, and assayer's clerk, $1600 each.

Assayer in charge of Denver mint, $2500; melter, $2250; assistant assayer, $1400; chief clerk, $1800; one clerk, $1600; one clerk, $1400.

Superintendent of the assay office at New York, $4500; assayer and melter and refiner, $3000 each; chief clerk, $2500; weighing clerk, $2500; paying clerk, $2000; bar clerk, $1800; warrant clerk, $2250; two calculating clerks, $1800 each; assistant weigh clerk, $1600; assayer's first assistant, $2250; assayer's second assistant, $2150; assayer's third assistant, $2000.

Assayer at Helena, M. T., $2500; melter, $2250; one clerk of class 1.

Assayer at Boise City, I. T., $2000; one clerk, $1000.

Assayer at Charlotte, N. C., $1500; assistant assayer, $1250.

Assayer at St. Louis, $2500; melter, $2000; one clerk, $1000.

Coast and Geodetic Survey.—Superintendent, $6000; assistant, $4200; consulting geometer, $4000; disbursing agent, $2500. There are also habitually employed upward of fifty so-called assistants, with salaries varying from $3750 to $1100, and about one hundred clerks, computers, draughtsmen, printers, engravers, etc., at compensations varying from $2000 per year down to $1.50 per day.

Revenue Marine Service.—Thirty-four captains, $2500; thirty-four first lieutenants, $1800; thirty-four second lieutenants, $1500; twenty-two third lieutenants, $1200; twelve cadets, $900; twenty-three chief engineers, $1800; eighteen assistants, $1500; twenty-seven assistants, $1200.

Alaska Seal Fisheries.—One agent, $3650; assistant agent, $2920; two assistant agents, $2190; travelling expenses, $600 each per annum.

Marine Hospital Service.—Supervising surgeon-general, $4000; sixty-five medical officers with salaries ranging from $3000 down to $1000 per year; ten clerks with usual clerical salaries.

National Board of Health.—Seven members, $10 per day; chief clerk, $2300; one clerk, $1800; two, $1600; two, $1200.

Steamboat Inspection Service.—Supervising inspector-general, $3500; twelve supervising inspectors, $3000; two inspectors of hulls, $2200; fifteen inspectors of hulls, $2000; two inspectors of hulls, $1600; three inspectors of hulls, $1500; twelve inspectors of hulls, $1200; one inspector of hulls, $900; five inspectors of hulls, $800; two inspectors of boilers, $2200; sixteen inspectors of boilers, $2000; five inspectors of boilers, $1600; three inspectors of boilers, $1500; fourteen inspectors of boilers, $1200; one inspector of boilers, $900; five inspectors of boilers, $800; six clerks, $1200; two clerks, $1000; clerk, $900.

Special Agencies of Customs.—Twenty special agents, per day, $8; eight special agents, per day, $6; sea island agent in Alaska, $3650; sea island agent in Alaska, $2920; two sea island agents in Alaska, $2190; two isthmus inspectors, $2500.

Internal Revenue Agencies.—Supervising agent, per day, $12; twenty-one agents, per day, $8; seven agents, per day, $7; six agents, per day, $6.

National Bank Examiners.—The number of these officers is not regulated by law. The banks examined pay the fees for examination. The examiners are chosen by the comptroller of the currency at will.

Secret Service.—Chief, $3500. This force is also variable, but consists usually of about forty detectives and a few clerks, paid at various rates, according to time employed and services rendered.

WAR DEPARTMENT.

Chief clerk, $2500; disbursing clerk, $2000; stenographer, $1800; two chiefs of division, $2000 each; five clerks of class 4, four clerks of class 3, four clerks of class 2, twelve clerks of class 1; one clerk, $1000.

Adjutant-General's Office.—Chief clerk, $2000; eleven clerks of class 4, seventeen clerks of class 3, thirty-five clerks of class 2, one hundred and fifty-one clerks of class 1; six clerks, $1000 each; thirty additional clerks of class 1; and twenty-five clerks, $1000 each; twenty-five clerks, $1000 per annum each.

Office of the Inspector-General.—One clerk of class 4.

Bureau of Military Justice.—Chief clerk, $1800; one clerk of class 3, one clerk of class 1.

Signal Office.—Two clerks of class 4 and one clerk of class 1.

Quartermaster-General's Office.—Chief clerk, $2000; seven clerks of class 4, nine clerks of class 3, twenty-four clerks of class 2, forty-eight clerks of class 1; twenty copyists, $900 each; engineer, $1200; draughtsman, $1200.

Commissary-General's Office.—Chief clerk, $2000; eight clerks of class 4, six clerks of class 3, nine clerks of class 2, one hundred and six clerks of class 1; fourteen clerks at $1000 each; anatomist, $1600; engineer, $1400; one hundred and twenty clerks, $1000 each.

Ordnance Office.—Chief clerk, $2000; four clerks of class 4, two clerks of class 3, three clerks of class 2, three clerks of class 1; one clerk, $1000; engineer in War Department building, $1200; assistant engineer, $1000.

Public Buildings and Grounds.—Clerk in the office of public buildings and grounds, $1400; public gardener, $1600; disbursing officer at the Leavenworth military prison, $150 per month; clerk in office of prison quartermaster, $116.66 per month.

NAVY DEPARTMENT.

Chief clerk, $2500; disbursing clerk, $2000; four clerks of class 4, three clerks of class 3; stenographer, $1600; four clerks of class 1; three clerks, $1000 each.

Bureau of Yards and Docks.—Chief clerk, $1800; draughtsman, $1800;

one clerk of class 4, one clerk of class 3, one clerk of class 2, one clerk of class 1 ; one clerk, $1000.

Bureau of Equipment and Recruiting.—Chief clerk, $1800 ; one clerk of class 4, one clerk of class 3, two clerks of class 2, two clerks of class 1.

Bureau of Navigation.—Chief clerk, $1800; one clerk of class 3, one clerk of class 2 ; one clerk, $1000.

Bureau of Ordnance.—Chief clerk, $1800; draughtsman, $1800; one clerk of class 3, one clerk of class 2.

Bureau of Construction and Repair.—Chief clerk, $1800; draughtsman, $1800; one clerk of class 4, one clerk of class 3, one clerk of class 2, one clerk of class 1.

Bureau of Steam Engineering.—Chief clerk, $1800; chief draughtsman, $2250; assistant draughtsman, $1600; one clerk of class 2, one clerk of class 1 ; one clerk, $1000.

Bureau of Provision and Clothing.—Chief clerk, $1800; one clerk of class 4, two clerks of class 3, two clerks of class 2, three clerks of class 1.

Bureau of Medicine and Surgery.—Chief clerk, $1800; one clerk of class 3, one clerk of class 2, one clerk of class 1 ; one clerk, $1000.

Judge Advocate General's Office.—One clerk of class 3; one clerk, $1000; superintendent of the building, $250; engineer, $1200; assistant engineer, $1000.

Naval Observatory.—Clerk, $1600; three civilian astronomers, $1500; instrument maker, $1500.

Hydrographic Office.—Clerk, per month, $120; draughtsman, per month, $191.63; draughtsman, per month, $175; draughtsman, per month, $133.33; draughtsman, per month, $120; two draughtsmen, per month, $108.33; two draughtsmen, per month, $100; two printers, per day, $4; two engravers, per day, $4; engraver, per day, $3.50; two engravers, per day, $3.

Nautical Almanac Office.—Two computers, $1600; two computers, $1500; three computers, $1200.

DEPARTMENT OF THE INTERIOR.

Assistant secretary, $3500; chief clerk, $2500, and $250 additional as superintendent of the Patent Office building ; seven clerks, chiefs of division, $2000 each; stenographer, $1800; six clerks of class 4, four clerks of class 3, four clerks of class 2, seven clerks of class 1 ; one clerk, $1000; captain of watch, $1000; engineer, $1200; assistant engineer, $1000.

Assistant Attorney-General's Office.—Law clerk, $2250; three clerks at $2000 each, and one clerk at $1300.

General Land-Office.—Commissioner of the General Land-Office, $4000; chief clerk, $2000; law clerk, $2000; recorder, $2000; three principal clerks, $1800; sixteen clerks of class 4, thirty clerks of class 3, forty clerks of class 2, sixty-two clerks of class 1; thirty clerks at $1000 each, and fifteen copyists at $900 each; draughtsman, $1600; assistant draughtsman, $1400; $450,000 is appropriated for the salaries and commissions of registers of land-offices and receivers of public moneys, not to exceed $3450 each.

Indian Office.—Commissioner of Indian affairs, $3500; chief clerk, $2000; financial clerk, $2000; principal book-keeper, $1500; four clerks of class 4, three clerks of class 3; stenographer, $1600; twelve clerks of class 2, ten clerks of class 1; thirteen clerks, $1000 each.

Pension Office.—Commissioner of Pensions, $5000; first deputy commissioner, $3600; deputy commissioner, $2400; chief clerk, $2000; medical referee, $2250; forty-five clerks of class 4, seventy-five clerks of class 3, one hundred clerks of class 2, one hundred and forty-eight clerks of class 1; ten clerks, $1000 each; thirty copyists, $900 each; one engineer, $1200; twenty-nine examiners, $2000 each; twenty clerks of class 3, twenty clerks of class 2, fifty clerks of class 1.

Patent Office.—Commissioner of Patents, $4500; assistant commissioner, $3000; chief clerk, $2250; three examiners-in-chief, $3000 each; examiner in charge of interferences, $2500; trade-mark examiner and examiner of designs, $2400 each; twenty-three principal examiners, $2400 each; twenty-four first assistant examiners, $1800 each; twenty-four second assistant examiners, $1600 each; twenty-four third assistant examiners, $1400 each; financial clerk, $2000; librarian, $2000; machinist, $1600; three chiefs of division, $2000 each; one clerk of class 4, five clerks of class 3, nineteen clerks of class 2, and forty-five clerks of class 1; forty-two permanent clerks, $1000 each; seventy copyists, $900 each; four draughtsmen, $1200 each; messenger and purchasing clerk, $1000; skilled laborer, $1200; five model attendants, $1000 each.

Bureau of Education.—Commissioner of Education, $3000; chief clerk, $1800; two clerks of class 4; statistician, $1800; one clerk of class 3; translator, $1600; two clerks of class 2, two clerks of class 1.

Auditor of Railroad Accounts.—Commissioner of Railroads, $4500; book-keeper, $2400; assistant book-keeper, $2000; railroad engineer, $2500; one clerk, $1400.

Surveyors-General.—Surveyor-general of California, $2750; Colorado, New Mexico, Idaho, Nevada, Oregon, Washington Territory, Montana, Utah, Wyoming, Arizona, $2500 each; Minnesota, Dakota, Nebraska, and Iowa, $2000 each; Louisiana and Florida, $1800 each.

POST-OFFICE DEPARTMENT.

Chief clerk, $2200; stenographer, $1800; appointment clerk, $1800; law clerk, $2250; three clerks of class 1; one messenger, $1200; topographer, $2500; one clerk of class 3; one clerk, $1000.

First assistant postmaster-general, $4000; chief clerk, $2000; three clerks of class 4, fifteen clerks of class 3, six clerks of class 2, twelve clerks of class 1; four clerks, $1000 each; superintendent of blank agency, $1800; assistant superintendent of blank agency, $1600; four assistants to superintendent of blank agency, $1200 each; two assistants to superintendent of blank agency, $900 each; one clerk, $1000; superintendent of free delivery, $2100; one clerk of class 2.

Second assistant postmaster-general, $4000; chief clerk, $2000; chief of division of inspection, $2000; superintendent of railway adjustment, $2000; eight clerks of class 4, thirty clerks of class 3, sixteen clerks of class 2, thirteen clerks of class 1; nine clerks, $1000 each.

Third assistant postmaster-general, $4000; chief clerk, $2000; chief of division of dead letters, $2250; chief of division of postage stamps, $2250; seven clerks of class 4, eighteen clerks of class 3, twenty-eight clerks of class 2, thirty-seven clerks of class 1; six clerks, $1000 each; ten female clerks, $1200 each; forty-seven female clerks, $900 each.

Superintendent of foreign mails, $3000; chief clerk, $2000; one clerk of class 4, three clerks of class 3, one clerk of class 2, one clerk of class 1; two clerks at $1000 each.

Superintendent of the money-order system, $3000; chief clerk, $2000; five clerks of class 4, seven clerks of class 3, five clerks of class 2, nine clerks of class 1; one clerk at $1000; five clerks at $900 each.

Chief of division of mail depredations, $2250; one clerk of class 3, one clerk of class 2, three clerks of class 1; one clerk, $1000.

Disbursing clerk and superintendent, $2100; one clerk of class 2; one clerk of class 1; engineer, $1400; assistant engineer, $1000; carpenter, $1200; assistant carpenter, $1000; captain of the watch, $1000.

Inspection Service.—Nine inspectors, $2500; nine inspectors, $1600 and $5 per day for expenses; six inspectors, $1600 and $4 per day for expenses; eighteen inspectors, $1500 and $4 per day for expenses; seven inspectors, $1200 and $4 per day for expenses; four inspectors, $1400 and $4 per day for expenses; inspector, $1400; inspector, $1200.

Railway Mail Service.—General superintendent, $3500; nine assistants, $2500; assistant superintendent, $1600 and $4 per day for expenses; assistant superintendent, $1500 and $4 per day for expenses; assistant superintendent, $1200 and $5 per day for expenses; assistant superintendent, $1200 and $4 per day for expenses; seventy-two route agents, $1000; three route agents, $980; forty-nine route agents, $960; eighty-five route agents, $940; twenty-six route agents, $920; eight hundred and ninety-four route agents, $900; forty-one railway postal clerks, $1400; three hundred and fifty-six railway postal clerks, $1300; four hundred and forty-three railway postal clerks, $1150; one hundred and seventy-eight railway postal clerks, $1000; sixty-nine postal clerks, $900.

Supply Service.—Three distributing agents for stamped envelopes, postage stamps, and postal cards, $2500; fifteen clerks, $1000 to $1800; delete clerk, $1800.

DEPARTMENT OF JUSTICE.

Solicitor-general, $7000; three assistant attorneys-general, $5000 each; assistant attorney-general of the Post-Office Department, $4000; solicitor of the internal revenue, $4500; examiner of claims, $3500; law clerk and examiner of titles, $2700; chief clerk, $2200; stenographic clerk, $1800; one law clerk, $2000; five clerks of class 4, one clerk of class 2, two clerks of class 1, five copyists; telegraph operator, $1000; solicitor of the Treasury, $4500; assistant solicitor, $3000; chief clerk, $2000; four clerks of class 4, three clerks of class 3, two clerks of class 2, two clerks of class 1.

Court of Claims.—Five judges, $4500 each; chief clerk, $3000; assistant clerk, $2000; bailiff, $1500.

Court of Alabama Claims.—Counsel, $8000; three judges, $6000 each; assistant counsel, $3500; insurance expert, $3500; clerk of court, $3000; disbursing agent, $2000; clerk, $2000.

DEPARTMENT OF AGRICULTURE.

Commissioner, $3500; chief clerk, $2000; entomologist, $2000; chemist, $3000; two assistants, $1200 and $1600; statistician, $2000; superintendent of gardens, $2000; superintendent of seed division, $1800; botanist, $1800; microscopist, $1800; six clerks, $1800; four, $1600; six, $1400; six, $1200; five, $1000; superintendent of folding-room, $1200; lady superintendent of seed-room, $900; engineer, $1200.

GOVERNMENT PRINTING-OFFICE.

Public printer, $4500; chief clerk, $2400; foreman of printing, $2100; foreman of binding, $2100; three clerks of class 4, each $1800; one clerk of class 2, $1400; three clerks of class 1, each $1200; nine assistant foremen, each $1800; two assistant foremen, each $1650; five assistant foremen, each $1200; engineer and two assistants, each $1300. About twenty-five hundred printers, binders, and other employés are engaged in this office.

DIPLOMATIC AND CONSULAR SERVICE.

Envoys extraordinary and ministers plenipotentiary to Great Britain, France, Germany, and Russia, $17,500 each; envoys extraordinary and ministers plenipotentiary to Spain, Austria, Italy, Brazil, Mexico, Japan, and China, $12,000 each; envoys extraordinary and ministers plenipotentiary to Chili and Peru, $10,000 each; ministers resident at Belgium, Netherlands, Sweden and Norway, Turkey, Venezuela, Hawaiian Islands, Argentine Republic, and the United States of Colombia, $7500 each; minister resident and consul-general at Bolivia, $5000; ministers resident accredited to Guatemala, Costa Rica, Honduras, Salvador, and Nicaragua, $10,000 each; minister resident and consul-general to Hayti, $7500; minister resident and consul-general to Liberia, $4000; charges d'affaires to Portugal, Denmark, Paraguay and Uruguay, and Switzerland, $5000 each; secretaries to the legations at London, Paris, Berlin, and St. Petersburg, $2625 each; secretary to the legation at Japan, $2500; secretaries of legations at Austria, Brazil, Italy, Mexico, and Spain, $1800 each; second secretaries to the legations at Great Britain, France, and Germany, $2000 each; clerk to the legation at Spain, $1200; clerk to the legation in Central America, $1000; secretary to the legation, acting also as interpreter, at China, $5000; interpreter to the legation at Turkey, $3000; interpreter to the legation at Japan, $3500; agent and consul-general at Cairo, $4000; charge d'affaires and consul-general of the United States in Roumania, at Bucharest, $4000; consuls-general at London, Paris, Havana, and Rio de Janeiro, each $6000; consuls-general at Calcutta and Shanghai, each $5000; consul-general at Melbourne, $4500; consul-general at Kanagawa and Montreal, each $4000; consul-general at Berlin, $4000; consuls-general at Vienna, Frankfort, Rome, Constantinople, and Halifax, each $3000; consuls-general at St. Petersburg and Mexico, each $2000; consul at Liverpool, $6000; consul at Hong Kong, $4000; Honolulu, $4000; Foo-Chow, Hankow, Canton, Amoy, Tien-Tsin, Chin-Kiang, and Ningpo, China, and Callao, Peru, $3500 each; Manchester, Glasgow, Bradford, Demare, and Belfast, Great Britain; Havre, France; Matanzas, Spain; Vera Cruz, Mexico; Panama, Colon, Aspinwall, United States of Colombia, Buenos Ayres, Argentine Republic; Tripoli, Tunis, and Tangier, Barbary States; Magaski, Osaka, and Hiogo, Japan; Bangkok, Siam, and Valparaiso, Chili, $3000 each; Singapore, Tunstall, Birmingham, Sheffield, Dundee, Nottingham, Marseilles, Bordeaux, Lyons, Cienfuegos, Santiago de Cuba, Antwerp, Brussels, St. Thomas, Hamburg, Bremen, and Dresden, $2500 each; Cork, Dublin, Leeds, Leith, Toronto, Hamilton, St. John, New Brunswick; Kingston, Jamaica; Coaticook, Nassau, New Providence; Cardiff, Port Louis, Mauritius; Sydney, New South Wales; San Juan, Porto Rico; Lisbon, Rotterdam, Odessa, Sonneburg, Nuremberg, Barmen, Cologne, Chemnitz, Leipsic, Crefeld, Trieste, Prague, Basle, Zurich, Acapulco, Matamoras, Pernambuco, Tamatave, Apia, Maracaibo, Montevideo, and Beirut, Smyrna, $2000 each; Bristol, Newcastle, Auckland, Gibraltar, Cape Town, St. Helena, Charlottetown, Prince Edward Island; Port Stanley, Clifton, Pictou, Winnepeg, Mahé, Kingston, Canada; Prescott, Port Sarnia, Quebec, St. Johns, Canada; Barbadoes, Bermuda, Fort Erie, Goderich, Canada West; Windsor, Canada West; Southampton, Ottawa, Ceylon, Nice, Martinique, Guadeloupe, Cadiz, Malaga, Barcelona, Fayal, Azores; Funchal, Verviers, Liege, Munich, Stuttgart, Mannheim, Aix-la-Chapelle, Amsterdam, Copenhagen, Geneva, Genoa, Naples, Leghorn, Florence, Palermo, Messina, Jerusalem, Tampico, Laguayra, Puerto Cabello, Bahia, Para, Manila, San Domingo, and Guayaquil, $1500 each; Gaspé Basin, Windsor, Nova Scotia; Bombay, Sierra Leone, Turk's Island, Stettin, Nantes, Algiers, Venice, Cape Haytien, Sabanilla, Batavia, Rio Grande del Sul, Ruatan and Truxillo, Mozambique, Guaymas, Nuevo Laredo, Piedras Negras, Zanzibar, Santiago, Cape Verde Islands; Tahiti, and Talcahuano, $1000 each.

Commercial agents at St. Paul de Loando, Levuka, and San Juan del Norte, $1000 each; interpreters: at Shanghai, $2000; at Tien-Tsin, Foo Chow, and Kanagawa, $1500 each; interpreters to the consulates at Hankow, Amoy, Canton, and Hong Kong, $750 each; interpreters to twelve other consulates at China, Japan, and Siam, $500 each.

DISTRICT OF COLUMBIA GOVERNMENT.

Two commissioners, $5000 (the engineer commissioner is detailed from the army); secretary to commissioners, $2160; clerk, $1500; clerk, $1400; clerk, $900; auditor and comptroller, $3000; book-keeper, $1800; clerk, $1000; three clerks, $1400; two clerks, $1200; clerk, $900; clerk of special assessments, $1800; clerk, $1400; clerk, $1000; two clerks of sinking fund, $1200; coroner, $1800; collector of taxes, $4000; clerk, $1800; clerk, $1400; clerk, $1200; attorney, $5000; assistant, $1900; special assistant, $960; clerk, $960; treasurer and assessor, $3000; assistant, $1800; clerk, $1600; two clerks, $1400; six clerks, $1200; clerk,

$900; inspector of buildings, $2400; assistant, $1700; assistant, $1000; inspector of gas and meters, $2000; assistant, $1000; two clerks of assessment, $1200; chief clerk engineer's office, $1900; clerk, $1600; clerk, $1400; clerk, $1200; two clerks, $900; computing engineer, $2400; draughtsman, $1000; three levellers, $1400 to $1600; inspector of pavements, $2400; inspector, $1500; two inspectors, $1200; superintendent of property, $1800; clerk, $1200; superintendent of streets, $2000; three supervisors of roads, $900; health officer, $3000; plumbing inspector, $1500; six sanitary inspectors, $1200; two food inspectors, $1200; pound master, $1200; clerks (number and salary fixed by the health officer), $7000; superintendent of public schools, $2700; superintendent of colored schools, $2250; four hundred and two school-teachers, $250 to $1650; eight school janitors, $32 to $1270; superintendent of police, $2610; inspector, $1800; property clerk, $1800; clerk, $1500; six detectives, $1320; ten lieutenants, $1200; twenty sergeants, $1140; seven sergeants, $1080; one hundred and twenty policemen, $1080; seventy-three policemen, $900; chief engineer fire department, $1800; assistant, $1400; superintendent fire alarm, $1500; two operators, $1200; eight foremen, $1000; six engineers, $1000; police justice, $3000; clerk of police court, $2000; deputy, $1000; superintendent of parking, $1200; market master, $1650; market master, $1500; intendant of poor-house, $1000; physician, $1200; water registrar, $2400; two clerks, $1440 and $1200; book-keeper, $1500; inspector and tapper, $1440; superintendent of reform school, $1500; assistant, $1000; warden of jail, $1800; deputy, $1200; clerk, $1200; physician, $1200; guards, $1000; engineer, $1400; assistant, $1200; superintendent of insane asylum, $208.33 per month; chief clerk, $108.33; surgeon freedmen's hospital, $166.66 per month; executive officer, $116.66 per month.

The clerk of the Supreme Court, the district attorney, marshal, register of wills, and recorder of deeds are compensated by fees. In addition there are connected with the district courts deputy clerks, marshals, bailiffs, etc., whose salaries vary from $2500 to $500.

TERRITORIAL GOVERNMENT.

Governor of Arizona, $2600; chief-justice and two associate judges, $3000 each; secretary, $1800; interpreter and translator in the executive office, $500.

Governor of Dakota, $2600; chief-justice and three associate judges, $3000 each; secretary, $1800.

Governor of Idaho, $2600; chief-justice and two associate judges, $3000 each; secretary, $1800.

Governor of Montana, $2600; chief-justice and two associate judges, $3000 each; secretary, $1800.

Governor of New Mexico, $2600; chief-justice and two associate judges, $3000 each; secretary, $1800; interpreter and translator in the executive office, $500.

Governor of Utah, $2600; chief-justice and two associate judges, $3000 each; secretary, $1800.

Governor of Washington Territory, $2600; chief-justice and two associate judges, $3000 each; secretary, $1800.

Governor of Wyoming, $2600; chief-justice and two associate judges, $3000 each; secretary, $1800.

INDEX.

www.ingramcontent.com/pod-product-compliance
Lightning Source LLC
Chambersburg PA
CBHW021113270326
41929CB00009B/855